M

SHELF No.

WITHDRAWN

301006413I

Sociology in its Place
and Other Essays

SOCIOLOGY IN ITS PLACE

and Other Essays

by

W. G. RUNCIMAN

CAMBRIDGE

AT THE UNIVERSITY PRESS

1970

MAGDALEN COLLEGE LIBRARY

Published by the Syndics of the Cambridge University Press
Bentley House, 220 Euston Road, London N.W.1
American Branch: 32 East 57th Street, New York, N.Y. 10022

© Cambridge University Press 1970

Library of Congress Catalogue Card Number: 75 120194

Standard Book Number: ██████████
521 07905 5

Printed in Great Britain
at the University Press, Aberdeen

Contents

Preface

These papers have all, except the first, been published before, but I hope that by being brought together in this volume they will lend support to some of the arguments of the opening essay. They are grouped under three headings. The first four are purely methodological; the second three, although they too are methodological in part, contain in addition some results of empirical research; the last four are philosophical, if only in the sense that they first appeared in journals of philosophy. I have made a number of minor amendments and added a prefatory note to each, but they are left in the main as they were originally written.

London   W. G. R.
October 1969

PART I

1. Sociology in its Place

Sociology is no longer described, as some textbooks used to describe it, as a branch of knowledge discovered in the 1820s by Auguste Comte. Comte's claim to have coined the term is not disputed. But on any plausible definition of it, he was not its founder. We need not even cross the Channel: historians apart, the contributions of Smith, Malthus and Bentham to the scientific study of social institutions and behaviour are not only earlier but in some ways more important than Comte's. Yet Comte is, nevertheless, the proper starting point for this essay because he was the first to attempt a systematic exposition of the relation of the study of social institutions and behaviour to the sciences as a whole. It is true that his views were never properly founded on or tested against empirical research. As was fairly said of him by John Stuart Mill, 'it appears as if, to his mind, the mere institution of a positive science of sociology were tantamount to its completion'.[1] The ideas for which he is best known are original as much to Hegel, Saint-Simon and even, perhaps, Herbert Spencer as to himself, and his hierarchy of the sciences, which put astronomy before physics and bypassed psychology altogether, is not one which contemporary philosophers or historians of science are likely to defend in detail. But he was the first to draw proper attention to the fact (however mistaken some of the conclusions he drew from it) that the science of social institutions and behaviour as we now think of it stands at the end not only of a historical but also—and more important—of a logical series.

It may be said that all distinctions between the sciences are purely matters of convenience; and so they are. The sciences stand in relation to one another in a number of different dimensions; these relations are by no means symmetrical; and the importance of the particular distinction to be drawn depends on the particular question that the researcher may have in mind. But to say that these are matters of convenience is not to say that they can be ignored. On the contrary: it is a besetting difficulty of the social sciences that questions of this kind seem intimately bound up with the practical problems of research. The scope and status of the

[1] *Auguste Comte and Positivism* (1865), pp. 119–20.

I

sciences of man are hard to establish satisfactorily in the absence of substantive achievements comparable to those of the sciences of nature; yet until their scope and status can be established, it remains difficult to see by what approach such achievements are best likely to be attained. I shall not, in this paper, do more than touch on the wider issues raised by an assertion of this kind: I shall assume without argument that scientific method is applicable to human behaviour, and I shall be concerned only with one aspect of the many controversies surrounding the relation of sociology to the other sciences of man. Within these limits, however, I shall argue that 'sociology' cannot be usefully distinguished in content from either anthropology or history; that it is not only a historical but an applied science in the sense that its explanations are parasitic on the laws of others; that this follows from the position which Comte himself assigned to it in the hierarchy of the sciences; and that to talk of looking for distinctive 'sociological' theories is therefore unhelpful and misconceived.

I

If this view is at all plausible, it raises an immediate question: how does it come about that sociology continues to be regarded as an autonomous subject? This question is partly logical, in the sense that there may be counter-arguments by which sociology's autonomy can be vindicated, and partly historical, in the sense that its autonomy may be the consequence of identifiable accidents of academic, or sometimes non-academic, organisation and research. To give an adequate historical answer would require a detailed discussion of the recent intellectual history of Europe and the United States such as would in any case be beyond my competence. But even a cursory look at the history of the subject in Britain reveals just how haphazard it has been. Indeed it seems almost to make the question more puzzling rather than less. So far from there ever having been a homogeneous tradition within which British sociology could be identified in terms of the common researches of its practitioners, there have for more than a century been four 'sociological' traditions (leaving historiography aside altogether) which have remained consistently separate from each other.

If labels are helpful, we might call the four traditions the evolutionary, the political-economic, the ethnographic and the administrative-reformist; or to identify them with the most obvious names, we might call them the tradition of Spencer, the tradition of Mill, the tradition of Tylor and the tradition of Booth. These labels should not be taken too strictly. But even if we go back as far as the 1840s, it is already striking how clearly the four traditions seem to be marked out. By the end of that decade, Spencer had brought out his *Social Statics* and Mill his *Political Economy*, the Ethnological Society of London had been founded for seven years and publishing its regular proceedings for two, and the Statistical Society had carried out and published its detailed quantitative survey of 'The State of the Poorer Classes in St George's in the East'. A hundred and twenty years later, the four are as easily distinguishable as ever. The evolutionary tradition has passed from Spencer through the so-called Social Darwinists to Hobhouse and his successor Professor Morris Ginsberg, and then, just when it appeared to be petering out altogether, has been revived in its biological rather than its philosophical expression in a manner best exemplified in the symposium held by the Royal Society in 1966 under the chairmanship of Sir Julian Huxley on the theme of 'Ritualization in Animals and Man'. The political economy of Mill has developed through Jevons, Marshall and Keynes into the economic theory of today, shedding the 'political' along the way for it to take root and flourish as a tradition of its own. The ethnographic tradition has passed from Tylor and Frazer through Malinowski and Radcliffe-Brown to Professor Evans-Pritchard and his pupils, acquiring in the process, thanks to Malinowski, a rigorous and distinctive professional technique. The administrative-reformist tradition of Sir John Simon, William Farr, the Statistical Society, the Royal Commissions and the factory inspectors has passed through Booth, Rowntree, Beveridge and the Webbs to contemporary 'Social Administration' in the manner of Professors Titmuss and Townsend. It is true that the four traditions sometimes overlapped in the past—notably in the Eugenists' combination of evolutionism, reformism, and questionable anthropology with admirably sophisticated statistical methods—and that they are in quite frequent contact at the present. The revival of the evolutionary tradition in its current form has circumvented the resistance of the ethnologists to anything which might smack of the discredited 'comparative method'; social administration is taught with increasing reference to wider social theory; economics, since becoming more and more preoccupied with problems of growth and development, has shown a greater willingness to look outside its conventional boundaries for the determinants of economic behaviour. But it would be a fruitless exercise to try to define something called 'British sociology' of which the four would be common derivatives. Although there has since 1903 been a professional association of British sociologists with all the trappings appropriate to an autonomous branch of learning, the

SOCIOLOGY IN ITS PLACE

circumstances of its founding hardly bear out a description of it in these terms: the fact is that 'a national society designed to promote sociology as an academic subject was the result of a temporary alliance between town-planners, eugenists, charity organisers and workers in the various social settlements'.[1] The proliferation of university appointments which has finally established sociology in Britain as an autonomous academic subject is a phenomenon of the 1950s which, so far from representing the triumph of a long-standing indigenous movement, was more the result of a conscious desire to imitate the United States. Its explanation must be sought not so much in the long and distinguished history of British social science[2] as in the reasons for which that history has deliberately been given an uncharacteristic turn.

It might then seem natural to try to answer the question in terms of what those who now call themselves sociologists in fact do. But this turns out to be almost as unrewarding as the attempt to answer it historically. If a general conclusion suggests itself from a survey of the teaching conducted under the heading of sociology in the major universities of Britain and the United States, it is that the subjects covered are not merely quite extraordinarily diverse but could in a great number of instances be equally well labelled something else, from economic history to statistical demography to clinical psychology to political science. It is as difficult to find a distinctive method as a distinctive content. In content, sociology as taught and practised ranges over virtually the whole field of social behaviour; in method, it can range from documentary research to participant observation to sample surveys to computer simulation. There does remain, in the great majority of universities or institutes of research, a departmental distinction between those concerned with small, preliterate societies and large industrial societies, if only because obviously different methods are appropriate to the study of each. But this hardly amounts to a difference of principle between 'sociology' and 'anthropology';

[1] R. J. Halliday, 'The Sociological Movement, the Sociological Society and the Genesis of Academic Sociology in Britain', *Sociological Review*, n.s. XVI (1968), 381.
[2] An interesting, and perhaps revealing, side-issue in this history has been the membership of the Royal Society by social scientists. Apart from Sir William Petty among the founding members, Malthus was an F.R.S., and so were Sir John Simon and William Farr among the administrators, Haddon, Pitt-Rivers and Seligman among the ethnographers and Jevons and Sir Robert Giffen among the economists. But the list does not extend to Marshall, Keynes, Malinowski, Radcliffe-Brown or Evans-Pritchard. This can largely be explained by the extent to which the work of those included was of a statistical or experimental kind, and it was in this light that the matter was in fact discussed in 1902 (see the Society's *Yearbook*, pp. 182–3—a reference which I owe to Dr H. O. Pappé). Yet why should, say, Keynes have been excluded when Seligman was elected as late as 1919?

4

it is merely a difference analogous to that between the study of England in the tenth and England in the twentieth centuries—a large difference, certainly, but not a difference between one science and another. It might, perhaps, be objected to this that my question was wrongly put in the first place, since a definition of the scope, method and content of either 'history' or 'anthropology' would turn out to be just as elusive; and perhaps it would. But the conclusion to be drawn from such an enquiry would not be that the autonomy of 'sociology' had been vindicated. On the contrary: it would be that sociology and history, like sociology and anthropology, come to much the same thing. If the dictum that 'anthropology is the science among social studies' is as old as Malinowski,[1] the dictum that 'history is the science of human societies' is at least as old as Fustel de Coulanges.

What, therefore, are the reasons for which sociology is so widely held to constitute an autonomous discipline? At the risk of oversimplification it can, I think, be said that there are two principal reasons which are connected to each other. Both are to be found in Comte, whether or not it is to his influence that their currency is due, and both are in part good reasons. The first is the evolutionists' reason: as biological systems have evolved from physical systems, so have social systems evolved from biological systems, and just as there is a science of biological systems— biology—so there must be a science of social systems—sociology. The second reason is the positivists' reason: if the explanation of human events is possible at all (and there is no good argument for thinking that in principle it is not), then there must be a corpus of laws by reference to which such explanations are vindicated, or in other words a science of societies which stands to history as pure to applied.

The evolutionists' reason is in one sense entirely sound; social systems have indeed evolved from biological systems and the study of man's capacity for the extra-organic transmission of information and its consequences is something very different from the study of his genetically transmitted capacities as a precultural species. What is more, social systems have properties which, although they may be reducible in principle to aggregations of the properties of the individuals composing them, must in practice be treated as predicates of the collectivity. I shall have to say something more in both this and the following section about the question of reduction. But even those who maintain that sociology is reducible in a strong sense to psychology need not be driven to conclude that sociology loses its *raison d'être* on this account, any more than the

[1] See Malinowski's preface to Raymond Firth, *We, The Tikopia* (1937), p. xi.

5

reducibility of chemistry to physics should be thought to enable universities to do without their departments of chemistry. What is more natural, therefore, than to say that sociology is the science of social systems, that its objective is to study the evolution, structure and workings of those social systems which are available to us for observation, and that the terms in which this objective is to be pursued is by establishing the lawlike relations between the properties of social systems as such?

Similarly, the positivists' reason can be stated in such a way as to leave it disputable only by those who wish to deny that human behaviour is amenable at all to the orthodox procedures of observation, hypothesis, and empirical test. Once it is accepted that scientific method can be and is being applied to human behaviour, it follows that to proffer any explanation of human behaviour at all is implicitly to appeal to lawlike generalisations under which the behaviour in question could be subsumed, whether or not these are explicitly stated or even precisely known. Different sociologists (or anthropologists or historians) may look in very different places for the influences or events which they believe to be decisive, and they may try to support their attributions of cause and effect on many different types of ground. But none of them seek to argue that the behaviour they are studying is merely random. To criticise sociologists, therefore, for being unable to state the laws from which their tentative explanations of designated items or sequences of behaviour are derived may be merely to say that sociology has not yet been as successful as one day it will. And when it is, shall we not become able to turn to it for the justification of our explanations and predictions of historical events, just as two or three hundred years ago we became able to turn to celestial mechanics and its laws to justify our explanations or predictions of the complicated interplay of the heavenly bodies?

Both these considerations are plausible, but misleading. Let us agree without further discussion that there are such things as social systems and that their workings are explicable in principle. But then let us ask, what exactly do social systems consist of and how in practice do we set about explaining their workings? It admittedly follows from the position of social systems in the *scala naturae* that they are the most general and complex systems, both materially and formally: materially, because they contain within themselves all the previous stages of evolution; formally, because associations, institutions and societies are all their logical subclasses. It may seem natural, therefore, to see them as comprehending, in some kind of Comtean sense, the totality of human behaviour and to argue from this that the explanation of human behaviour, and therefore

6

human history, is to be derived from our knowledge of the laws by which the workings of social systems are governed. But this is just where Comte goes astray. It is perfectly fair to represent the study of sociology (or history), as Spencer likewise does, as 'the study of Evolution in its most complex form'.[1] But the temptation which has to be resisted, once we have agreed with Comte and Spencer that the science of social systems is in this sense the topmost branch of human knowledge, is then to talk as though the 'lower' disciplines concerned with the study of man are somehow derivable from, or subordinated to, or to be justified only in terms of, the 'higher'. This, at least, is what Comte himself seems sometimes (although, to be fair, not always) to have meant when he talked in such phrases as sociology 'completing our contemplation of reality' or the 'systematization of biological science which sociology alone can effect', and it is likewise what some of his successors seem to mean when they talk of a 'general sociological theory' of which the theories of the specialised social sciences are to be viewed as special cases. The error in this is to draw from the self-evident sense in which social systems comprehend all others the implication that the relationship of explanans to explanandum operates in the opposite direction to that in which it actually does. If there are lawlike generalisations (and why should there not be?) linking logically unconnected properties of social systems, their theoretical justification must be sought not from above but from below. They do not vindicate lawlike generalisations of other kinds, but call to be vindicated by them. If there is a science which stands to human history as pure to applied, it is not the science of social systems as such, but the science which Comte tried to bypass—psychology. Comte, in other words, should be stood on his head.

It may be that no one, not even the most committed disciple of Durkheim or Comte, wishes actually to question that the assertion that the subject-matter of sociology is social systems is not a denial that its subject-matter is still the behaviour of individual human beings. Indeed, it is often remarked that the so-called doctrine of 'methodological individualism' is in this sense trivially true. But if it is, then it is all the more remarkable that so many sociological writers should in practice have written as though it were not, or that they should at any rate have failed to draw the conclusion that sociology cannot be autonomous in the sense that Comte, and subsequently Durkheim, wished to maintain. For when we talk of the properties of social systems as the variables of the kind with which sociologists deal, we are still talking about individual beliefs

[1] Herbert Spencer, *The Study of Sociology* (1873), p. 350.

and actions; we are not attributing beliefs or actions to anyone or anything other than individual men and women; and even those who suggest that there are laws about social systems which are not derivable from laws about individuals cannot claim that a social system is an entity of which beliefs and actions are directly predicable. Whatever sociologists, anthropologists or historians may hold to be the constituents of social systems—whether institutions, or roles, or norms and sanctions, or actual social relations in the sense of Radcliffe-Brown, or forms of social relations in the sense of Lévi-Strauss—they are still dealing with the behaviour of persons towards each other. This is not to say that statements about a social system can always be translated into statements about designated individuals: a society's language, to take the example most commonly invoked, is more than the vocabulary and syntax of Messrs $A, B \ldots Z$. But at the same time, it is only by individual persons that language is used, and only upon their uses of it that any assertion made about it by the observer can be based. Whatever view, therefore, is to be taken of the several disputes between 'individualists' and 'holists', whether the issue between them is the reducibility of concepts or the reducibility of laws, the sense in which social systems can be claimed to be more than the sum of their constituent members is not the same as that in which (at the level below) a statement about the behaviour or properties of an organism can be claimed to be more than a statement about the sum of its physiological parts. To explain the origins and workings of social systems is to explain the thoughts and actions of men. Such explanations, to be sure, will depend to a large degree on the properties of those social systems of which the individual is a member. Durkheim's dictum that 'les phénomènes sociaux prennent naissance non dans l'individu mais dans le groupe' is entirely correct if it is understood to mean, in our contemporary jargon, that very little of social behaviour can satisfactorily be explained in terms of variables endogenous to the personality system itself. But once again, whether the properties of social systems are taken as the dependent or the independent variable, when we are talking of the properties of social systems (as distinct from the ecological properties of their environment) we are talking of what individual human beings may be shown to think, say and do.

Now there is nothing to prevent us, if we wish, from classifying the sciences in terms of independent instead of dependent variables. Once, indeed, we were so fortunate as to have general and well-confirmed causal laws, you could say that it would merely be a matter of looking at the same thing from the other end. From such a viewpoint, sociology becomes the science of whatever is explained by variations in the properties of social systems, just as astrology is the science of whatever is explained by the conjunctions of the stars. But how useful a demarcation does this yield? It is possible that a researcher may stumble on the fact that what he thought was the cause of one thing is in fact the cause of another, or, more deliberately, that he may make an interesting discovery by looking about for facts that will fit his model rather than a model that will fit his facts: attempts by economists and demographers to fit stochastic process models to the statistics of income distribution or occupational mobility, furnish perfectly respectable examples. But this is not an adequate basis for demarcating the different social sciences. Such questions as 'what are the consequences of industrialisation?' or 'what will result from a change in the traditional rules of sexual morality?' are admittedly not meaningless: important decisions of social policy may depend on the answers to them. But they are questions to which no single and clearly defined answer is available precisely because so much is involved in accounting for the behaviour of the dependent variables. Once we recognise that all our talk about the properties of social systems is still talk about individual behaviour, it becomes apparent once again that to search for social laws in the sense of one-to-one correspondence between specified properties of social systems as causes and whatever other kinds of behaviour are observed to covary with them as effects is to turn the normal procedure of explaining behaviour back to front.

If, accordingly, we follow the more natural course of demarcating academic subjects in terms of the categories of dependent variables which they seek to subsume under some set of connected, disconfirmable laws, we shall want to say that sociology is the science of social systems in the sense that its laws explain how social systems behave. But this is still unsatisfactory. The 'behaviour of social systems' covers individual beliefs and actions of such different kinds that some further classification is immediately necessary. To account for any specified property of a social system requires that the relevant category of human behaviour and institutions is identified and linked to the antecedent conditions by reference to which its occurrence could in principle have been predicted. This requirement both explains and justifies the development of the specialised social sciences such as criminology, economics, demography, political science and the rest. It is not a coincidence that Smith, Malthus and Bentham, whom I cited as having made more important contributions to the scientific study of social institutions and behaviour than Comte, should be able readily to be assigned to specialised disciplines in a way that Comte cannot. It is natural to say that Smith contributed to economics, Malthus to demography and Bentham to jurisprudence because of the value of the attempts which they made to explain respectively markets, populations and the operations of the criminal law. We may label them all sociologists if we choose. But what will the label signify? The choice is effectively put by Hobhouse in an encyclopaedia article on 'Sociology' which he wrote in 1920: 'In a wider sense, sociology may be taken to cover the whole body of sociological specialisms. In a narrower sense it is itself a specialism, having as its object the discovery of the connecting links between other specialisms'.[1] But the first alternative, if it does not simply make sociology synonymous with the sciences of man in total, makes it then indistinguishable from anthropology and/or history; and the second alternative merely makes it an anthology drawn from the specialised social sciences, since the 'connecting links' are only discovered by a demonstration that among the independent variables needed to explain the subject-matter of one social science there are almost always included some of those which belong to one or more of the others. From either viewpoint, it is equally implausible—although almost universally done—to speak of sociology as though it were itself a distinctive social science co-ordinate with economics, demography, political science and all the other established 'specialisms'.

A defence of the autonomy of sociology on the grounds that it is the science of social systems is thus misconceived for the simple reason that there are not and cannot be laws of social systems as such. Sociology (together with history and anthropology) is a consumer of laws, not a producer of them. 'Sociological' laws can only be the laws of such specialised social sciences as may be defined in terms of one distinguishable category of collective behaviour which is shown to vary consistently in accordance with a specified range of necessary and sufficient conditions. To be sure, any individual action may be viewed from a number of different aspects. There are few items of human behaviour, even the simplest, which are exclusively economic or religious or political or what you will, and the explanation of any particular item of sequence of behaviour is likely, as I have just remarked, to invoke independent variables of several different kinds. But this is to say no more than that the social sciences are all, in the late Professor Pantin's term, 'unrestricted' sciences.[2] The economist or political scientist, in other words, is in the same situation as the geologist. He is not dealing with a closed and complete system of laws

---

[1] Reprinted in *Sociology and Philosophy* (ed. Ginsberg, 1966), p. 27.
[2] C. F. A. Pantin, *The Relations between the Sciences* (1968), ch. 1.

within which he can deductively predict or retrodict the class of occurrences in which he is interested (nor, incidentally, is he any better able
to conduct his own experiments). Instead, he must be prepared to draw
on any adjacent discipline, from meteorology to population genetics,
which will in fact help him to account in retrospect for what is puzzling
him. The economist seeking to explain variations in the price of food-
stuffs or the political scientist seeking to explain the results of parliamentary elections are both looking for whatever set of antecedent conditions
of whatever kind will in context do the job which they want done.
Economics is one sort of applied psychology just as geology is one sort of
applied physics; and since the history of the British (or any other)
economy, just like the history of the Carmarthenshire (or any other)
plateaux, is a complicated business, the researcher who chooses things
of this kind as his subject-matter must take help from wherever he can
find it.

Sociology, in fact, is without laws in a double sense. Not only are there
no laws of social systems as such because, in the words of Mill, 'the mode
of production of all social phenomena is one great case of intermixture
of laws'.[1] In addition, there is a sense in which no social science, and
indeed no biological science, however demarcated, can have laws of its
own any more than geology can. This derives from their congenital status
as historical sciences, and it is perhaps best brought out in the analogy
which has been drawn by Professor Smart between biology and radio-
engineering: 'From a logical point of view,' says Smart, 'biology is
related to physics and chemistry in the way in which radio-engineering
is related to the theory of electromagnetism etc. . . . Just as the radio-
engineer used physics to explain why a circuit with a certain wiring
diagram behaves as it does, so the biologist uses physics and chemistry to
explain why organisms or parts of organisms (e.g. cell-nuclei), with a
certain natural-history description, behave as they do. . . . So while,
roughly speaking, radio-engineering is physics plus wiring diagrams,
biology is physics and chemistry plus natural history.'[2] The applicability
of the analogy to sociology is obvious. It should not be pressed too hard,
since the reducibility of biology to biochemistry and biophysics is such a
different matter from the reducibility of sociology and the special social
sciences to psychology. But just as biology can be described as physics
and chemistry plus natural history, so can sociology be described as
psychology and ethology plus social history. This does not, of course,

[1] *System of Logic* (1843), VI, ix, 2.
[2] J. J. C. Smart, *Philosophy and Scientific Realism* (1963), p. 57.

imply that social behaviour cannot be studied scientifically, any more than this could be said of radio-engineering. But it does imply that any attempt to axiomatise sociological theory will be mistaken from the outset, and that a distinction between sociology, anthropology and history will have meaning only in terms of incidental differences of technique.

In practice, although Smart's argument is perfectly sound, it is probably useful to continue to talk about 'laws' in psychology and the specialised social sciences, not because it is not demonstrable that there can never be laws in this field which will stand comparison with the laws of chemistry and physics but because it is important to make the further distinction, stressed by Mill and many others since, between 'laws' in a somewhat looser sense and empirical generalisations. It is possible that sociologists (or anthropologists or historians) may discover any number of consistent correlations of the form 'whenever X, then Y' where X and Y are logically distinct properties of some sub-class of social systems. But it would be misleading to describe them as laws even in the loose sense unless it can also be asserted both that the connection between X and Y is causal and also that this connection can be fairly precisely formulated;[1] and once this is so, then the empirical generalisation becomes a causal 'law' within the specialised social science to which Y is to be assigned. These things may be said to be no more than terminological conventions.[2] But the usefulness of such conventions is that they can preserve important distinctions of substance. The quasi-universal propositions of 'if . . . then' form for which the specialised social sciences are searching do not simply assert a concomitance of X and Y, however statistically significant; they assert that given a specified background of necessary conditions X will be sufficient for the occurrence of Y. It is perfectly true that no set of laws of this kind will have the closure and completeness of the related sets of laws of classical physical theory. But it seems unnecessarily stringent to deny them the title of 'laws' altogether because they can only, in Smart's sense, be applications of the laws of physics and chemistry. Perhaps it is true that in principle (whatever that is worth) the whole of chemistry, physiology, biology and social science

---

[1] I make no attempt to say what exactly is meant by 'causal', except that it is to be taken not in a restricted or 'mechanistic' sense but a sense broad enough to include interdependence or feedback, and not merely links-in-a-chain.

[2] In actual usage, the situation is doubly confused, since some empirical generalisations in the natural sciences have been accepted as 'laws', such as Galileo's, Kepler's and Boyle's laws, before they have received 'theoretical grounding' (Carl G. Hempel, *Philosophy of Natural Science* (1966), p. 58), and some social scientists still disagree completely with others about what is meant by 'law' in science in general (cf. e.g. J. Beattie, *Other Cultures* (1966), pp. 45–6, taking issue with Radcliffe-Brown).

could be described in terms of the application of laws governing the behaviour of the elementary particles; but that is not of the smallest interest to the practising social scientist even of the most physicalist bent of mind. The social scientist is concerned to apply, and perhaps discover, the putative 'laws' of human behaviour in the various kinds of social context in which it may be observed. As long as there is an implicit claim that first, there is a causal connection between the variable designated as dependent and the antecedent conditions specified, and second, this claim is (at least within fairly broad limits) generalisable,[1] then it is, I think, reasonable to speak not only of a distinctive discipline to which, according to the dependent variable in question, this proposition may be assigned but in addition to speak of the proposition as a (provisional) law.

Two objections of a different kind, however, might be raised at this point against my argument that although the specialised social sciences may be said to be autonomous in a limited sense, 'sociology' itself can not. The first of these is argued by Professor Alex Inkeles in a recent introductory textbook: 'If', says Inkeles, 'the long continuing process of differentiation and specialisation in scholarship were to go so far that all the sub-fields of sociology came to be established as separate disciplines, would sociology then cease to exist as a discipline in its own right? We can properly say 'no' only if we can point to a distinctive subject-matter which would remain for sociology. Happily we can. Indeed . . . we may propose several distinctive subject-matters to which sociology could still lay claim. They are, in decreasing order of size and complexity: societies, institutions and social relationships.'[2] Now it is true that there are many areas of social behaviour which have not yet been appropriated by any specialism which could claim to be 'a discipline in its own right'. But in recognising what is implied by the claims of those specialisms which *have* succeeded in establishing themselves, Inkeles is driven back onto precisely the sort of defence of the alleged autonomy of sociology which I am concerned to criticise. His first two suggested subject-matters, societies and institutions, cannot have laws of their own for reasons which I hope are by now clear, and so far from being the exclusive subject-matter of a single specialism, they are common at once to history-cum-anthropology and to the specialised social sciences dealing with their selected

---

It is worth remembering that, for example, Boyle's Law breaks down over certain temperatures and Galileo's Law over distances not negligible by comparison with the radius of the earth; which perhaps offers some (although not much) comfort to social scientists concerned about the limited scope and precision of their few non-vacuous generalisations.

[2] A. Inkeles, *What is Sociology?* (1964), p. 13.

sub-classes. There is perhaps a sense in which social relationships could be said to belong to a science of their own in a way that societies and institutions, although made up of combinations of social relationships, do not, and that is the sense in which social relationships belong to psychology, suitably defined. But this is not at all the point that Inkeles wishes to make. It is a perfectly valid point, as I shall hope to make clearer in the following section. But so far from helping to maintain the autonomy of sociology as a specialism, it reinforces the quite different distinction between first, sociology, anthropology and history taken together, second, the specialised social sciences defined in terms of their distinctive dependent variables, and third, psychology as the science of individual human behaviour on which all the social sciences must be presumed to depend.

The second objection which might be raised is to say that by attempting to assimilate both sociology and anthropology to history I am overriding an important difference of a kind which, although more a difference of method than of subject matter, nevertheless gives sociology a status of its own. This is the distinction between the explanation of unique and particular narrative sequences of the kind with which historians are customarily concerned, and the explanation of large-scale regularities, which are the province of sociologists (and perhaps anthropologists). Now it is certainly true that to try to explain why Caesar crossed the Rubicon is a different sort of exercise from trying to explain why all industrial societies have sectional conflicts over the distribution of surplus resources. But the difference applies within sciences just as much as between them. Once given a well-tested body of theoretical knowledge connecting empirically disconfirmable sets of laws, it may be invoked either, on the one hand, to explain a unique event by showing it to follow from a specified conjunction of antecedent conditions or, on the other, to justify an observed regularity for which quasi-universal generalisability has been claimed. It is merely a matter of what procedure is appropriate to the question the investigator has chosen to ask. It was at one time fashionable to distinguish all the natural from all the physical sciences in these terms. But a physical scientist may be concerned to account for a unique event or sequence, just as a social scientist may be concerned to account for a consistently confirmed generalisation. To claim that sociology is the 'nomothetic' where history is merely the 'idiographic' science of man is therefore doubly mistaken. It confuses an intra-disciplinary with an inter-disciplinary difference of method; and it presumes once again that the regularities which sociologists may discover will be causal laws belonging to some autonomous discipline distinct from the specialised social sciences defined in terms of their own dependent variables. The distinction between 'idiographic' and 'nomothetic' explanation does have its usefulness; but this usefulness does not lie in its furnishing a criterion for distinguishing a 'history' without laws from a 'sociology' with them.

Once it is clearly recognised that for all these reasons sociology cannot be more than an application, or in Mill's term an 'intermixture', of the specialised social sciences (which are applications of psychology in their turn), it becomes easier to understand why the attempt to define it in terms of what self-styled sociologists do yields so diverse and confusing a reply. It is simply a result of the fact that 'sociology' is a residual term. Once it is not being used generically to cover all the specialised social sciences, it becomes a label most readily applied either to those empirical generalisations which cannot yet be effectively related to the causal laws of a specialised discipline, or else to one of Mill's cases of 'intermixture' where it so happens, for reasons of academic convention, that the explanandum is not within a category such as to be more naturally labelled 'anthropology' or 'history'. If we are puzzled how it happens that certain sorts of research into human behaviour are typically called 'sociology' by practitioners and laymen alike, we shall discover on investigation that it tends to be for one or other of five broad and sometimes overlapping reasons: first, because there is not (or not yet) a specialised social science to which it can be assigned;[1] second, because it is too nearly contemporary, or contains too little narrative, to be easily called 'history';[2] third, because it concerns too large and highly developed a community or society for the 'anthropological' method of participant–observation to be appropriate to it; fourth, because it is formulated at so high a level of generality that its empirical content is in doubt; fifth, because it is 'applied' in the still further sense of being concerned with the diagnosis and if possible the cure of some recognised social ill.

In the last two of these categories, 'sociology' becomes more or less synonymous with the philosophy of history on one side and practical social administration on the other. But the other three categories do provide the answer to the question how it comes about that 'sociology' is talked of as though it were a special social science on its own. It is, of course, perfectly possible that the work done under the label of sociology

---

[1] The study of hierarchies of rank in human societies is a good example of a specialised topic which is still on the borderline: see chapter 4, below.

[2] Cf. e.g. chapters 5 and 6, below.

will be just as interesting and important as that done under the label of history, anthropology or one of the specialised social sciences. But once the impossibility of an autonomous science of social systems has been recognised, it becomes easier not only to understand why this seems so seldom to be the case, but at the same time to account for those apparent failings of academic sociology on which its critics most frequently pass censure—the unconvincingness of its claims to 'theory'; the ambiguity of 'sociological' as a descriptive (or sometimes evaluative) term; its propensity to jargon; and its preoccupation with questions which seem to be formulated in a way which makes them incapable of decisive answer.

The unconvincingness of its claim to 'theory' is a natural consequence of the impossibility of sociological laws. Very different things may, of course, be meant by the terms 'theory' and 'theoretical', and sociologists are by no means alone in using them in unclear and conflicting senses. But if we may take a theory to be a set of connected, disconfirmable laws in terms of which a defined category of explananda can be shown to follow from specified initial conditions, it becomes clear that in the writings of many sociologists the term is grossly abused. It may be used to mean empirical generalisation, or taxonomy, or generalised description, or quantification, or extrapolation to a hypothetical limiting case, or simply explanation in a sense not further defined; and while all these have their uses, it is hard to resist the conclusion that the tendency of sociologists to talk of them as 'theory' is itself a further symptom of the lack of 'sociological' laws of such a kind as would constitute a 'theory of social systems' in the proper sense.

The claim that there is, or will be, a 'general theory' in sociology is associated particularly with the work of Professor Talcott Parsons and his followers. But it rests on so blatant a confusion of explanation with taxonomy as to make it puzzling that it should be taken as seriously as it has. It is not that Parsons has lacked critics. To take only two of the most distinguished, his colleague Professor Homans has credited Parsons's work with 'every virtue except that of explaining anything';[1] and Professor Max Black, when invited as a philosopher to express his views on Parsons's 'social theory' was forced to record his 'dismay at the conceptual confusion which in my judgement pervades the entire structure'.[2] But

---

[1] G. C. Homans, *Social Behaviour* (1961), p. 10.

[2] 'Some Questions about Parsons' Theories', in Max Black (ed.), *The Social Theories of Talcott Parsons* (1961), p. 288. Black's criticisms are, if anything, confirmed by Parsons's rejoinder (*ibid.* pp. 311–63).

although Parsons may seem to communicate to some of his readers a sense of spurious intellectual achievement by inventing some abstruse-looking labels, attaching them where they belong by definition, and then misnaming the operation 'analysis',[1] his claims still cannot be dismissed quite so quickly. The real answer to the puzzle is that such claims can continue to seem plausible to the extent that it is not clearly understood why there can be no laws of social systems as such.

There is, after all, nothing wrong with taxonomy. It is not to be confused with explanation, but it is in some form a necessary preliminary to it. By attempting a very general taxonomy of social behaviour, Parsons has brought together a number of ideas which, however obvious in themselves, may in this form help other investigators to ask specific questions about a society or institution and its development which have a genuine empirical content and might otherwise not have occurred to them. The exercise is misleading, however, because Parsons fails to disavow the implication that his taxonomy is in itself of explanatory value, rather than leaving, as it does, the social institutions and behaviour classified in terms of it still to be explained in any way at all. The result is that he gives the quite erroneous impression that if and when such explanations *are* produced, they somehow exemplify or contribute to 'general sociological theory'; and although this may serve to minister to the wish of practising sociologists to feel that they are united in the pursuit of a common goal analogous to the great synthesising achievements of natural science, it has, unfortunately, no other justification. Instead, it is likely, as much of Comte's writing has done, to distract attention from the proper foundations of sociological explanation in the laws by which individual thoughts and actions of different kinds are governed. It is only fair to Parsons, as to Comte, to say that he sometimes appears to recognise this.[2] But this recognition is never followed up. Only when the logic of sociological explanation has been spelt out in a very much more rigorous manner than Parsons ever (as far as I am aware) attempts, does it become possible to see both why his claims are so misleading and why nonetheless they have had such influence as they have.

At the same time, it will become easier to account for the ambiguity

---

[1] For a characteristic misuse of 'analysis' and 'theory' taken from one of Parsons's most recent books, cf. *Societies* (1966), pp. 111–12: 'In the area of theory, there has now been sufficient advance so that most of the difficulties of Weber's 'type atomism' can be avoided. To a much greater degree, variability can now be analysed as a function of different combinations of the same analytically defined components.'

[2] See his *Essays in Sociological Theory* (rev. ed., 1954), p. 233: 'The ultimate foundations of such a theory must certainly be derived from the science of psychology.'

MAGDALEN COLLEGE LIBRARY

not merely of 'theory' but of 'sociological' itself. The term is (naturally enough) often used by self-styled sociologists, and it is found with perhaps the greatest frequency in the review columns of the academic sociological journals, where it is common to see books assessed for the degree to which they qualify for the epithet 'sociological' in an evidently commendatory sense. Once again there is nothing which is necessarily mistaken in this. Indeed, where the charge that a book is 'un-sociological' means that its author has neglected such broader causes of a demographic, or economic, or cultural kind as would have helped him to a better explanation of what he is writing about, then it has a wholly respectable evaluative use, much as 'un-historical' can have. The ambiguity arises, however, because 'sociological' is often so used as to imply not merely that a piece of work does or does not take account of the multifarious causes of a 'social' kind by which a particular sequence of events may have been influenced, but also that there is something distinctive in method or doctrine about a 'sociological' approach. But as soon as we ask in what this distinctiveness lies, the answer is as elusive as ever. The term may, in context, be used to mean that there is a lack of a distinctive method as, for example, when a generalisation about a country or a region is put forward without any reference to the criteria of statistical sampling; or it may mean that there is a neglect of some appropriate doctrine, as when social history in the manner of, say, G. M. Trevelyan is dismissed for its neglect of economic and technological causes. But neither of these is a vindication of the claim that sociology is an academic subject of its own. They mean merely that historical explanation is not so simple a matter as some of its practitioners have thought. If a historian or anthropologist ought to have had recourse to the methods of statistical sampling or the doctrines of economic theory, it is perfectly fair to criticise him on those grounds. But it is misleading to frame the criticism in such terms as to imply that he has neglected the findings of a specialism called sociology in the way that someone who proferred an explanation of the heating of a gas under pressure without reference to molecular movement could be said to be neglecting the findings of a specialism called thermodynamics.

The point is, perhaps, a rather trivial one; but both it and the related point about 'jargon' are symptoms of the misconception which I am concerned to correct. The issue of jargon, it might be said, is a matter purely of style and not of substance: the elegance or inelegance of the technical vocabulary of a subject should have nothing to do with the validity or importance of its discoveries. But inspection of the charges levelled

18

against sociologists' jargon does not so much demonstrate that writers concerned with the explanation of social behaviour write less well than other people as confirm that 'sociology' is a residual label. The term 'jargon' is in practice applied only to those 'sociological' writings which aspire to a greater precision and generality than the language of common sense but have not so far succeeded in this as to establish themselves within a specialised social science which has to be acknowledged as such. The ostensible question of style has really nothing to do with it. Much of the language of economics, or demography, or linguistics, or psychological medicine, is, like much of the language of the physical sciences'and indeed of philosophy, just as cumbrous and unpleasing to the ear as the language of 'sociology'. The reasons why the charge of jargon is so often levelled against an author such as Parsons is not that his style is ugly or even that it is obscure but that it is redundant. It is 'jargon' because it cannot convincingly be claimed to belong either to the glossary of common literary terms or to a distinctive and rigorous specialism which can only account for its own dependent variables by employing neologisms. A sociological term like 'industrialisation' is not jargon because its descriptive use is so universally familiar and convenient; a sociological term like 'consumption function' is not jargon because, by contrast, it has a place in a reasonably well-tested generalisation belonging to a specialised social science. In between remain the terms which add nothing to the ordinary descriptive language of common sense but which cannot (or at any rate not yet) be justified by a demonstration that there is some dependent variable which with their help can at last be brought within the scope of a testable theory.

Of all English-speaking social scientists, the author who furnishes the best illustrations of this is perhaps Bentham. He was at least as prone to neologism as any sociologist of the present time, and the varying fate of his neologisms is instructive. It will be enough to cite three: 'international' has been so far vindicated by general use that it needs an effort of the imagination to think of it as a neologism at all; 'utility', as Bentham sought to adapt it, has been vindicated not in terms of his own would-be general psychology of pleasures and pains but in the specialised use given to it by Jevons and others in specifically economic theory; 'epistemo-threptic' has been vindicated neither by common descriptive usage nor by its application within a well-tested theory and has accordingly fallen into a deserved oblivion. 'Jargon', in other words, is merely technical language which is unsuccessful, or at least unproven; and sociologists are accused of it more often than others merely because once their technical language

MAGDALEN COLLEGE LIBRARY
LIBRARY
COLLEGE

does succeed in establishing itself it is unlikely to continue to be called sociology. Either, like 'liberalism, 'charisma' or 'taboo', it will cease to be regarded as technical at all, or, like 'matrilocal', 'factor price' and 'age-specific fertility' it will be acknowledged to belong to a specialism sufficiently successful to be allowed to use what language it likes.

The propensity to jargon is linked in turn to the final failing which I listed—sociology's apparent preoccupation with questions incapable of decisive answer. This is not in itself a reason to be dismissive of it. It is sometimes difficult in the physical as well as the social sciences to see how a question might be decisively answered either because of the impossibility of designing a crucial experiment or collecting evidence equivalent to it or because the distinction between an empirical and logical question is not always so easy as it seems. In sociology, however, the amount of literature concerned with questions not directly answerable in the terms in which they are put seems often to spring from a determination to preserve, at whatever cost, a distinctive subject-matter of some sort or other. Thus it has been claimed that the 'central problem' of sociology is the 'problem of social order'[1]—in other words, the problem of how society persists at all. But what sort of question is this? It is not, one must suppose, unanswerable. But neither is it answerable in terms of the short list of 'sociological' causes or conditions which the form of the question appears to presuppose. Not only is it a historical question in the sense that the explanation of any particular instance of order or disorder, stability or change requires a narrative which will be very different from case to case, but to the extent that it is capable of a general answer it will be derivable not from any laws about society but from laws of a psychological and biological kind by reference to which the individual actions which bring about a particular social state can be shown to follow from specified genetic and environmental conditions. Few, however, of the answers debated in the sociological literature are of this kind. On the contrary, the argument tends to be couched in terms of the sweeping claims of one or more ostensibly exclusive rivals: social order is to be explained either by 'value-consensus' or by 'coercion'; social change is to be explained either by 'conflict theory' or by 'functional adaptation'. These claims are not merely inconclusive but misconceived. In the first place, they are often so framed as not to be susceptible to empirical refutation at all; and in the second, where they are, they are often so used as to conceal rather than to emphasise that one such 'theory' may in fact be perfectly compatible with another.

[1] Percy S. Cohen, *Modern Social Theory* (1968), p. 16.

At this point, it is no defence to say that it may not matter that an argument is either of uncertain empirical status or even demonstrably not empirical at all. It is true that this applies to the fundamental proposition of Newton's general theory as well as of Keynes's. But the test of a theory's capacity for explanation lies in the relation of its non-empirical to its empirical content, and it is here that 'sociological theory' is so often exposed as factitious.[1] There might, from a different standpoint altogether, be a justification for it of another kind, since much of traditional 'political theory' may be found illuminating even if it is not and does not pretend to be directly testable against the evidence in the manner of empirical science. But this is irrelevant to the present argument, if only because it is the typical claim of sociologists from Comte to the present to have superseded the traditional political theorists by substituting science for philosophy. Even if, therefore, there is still enlightenment to be derived from a reading of Hobbes or Burke, this will not serve to justify the current disputes among sociologists between the partisans of consensus and the partisans of conflict. These disputes are justifiable only to the extent that the disputants can specify what sort of evidence—even if the evidence itself is not presently available—would disconfirm their respective claims. But there is no evidence which can demonstrate that human society is 'fundamentally based' on either conflict or consensus. A 'theory of conflict' which claims scientific status, as can the mathematical theory of games in some of its applications, will recognise the fact of consensus as well,[2] just as a 'theory of functional adaptation', if such a thing can be adequately formulated beyond the confines of biology, will incorporate a recognition of the 'function' of conflict. To retain the 'problem of social order' and its obverse the 'theory of social change' as the distinctive concern of sociologists risks the maintenance of their academic autonomy at the price of their claims to empirical science.

C. Wright Mills, in a well-known polemical essay published in 1959, criticised the tendency of sociologists to concentrate their efforts at one or other of the two opposite poles which he called 'grand theory' and

---

[1] Cf. e.g. the criticism of the so-called 'theory of status consistency' in chapter 7, below. The same can, of course apply to 'theories' formulated within the specialised social sciences: cf. e.g. David Easton, *The Political System* (1953) and *A Framework for Political Analysis* (1965), and the effective dismissal of the second by Ralf Dahrendorf, *Essays in the Theory of Society* (1968), pp. 142–4.

[2] Cf. the discussion of one topic in games theory, and its relation to a traditional problem of political philosophy, in chapter 11, below (and for some interesting empirical work, A. Rapoport and A. M. Chammah, *Prisoner's Dilemma* (1965)).

'abstracted empiricism',[1] and Professor T. H. Marshall drew attention to it likewise a decade before when he spoke of sociologists choosing either 'the way to the stars' or 'the way into the sands'.[2] It would no doubt be an exaggeration to suggest that all the work being done either then or now in departments or institutes of sociology could be assigned to either the one category or the other. But there is certainly substance to the charge; and the tendency, so far from being a matter for surprise, could be confidently predicted on the basis of the argument I have been advancing here. It arises partly because the label 'sociology' tends to attach to research which is either too sweeping or too incoherent to be called anything else, and partly because sociologists themselves tend to mark out a distinctive area of their own by selecting topics for study which not only lie outside the province of any specialised social science but in addition are either too general or too apparently trivial to be already covered by anthropologists or historians. This will not necessarily turn out to be a mistake: generalisation is a perfectly proper pursuit, and what is trivial in the view of one person may turn out to lead to an important discovery in the work of another. But the quest for a distinctive 'socio-logical' subject-matter combined with a quest for general laws can only yield propositions so hedged about with *ceteris paribus* clauses as to defeat their original purpose. If a hostile critic asks what interesting discoveries twentieth-century sociology can claim to its credit, it will be no use looking for laws or even empirical generalisations which will satisfy him. The best answer will be to point to some much more specific finding such as Max Weber's discovery (since drastically modified) of the relation of the Protestant ethic to the evolution of European capitalism, or Evans-Pritchard's discovery of the role of the feud in the political and social system of the Nuer. But these are in no sense discoveries of either theories or laws such as the 'grand theorists' or 'abstracted empiricists' are ostensibly looking for. On the contrary, they illustrate how difficult it is to draw a distinction between sociology or anthropology on one side and history on the other. Indeed, it may be relevant to notice that Evans-Pritchard himself is one of the most emphatic proponents of the view that studies such as his should be classified with history and not with a 'natural science of society' such as was hopefully proclaimed by Radcliffe-Brown.

It may well be that the uncertainty over the nature and place of

---

[1] *The Sociological Imagination*, chs. 2 and 3.
[2] In an Inaugural Lecture delivered in 1946 and reprinted in *Sociology at the Crossroads and Other Essays* (1963), p. 14.

sociology among both its practitioners and its critics will not continue for very long. The anthropologists, after all, were at one time at least as divided and uncertain as the sociologists are now: the gulf between grand theorists and abstracted empiricists was at least as wide, and their concerns ranged as indiscriminately from extravagant philosophies of history to the haphazard accumulation of physical-anthropological detail. But they have succeeded, whatever the reasons, more quickly than the sociologists have done in channelling their efforts in one or other of the two viable directions—either, that is, towards careful studies of selected individual societies from what we may call the historian's point of view or towards contributions to the specialisms of language, kinship, religion, law, or political organisation out of which adequate cross-cultural generalisations may eventually be expected to emerge. Perhaps, therefore, in a century from now the sociological journals of today will look as eccentric, superficial and confused as the early issues of the *Anthropological Review* or *Journal of the Royal Anthropological Society* look to us now. Or even if the parallel with the anthropologists cannot be too closely drawn, it may at least be reasonable to suppose that as the social sciences progress the relations between them will become steadily less controversial. Yet it would be rash to regard this happy state of affairs as so imminent and inevitable that the natural course of research can be left to bring it about. As I observed at the beginning, these controversies assume so much importance in the sciences of man precisely because the course of research can be decisively determined for better or worse by the answers which are given to them. The question 'what is sociology?', put that way, is perhaps not particularly helpful. But the question which, I suggest, can usefully be put in its stead is rather: is there any distinction which needs to be drawn among the sciences of man beyond the distinction between first, psychology, second, the specialised social sciences, and third, sociology, anthropology and history taken together?

II

It will be evident from what I have said so far that I believe this question should be answered in the negative. But to justify this answer, I shall have to say something more not only about how 'psychology' is to be defined for the purpose but also about the form which an adequate explanation of human social behaviour must take. To be sure, this second topic raises a host of long-standing and intractable philosophical controversies. But for the purposes of this paper, it is not necessary to be able to pretend to resolve them. It is true that philosophical problems arise in the sciences of man from which the sciences of nature are spared;[1] that as our behaviour becomes progressively better explicable our traditional vocabulary of human action requires increasingly to be modified;[2] and that even if the sciences of man are as value-free in principle as the sciences of nature, there is still an indissoluble connection between the judgements of value that we do all in fact make and our beliefs about society and the world. But it is an empirical matter how far human behaviour can actually be explained; and this will resolve itself independently of the philosophical debates which the results of empirical research will continue to provoke. The test of the demarcation of the sciences of man which I am defending, and of the model of explanation which I shall be suggesting to go with it, is whether or not it turns out to be justified by the future course of social-scientific enquiry. I do not believe that anyone is ever going to discover a system of 'sociological' laws of a Comtean kind which will not be either fallacious or trivial. But if someone does, then my case collapses at once, and no amount of *a priori* argument will build it up again.

Accordingly, it should be possible to sketch in outline at least how an adequate explanation of the phenomena with which sociologists concern themselves should be constructed, even if the stock of such explanations is so far exceedingly small and the stock of 'complete' explanations (whatever that may mean) non-existent. Whatever the philosophical difficulties which the concept of explanation raises, in the physical no less than the biological and the biological no less than the social sciences, it is still possible at least roughly to set out the conditions which a successful explanation must satisfy. It must identify the explanandum as a member of an appropriate class; it must link its occurrence to initial conditions from which events of that class are known to follow; it must specify these initial conditions, both necessary and sufficient; and it must account for the connection between these conditions and the explanandum and its class in terms of laws whose connection to yet other laws constitutes the 'theory' which gives the explanation its grounding. It does not follow from this that explicability entails predictability in actual practice. Not only can we sometimes predict although we cannot explain: innumerable cures in medicine have been successfully achieved under these conditions,

---

[1] Cf. chapters 8–10, below.

[2] As is forcefully brought out by Isaiah Berlin in the 'Introduction' to *Four Essays on Liberty* (1969), pp. x–xii; what is less certain is how far the entrenchment of our traditional vocabulary of responsibility and free will is, as Berlin suggests, evidence for its validity.

to say nothing of success in forecasting the weather by the feeling in one's bones. In addition, we can often explain an event such as the outcome of a battle or the disintegration of an aeroplane in mid-air which we could not possibly have predicted. But both these are merely the reflection of our ignorance: there *is* an explanation connecting the weather with the feeling in my bones, did I but know it; and had I known enough about the state of the aeroplane (which I could not) then I *would* have detected metal fatigue before the appearance of the crack which caused it to disintegrate. 'Predictability in principle', which is rightly said to be logically tied to scientific explanation, is sufficiently vindicated by explicability in retrospect. The important question for the theorist (as opposed to the practical reformer) is not 'to what forecasts can we commit ourselves?' but 'what sort of initial conditions and laws will properly account for what can already be observed?'

In answering this question, it is sometimes difficult, despite all the warnings of philosophers of science, not to confuse the actual sequence of research with its justification. A discovery may, as I have remarked already, be arrived at as well from one end as the other, and there is no reason to suppose that any sociologist, anthropologist or historian need ever follow in practice the purely logical steps in terms of which his inquiry is described by the philosophers of science. But if this caveat is properly heeded, an exposition of social-scientific explanation can safely begin at the point where the researcher is confronted with something for which he is unable to account to his satisfaction. Even before this point has been reached, there is already an elaborate process of enquiry which must take place if his explanandum is to be identified at all. Observation is not the simple matter that crude empiricism used to make out, and no philosopher of science would nowadays deny that the description of what requires to be explained is itself a 'theory-laden' affair: to identify a bodily movement as a salute rather than a wave, threat or benediction is already to start explaining its occurrence. But within what is sometimes called his 'paradigm', the sociologist may be taken as starting from the observation of a phenomenon which he will initially describe in 'theory-laden' but at this stage uncontroversial terms: an economic depression, a religious creed, a parliamentary election, a rising (or falling) birth-rate, a tribal rebellion, or what you will. His 'observation', taken literally, may be in any one of various forms: it may be by heresay or the study of written records just as much as by participant-observation, in the same way that the observations of the physical scientist may consist in graphs or pointer readings just as much as the evidence of his own eyes. But whatever the nature of the evidence he may be using in the given case, the sociologist will start from an observation which he believes to be reliable and which, if it is, any competent fellow-observer would be willing to describe in equivalent terms.

Explanation, however, only gets fully under way with the formulation of some empirical generalisation appropriate to the explanandum: that is, an empirical generalisation in which the explanandum is described and classified by reference to an aspect or property of it which can be shown to be consistently related to something else. This stage is discretionary in two ways. First, the choice of putative correlations is very wide—one researcher may wish to link to sunspots what another wishes to link to customs of child-rearing and a third to the teachings of the church—and only further research will enable the choice to be narrowed. Second, the notion of explanation presupposes the possibility of the *non*-occurrence of the explanandum, and there is such a multiplicity of antecedent necessary conditions of the explananda which I have listed that the number of contrasts to be drawn is almost unlimited: the investigator may be asking himself about remote constitutional origins, or about the long-term influences of geography and climate or about psychological predisposition or conditioning, or about very particular events immediately preceding the time of his inquiry. But neither of these considerations diminishes the objectivity of his research. He will have to set out the assumptions on which the particular contrast which he draws has been based; but these assumptions, and likewise the hypotheses which he goes on to frame on the basis of them, are all open to the scrutiny and test of any other researcher who chooses to challenge them.

It is possible that the explanandum will itself be an empirical generalisation already; and in these cases the distinction between 'nomothetic' and 'idiographic' may seem appropriate once again. But this difference does not affect the logic of social-scientific explanation any more than (as I argued earlier) it affects the classification of the social-scientific disciplines. Many social-scientific enquiries do in practice begin not with singular events but with empirical generalisations: the rate of suicide is higher among Protestants than Catholics; girls cluster closer, but to a higher mean, of reading ability than boys; the distribution of wealth is more unequal the larger the total social product; and many more. But they differ from 'unique' explananda only in that the contrast in the investigator's mind is already more clearly formulated on the strength of the findings which he takes for granted already. Generalisation is implicit in the explanation of 'singular' events just as much as in the explanation of observations already generalised. No singular event can even be described, let alone explained, except in terms of characteristics which it shares with others. It is only the combination of characteristics which is singular, and to proffer an explanation of it is necessarily to claim that its occurrence is in principle replicable. It is true that there is a difference of another kind between the attempt to formulate a generalisation with some implicit causal content and the attempt to select which of a number of quasi-causal generalisations already available will fit the particular case at hand: taken in this way, the nomothetic/idiographic distinction is, as we shall see in a moment, perfectly sensible. But in either case, explanation is achieved only where a particular kind of generalisation can be vindicated—one which links an identifiable category of observable conditions or events to one or more specified initial conditions. If (still without hazarding a definition of 'cause') we can claim that this link is broadly speaking causal, then the generalisation is a candidate for a 'law' in the sense which I have adopted in this paper; and if the claim that it is causal can in turn be justified by reference to other laws, then (and only then) shall we be able to talk about a 'theory'.

In practice, this schema will work out in a variety of different ways, as may be seen easily enough from the examples I have already used. If we consider a precise and universal relation supposed to have been discovered between distribution of wealth and size of total product,[1] it is clear that this would already amount to the provisional formulation of an economic law. This law would have to be connected to other laws, both ecological and psychological, such as would enable us to say *why* the size of the total product determines its distribution, and even then would be taking for granted a whole history of antecedent conditions of many different kinds. But in the absence of counter-examples not covered by a previously formulated exception-clause, economists could fairly claim to have discovered a law 'governing' the distribution of wealth, even if they could not be expected to list all of the assumed antecedent conditions and even if they had only a hazy idea of the supporting laws from which this putative law of theirs might be derivable. But the law in question could be held to deserve the name just as well as (to take Professor Hempel's example again) Boyle's law did before it received its 'theoretical grounding'.

In the same sort of way, the consistently different suicide rates of Protestants and Catholics (for which there is much evidence) might turn

---

[1] This is in actual fact implausible, but by no means entirely so: see e.g. M. D. Sahlins, *Social Stratification in Polynesia* (1958), and G. E. Lenski, *Power and Privilege* (1966).

out to deserve lawlike standing if they could be linked to some underlying generalisation which showed the connection between religious affiliation and propensity to suicide to be a causal one. Indeed, it is one of the most famous empirical generalisations in the literature of the social sciences because of Durkheim's attempt to link it to what is in fact (however reluctant Durkheim would be to have it so phrased) a presumptive psychological law governing this widespread and reasonably well definable phenomenon of individual human behaviour. But the example may also serve to illustrate the hazards of assuming too soon that what is, at best, a limited empirical generalisation is authentically causal and is not, on the contrary, a case of spurious correlation which will dissolve on the introduction of some other generalisation of a quite different kind. Perhaps the statistical records of Catholic countries underrepresent the deaths which ought in fact to be classed as suicides because of the moral and religious stigma which attaches to it; perhaps the Catholic priesthood are able by the invocation of overt religious sanctions effectively to instil in their parishioners a reluctance to commit the sin of *felo de se* ; perhaps a propensity to suicide is genetically transmitted within demographic isolates which happen, for quite other historical reasons, to be Protestant. One way, after all, of explaining an ostensibly causal generalisation is to explain it away.

On the other hand, let us suppose for convenience that my third example—the difference in reading ability between girls and boys—could be explained by showing that reading ability is a sex-linked characteristic genetically transmitted. This fact of human behaviour would then be subsumed in a single move under a body of connected laws which would furnish not only the link between specified initial conditions and the explanandum but also the theoretical grounding which would entitle us to regard the explanation as, for practical purposes, complete. The example is again a fanciful one. But there is no doubt that some aspects of human behaviour can be explained in this way by jumping, so to speak, two branches at a time down the tree of knowledge. The field of psychological medicine already furnishes a limited number of examples. It is, of course, possible that a genetic hypothesis of this kind should have been arrived at on purely statistical grounds by a researcher ignorant of the theoretical grounding provided by modern biology and its improved knowledge of the mechanisms of inheritance. But in this case, the situation would again be that of Boyle's law at the time of its discovery. If the hypothesis can be adequately tested against a sufficiency of evidence, and does not rule out anything which an already accepted theory requires us to hold, then we shall want to call it a (putatively causal) law even if the question 'why is it that these initial conditions yield the predicatable variations observed?' cannot yet be satisfactorily answered.

Now the three examples which I have used are all hypothetical, in the sense that although the problems are authentic the solutions have yet to be found. But this is a fair representation of the present situation of the sciences of man. There is no lack of interesting discoveries; however trivial the achievements of some of the 'abstracted empiricists', it would be absurd to deny that we know enormously more about forms of political organisation, rules of kinship, price fluctuations in a money economy, witchcraft and sorcery, the structure of language, patterns of child-rearing, or the symbolism of religious ritual than we did even a few decades ago. The lack is a lack of theories—that is, of connected sets of laws into whose framework our discoveries could be fitted.[1] As it is, where precise and sophisticated models have been constructed, they can seldom be satisfactorily matched to the observable facts, and where generalisations can be framed which take account of a reasonably broad range of observations they have to be so heavily qualified as to become increasingly unenlightening. In this situation, it is tempting to draw one or other of two opposing conclusions, of which both are mistaken. The first is to assume that it is simply a matter of refining such generalisations as we have until they turn into laws in the end. The second is to assume that the attempt at 'scientific' explanation must be misconceived from the outset, and to substitute 'understanding' in its place.

I shall not comment here on the controversies raised by this second conclusion except to say that it confuses explanation with the identification of what it is that requires to be explained. Because, to borrow the words of Marc Bloch, 'historical facts are in essence psychological facts', the discovery of such facts cannot but raise difficulties, both technical and theoretical, which neither the physical nor the biological scientist has to face. But it is possible to agree with almost all of what is said, for example, by Collingwood about the problem of establishing what exactly Plato or Napoleon did think, or say, or mean when they said it, without denying that it may be just as explicable in principle in terms of necessary and sufficient conditions as anything else. The mistake of Collingwood

[1] There are, as is to be expected, better examples within the specialised social sciences which have established themselves than within 'sociology' in particular. Some theories in economics, although they may not fit as close to the observed facts as one might wish, still seem sufficiently precisely formulated and plausibly related to underlying psychological assumptions, that the term is not altogether misplaced.

and those who think like him is to suppose that to ascertain the 'psychological facts' absolves the investigator from any further attempt to account for them. 'Understanding' is, of course, a prerequisite for the explanation of a person's thoughts and actions, since if I cannot grasp the meaning and purpose of what you are saying, I cannot even begin to discover why it is that you are saying it; but it does not follow that this understanding either constitutes or replaces explanation. This, however, is merely an aside to the present argument in which, as I said at the beginning, I take explicability in principle for granted. The other mistake—that of assuming that 'sociological' laws are to be sought by the progressive refinement of our existing generalisations—is in practice the more harmful one; and it springs directly from the misconceptions which this paper is concerned to criticise. By forgetting both that the social sciences are historical sciences and also that explanation must always be justified from beneath, it misconceives not only the nature of such laws but also their function.

Ever since the publication in 1942 of a now celebrated paper by Professor Hempel on 'The Function of General Laws in History',[1] argument has continued over whether the explanations of historians should be regarded as would-be lawlike 'explanation sketches' which could in principle be 'filled out' by means of a 'gradually increasing precision of the formulations involved' or whether historians, so far from being unable to justify their explanations by reference to initial conditions and general laws, do not need to invoke them at all. Those who take the alternative view have so far failed to produce an adequate account of 'historical' explanation without laws (partly, perhaps, because of the confusion between identification and explanation which I have attributed to Collingwood). But their arguments have been strengthened by a serious weakness in the presentation of Hempel's case. Hempel's chosen example is the migration of Dust Bowl farmers to California, which he suggests is explicable by reference to 'some such universal hypothesis as that populations will tend to migrate to regions which offer better living conditions'.[2] But why suppose that the law which underlies the 'explanation sketch' is a law about migration as such? Hempel's example of a physical explanation is the explanation of the cracking of an automobile radiator on a cold night by reference to the known laws of physics. But as one of his commentators has very sensibly reminded him, 'there is not a word about radiators in the laws by means of which the cracking of the radiator is to

[1] Reprinted in P. Gardiner, ed., *Theories of History* (1959), pp. 344–56.
[2] *Ibid.* pp. 349–50.

be explained'.[1] The case is in one way similar to that of the connection between religious affiliation and suicide. We may agree with Hempel that there must somewhere be relevant laws if any suggested explanation is to be vindicated; but we should not expect a migration to be explained by a law about migrations any more than a revolution by a law about revolutions or a radiator by a law about radiators or a rainbow by a law about rainbows. On the contrary, what is remarkable about our explanations of rainbows is that we explain them by reference to the same electromagnetic theory from which other special laws can be derived which explain (in the words of Professor Ernest Nagel, from whom the example is taken) such 'undeniably quite dissimilar occurrences' as lightning storms, the motions of a mariner's compass, and the formation of an optical image under the range finder of a camera.[2] It is characteristic of the successful sciences that their explananda are linked to the relevant laws by a redescription of a kind which to the untutored observer will be as surprising as it is remote. To explain the boiling of water, it would be fruitless to construct ever more elaborate generalisations about the antecedent and concomitant circumstances under which it has been witnessed by successive generations of observers; only when it has been seen as an instantiation of underlying laws about (among other things) atmospheric pressure can it be properly accounted for. In such cases as the movements of populations and the outbreak of revolutions, we are no doubt very far indeed from being able to fill our explanation sketches in. But we shall never succeed in doing it at all if we suppose that the discovery of the relevant laws will automatically follow from the sort of dogged inductions about the precise connection between migration and better living conditions which Hempel proposes. What is more, such a misunderstanding of the nature of the laws which are needed is likely to lead in turn to a misunderstanding of the function of empirical generalisation. As we have seen, the generalisations which the sociologist (whoever that term is used to refer to) is seeking may themselves be candidates for causal laws, if they can be theoretically grounded; or they may merely give him the clue to a generalisation of a different kind in which some alternative description of the explanandum furnishes the 'grounded' causal connection with the initial conditions specified. But in either case, the generalisation must be both precise and well-confirmed, and although the invocation of *ceteris paribus* may be legitimate (just as in the physical sciences) it must

---

[1] M. Mandelbaum, 'Historical Explanation: the Problem of "Covering Laws" ', *History and Theory*, I (1961), 154.
[2] E. Nagel, *The Structure of Science* (1961), p. 462.

be supported by an adequate specification of when other things can, and when they cannot, be taken to be equal. This is likely to be a complicated task; the necessary specification can usually be provided in experimental or quasi-experimental situations, but even here it is likely to rest on some fairly intricate statistical reasoning. On the other hand, it is only too easy to point to examples where the necessary specification is *not* provided, and the empirical generalisation vindicated only at the cost of such limited explanatory value as it might at first have appeared to possess.

Let me take just one example, which I choose because it has in fact been cited as an example of an explanation which furnishes a test of the 'sociological theory' in question. The generalisation is to the effect that social interaction promotes friendliness, and the work in which it is cited (and credited to Professor G. C. Homans) is Professor H. L. Zetterberg's *On Theory and Verification in Sociology* (1954). Zetterberg defines theories as 'systematically related' propositions resulting from the effort to discover 'general' propositions, and then goes on to say: 'Only at this stage does it make sense to speak of "testing a theory", "derivation" and—most important of all—"explanation". To "test" a theory, we check how well each of its propositions conforms to data and how well several propositions in conjunction with each other account for the outcome of a given situation. If such a "derivation" (or prediction) is successful, we call the outcome "explained"; that is, we claim that observed events conform to known propositions. Thus, Homans is able to explain the friendly feelings between brothers on the island of Tikopia by a reference to his already established proposition that a higher frequency of interaction results in a greater degree of liking.' But is this really an explanation? It is, after all, just as easy to cite well-documented cases where liking *de*creases with interaction —for example, in overcrowded prison camps. This does not mean that it is not perfectly possible that one reason why Tikopian brothers like each other so much is because they see so much of each other. But to show that this is so will require a detailed account of the social conditions and history of Tikopia rather than an ostensibly precise generalisation plus a long list of exceptions—clauses including the specification of a minimum of physical distance. If we could set out in psycho-physiological and ethological terms the necessary and sufficient conditions of mutual liking and *then* specify the social and institutional conditions under which these will be realised, we could indeed talk in Zetterberg's terms. But for the present, at least, we cannot. The empirical generalisation that interaction promotes liking is neither sufficiently precise nor sufficiently

32

'grounded' to be a serious candidate for a causal law. It should instead be compared to the sort of empirical generalisations which abound in the essays of Bacon or Montaigne. These can, no doubt, be very illuminating —many readers would say, much more so than Homans's. But they are illuminating because they bring home to the casual reader not what always does happen but merely what *can* happen more often than he has realised or might otherwise suppose.[1]

It is, indeed, this difference which accounts for the most important and characteristic feature of the 'explanation sketches' of sociologists, historians and anthropologists. Whatever situation or event the researcher had identified and thereafter seeks to explain, his question 'why?' will turn into the question 'how did it come about'. And in practice, he will always have to recognise that there are a number of possible answers, even once he has made up his mind which particular contrast he is interested in. If his evidence is adequate, he may have every hope of being able to rule out some or all of the rival possibilities which suggest themselves; to this extent, those who point out that historians do offer successful explanations without reference to laws are perfectly correct. But it does not follow from this that there are no laws, or even that these successful explanations do not presuppose their existence. It is rather that historians, sociologists and anthropologists often cannot do better than demonstrate that one particular weak and partial generalisation is all that is needed for the given case. It may be conceded that this generalisation cannot yet be accounted for in its turn. But it must nonetheless *be* capable of precise formulation and explanation if it is to be claimed to be able to perform the job in hand.

The parallel sometimes drawn between historians' researches and courts of law is useful here, as long as it is not pressed to the point where the researcher is thought of as concerned to deliver either a legal or a moral verdict. The judge needs, to take a well-worn example, an explanation of how two particular cars came to collide at a designated junction on a given date. The possibilities are myriad. Perhaps one car's brakes failed; perhaps one driver had a heart attack; perhaps there was ice on

---

[1] It is only fair to Homans to point out that whatever the weaknesses of the generalisation about friendliness, he is rightly insistent that generalisation in any social science (of which sociology is, to him, one among the rest) rests on implicit appeal to psychological theory: see his *The Nature of Social Science* (1967), ch. 2. His own preferred form of such theory—behavioural psychology in the manner of B. F. Skinner—may not be the most promising; perhaps more rewarding will turn out to be the sort of approach sketched by John Bowlby in *Attachment and Loss*, vol. I (1969). But this can only be settled by the course of research.

the road. This is the sort of inquiry in which it is natural and legitimate to speak of 'the' cause, and the contrast between 'idiographic' and 'nomothetic' explanation is most plainly visible. But although no mention will be made of scientific laws, let alone of the derivation of such laws within a more general theory, their existence is (unless the event is to be dismissed as random) an implicit presumption of the whole procedure. For to isolate, say, the ice on the road is to presume a lawlike connection between some property or other of ice and some property or other of the material of which the wheels are made which, when conjoined with a narrative specifying the weight, velocity and direction of the vehicle to which the wheels belong yields the necessary justification of the connection drawn between the explanandum and the stated initial conditions. It may so happen that the judge knows his textbook science, and can interject questions to the expert witnesses about temperatures, frictions and impacts. But even if he is an ignoramus in such matters, this will not disqualify him from assessing the evidence and arriving at the one right answer which does explain why the cars collided when they did. He needs only to know that certain things *can* happen if certain conditions are fulfilled; the laws that this may exemplify are indifferent to him.

One way of putting this more generally is to say that sociologists, anthropologists and historians aren't concerned to specify the necessary and sufficient conditions of their explananda so much as to isolate the 'contingently sufficient'[1] conditions which will account for the difference between the event or situation actually confronting them and the contrasting state of affairs which they would be observing otherwise. The explanandum is not directly related to laws and initial conditions; instead, it is related to an empirical generalisation which, although it may be a provisional candidate for lawful status, is more likely merely to be presumed to be explicable in turn by reference to still unformulated laws. As long as this presumption can be shown to be plausible, the generalisation, however far from the range and precision of a law, can suffice to demonstrate how the explanandum might have come about and therefore, by exclusion, did. It is this procedure which, together with the differences between the 'restricted' and the 'unrestricted' sciences, makes so-called 'historical' explanation more than trivially distinctive. There is still a difficulty of terminology because of the ambiguities of 'historical':

I owe the phrase to Michael Scriven, 'Review of Nagel, *The Structure of Science*', *Review of Metaphysics*, XVII (1964), p. 408, although the idea is of course not new and can be found in other terms in, for example, Weber and Mill. But see further, chapter 3, section II, below.

classical astronomy, for example, is a historical science in any common-sense definition, yet it does not need to invoke the notion of 'contingent sufficiency', since its laws are both complete and (as their algebraic form implies) time-reversible. Accordingly, the terms 'idiographic' and 'nomo-thetic' are probably the most useful after all, on condition that they are not used either to try to distinguish the *Geisteswissenschaften* from the *Naturwissenschaften* or to obscure the necessary replicability and therefore generalisability of all scientific explanation. The reason for retaining them is, on the contrary, to bring out two typical features which the sciences of man share in part with some (although by no means all) of the sciences of nature.

To illustrate this more specifically, it may be worth suggesting a com-parison between a sociologist trying to explain the origin of the Industrial Revolution and a biologist trying to explain the origin of life. Neither is likely to say, in the mid-twentieth century, that what he is studying is inexplicable. But both would freely admit that they are studying some-thing which is not retrodictable in any classical mechanistic way. The complicated and not very probable concatenation of circumstances which, in both cases, started the whole thing off might have occurred in other places or at other times from where they did. The antecedent conditions which need to be specified are numerous, 'unrestricted' and in some important instances very elusive—it may be as unfortunate that we are ignorant of the details of child-rearing practices in eighteenth-century England as that we have no adequate fossil record for the pre-Cambrian era. The best that we can do is to show that if certain combinations of circumstances *did* occur, then they *could* have produced the necessary effects; and if only one such combination appears to be plausible, then that must presumably be the one we are after. Despite the difficulties, it is not wholly impossible that within a few decades both problems will have been solved to the satisfaction of other workers in the field. It is more likely that there will be agreement about life than the Industrial Revolution, since the Industrial Revolution is, although much more recent, also (and for that very reason) much more complicated an affair. But in both cases, we may be able to isolate specified antecedent con-ditions which are connected, at least presumptively, to supporting laws, and which can accordingly show why (or in other words, how) the explanandum did in fact occur. We have known experimentally since 1953 that an electrical spark *could* have produced several kinds of amino acids in an atmosphere containing no oxygen but ammonia, methane and water vapour; and there are good grounds for thinking that the primitive atmosphere was probably composed of these. Since then, it has further been established that adenine is spontaneously formed in solutions of ammonium cyanide, which is a plausible component of the primitive sea, and that other elements of the all-important deoxyribonucleic acid can be produced by similarly simple chemical reactions. Accordingly the steps leading to the emergence of a self-reproducing molecule can now be given a precise and plausible formulation. These presumptions are all grounded in the known laws of chemistry and physics and can (unlike the sociological example) be furnished with direct experimental support. But even without the laws, it would be enough to have established the empirical generalisations from which could be constructed a conjectural account of the contingently sufficient conditions of the genesis of self-reproducing molecules encased in semipermeable membranes. And once that step is accounted for, we are a long way towards a satisfactory narrative of the whole long progressive decrease in entropy which continues through biological and then cultural evolution down to the Industrial Revolution and beyond. The analogy to the explanation of the Industrial Revolution is not meant to be pressed too hard; it would be foolish to try to identify the form of economic organisation which would be analogous to the genetic material, or anything of that kind. But the complicated story of antecedent necessary and contingently sufficient conditions which would furnish an adequate explanation of the Industrial Revolution would match in logical outline an adequate explanation of biogenesis. There are no laws *of* biogenesis, and no laws *of* industrial revolutions. But both are explicable in principle, and both explanations rest on the presumption of laws of *some* kind; and their difference from mechanistic explanations of a Laplacean kind has nothing to do with the difference between the sciences of man and the sciences of nature.

Accordingly, it should now be possible to summarise the relevant features of social-scientific explanation by referring back to the two senses of 'law'. In the strict sense, as we have had to concede, there are laws only of physics and chemistry. But it is useful to relax this strict sense a little. Lawfulness is a relative matter. There are limited, 'historical' laws in the social and the biological (and some of the physical) sciences; and the laws of any supporting science are not only more general than, but also historically relative to, the feebler laws or empirical generalisations of the 'superior' science. When we come to the top of the Comtean ladder, there are no laws at all, even in the most loose and generous sense. The case against 'historicism' in this form is incontestable. But explicability does not break down in some mysterious way because of it, any more than it breaks down, as the 'vitalists' used to believe, between the inorganic and the organic. The mistake which has been shared by some of the most sceptical opponents and some of the most committed defenders of the sciences of man is to suppose that if human behaviour is explicable by reference to causal laws, these must be causal laws of a Laplacean kind. But the idea of Laplace's Demon, able to predict from his knowledge of the classical dynamical laws all the future states of the universe, has been made to look hopelessly naive by the discoveries of nineteenth and twentieth century physical and biological science. Even the untutored layman now realises that not merely quantum mechanics but chemistry, thermodynamics and genetics all rest on a foundation of statistical probabilities quite different from the sort of Newtonian axioms and derivations with which Laplace supposed his Demon to be equipped.[1] It is true that some opponents of the social sciences have seized upon this (and particularly on what they may have read about the Heisenberg uncertainty relations) to argue that since predictability has been undermined in the world of nature, it must *a fortiori* have been undermined in the world of man. But this is merely to repeat the error of taking predictability in a Laplacean sense. In that sense, the state of the world is not predictable and never will be. But this discovery does not bring the sciences to a halt. Scientific explanations can still be offered, and are; and these are still linked in principle to predictability not in the sense that I could ever attach to this book an appendix foretelling what you will do when you finish reading this page, but in the sense that antecedent necessary and sufficient conditions could in principle be specified once it is possible to observe what you do in fact do. To extend still further the formulation of Professor Smart: the biological sciences are natural history plus physiological diagrams explained in terms of chemistry and physics; the social sciences are cultural history plus communications diagrams explained in terms of psychology and ethology. They are not Laplacean sciences, but they are not the less 'scientific' for that.

When, therefore, we credit the specialised social sciences with laws in the weak sense, the status of these laws must be seen in relation to the position of these sciences in the hierarchy of the sciences as a whole. Explananda which cannot be assigned directly to any one of the specialised social sciences belong to sociology in its residual and proper sense, distinguishable only by convention from either anthropology or history, and their explicability is thus bound to be 'idiographic'. The specialised social sciences, by contrast, stand midway between sociology, history and

[1] Cf. David Hawkins, *The Language of Nature* (1964), ch. 10.

anthropology on one side and psychology on the other; but although they too are not only historical but unrestricted, the fact that their causal generalisations are putatively derivable from psychological theory on the one hand and putatively applicable within the complex concatenations (or 'intermixtures') of history on the other makes the term 'law' defensible. It is true that psychology in its turn is an unrestricted and historical science relative to physiology, on whose theories it must be presumed to depend. But this relative lawfulness operates all the way down (or up) the hierarchy of the sciences, and it is this inter-connection, not some grand Comtean synthesis, which gives the enterprise of theoretical grounding its purpose and justification. Comte must, as I conceded at the very beginning, be credited with the correct perception that the historical and logical order are connected: it is no coincidence that a century after his death we can effect a satisfactory reduction of physics to chemistry, while the reduction of psychology to physiology is still little more than a hope. But it is not the long-awaited emergence of sociology which has made this hope plausible; it is the progressively more successful achievements of the sciences lower down Comte's evolutionary scale.

At this point, however, something more must be said not only about what may be meant by 'psychology' but about the sense in which the specialised social sciences are to be taken to be reducible to it. I do not necessarily mean by 'psychology' what is taught in university departments under that name. The achievements of psychology so defined are certainly as impressive as those of any other branch of the sciences of man: unmistakable advance has been made in the study of learning, memory, measured intelligence, perception and certain mental disorders since the days of Wundt, Freud and William James. But the psychological laws which would furnish the social sciences with their theoretical grounding will have to be of much wider scope than this. They will have in effect to furnish precise generalisations about individual responses in the widest sense of that word, so that behaviour which may be assumed to be influenced not merely by genetic or other endogenous variables or local stimuli such as can be experimentally applied but by variables of a complex institutional and cultural kind can be shown to be explicable by reference to them. So stated, the goal sounds Utopian. But it follows from the remarks which I made in the previous section about 'methodological individualism' that this must *be* the goal of the social sciences, whether or not they will ever be able to come near to achieving it. This is so quite irrespective of how much of human behaviour is in fact explicable by reference to genetic and how much to cultural influences. The theoretical grounding of a law of any designated category of social behaviour can only be a more general statement about human responses which justifies the assertion that within a specified set of institutional and historical circumstances the behaviour (or specified probability of behaviour) of the individuals in question did follow from the initial conditions listed.

Now it is sometimes said that to accept the (trivial) truth of the doctrine of methodological individualism does not commit one to accepting the reducibility of the *laws* of the social sciences to the *laws* of psychology. But this is itself an ambiguous assertion. It is true that the trivial sense of methodological individualism does not entail the claim that the subject-term of any social-scientific law is definitionally equivalent to a set of terms of individual psychology in the way that, for example, the term 'vixen' is definitionally equivalent to 'female fox'. But for the reducibility of sociology (or anthropology, or history) to psychology, it is enough to be able uncontroversially to say that any empirical connection asserted between the terms of a social-scientific law can be tested only against the behaviour (including, of course, the verbal behaviour) of individuals. It follows that these social-scientific terms must be capable of operational redescription in psychological terms; and it follows in turn from this that for each such particular case the psychological description is, after all, equivalent to the sociological. In practice, therefore, reducibility of social-scientific laws must be the implicit presumption of *any* explanation of social behaviour which claims 'theoretical' justification. It is true that social scientists can continue to do useful work by testing empirical generalisations (including those which they hope are causal) which are formulated entirely in sociological terms. It is also true that the way in which these terms are related to individual behaviour may be widely different in different contexts. Economists generalising about prices, anthropologists generalising about marriage rules, political scientists generalising about legislatures and demographers generalising about birth-rates are all using terms which for most of their purposes they need not explicitly break down at all and which, indeed, would be no more useful to them if they did. Furthermore, there is the difference within any social science between generalisations about actual aggregations of individuals—in other words, face-to-face groups or crowds—and institutional aggregations such as churches, trade unions, or political parties. But none of this modifies the dependence of sociological explanation on psychological. Explanation—to repeat yet again—is a matter of 'theoretical grounding'; and as Hempel's choice of metaphor serves to emphasise, it must come from below, not from above. This should be clearest of all in the relation of the social sciences to psychology, since this relation is, in effect, the last link in the Comtean chain once Comtean sociology has been seen to be incapable of properly lawlike generalisations of its own. Sometimes, it is possible for one of the later sciences to progress independently of supporting discoveries in the earlier; the chemical revolution of Priestley and Lavoisier did not depend upon a revolution in physics, and the Darwinian revolution, if it may be so called, in biology preceded the discoveries about the genetic mechanism which subsequently gave it its grounding. In the same way, economics, for example, has made considerable progress without waiting for a satisfactory account of the exact psychological mechanisms by which individual buyers and sellers are motivated to buy and sell. But theoretical grounding depends in the end on there somewhere being such underlying support. Without it, empirical generalisations can never become causal laws, and causal laws can never be built up into theories. In fact, to talk of 'social theory' at all is to presuppose psychological discoveries which, for the most part, have still to be made.

I hope it will be clear that the reducibility of the social sciences to psychology as I have described it does not involve the 'psychologism' for which Karl Popper, in particular, has criticised Mill. Some commentators have in fact found it difficult to detect just where 'methodological individualism' breaks off and 'psychologism' begins. But the error which it is necessary to guard against—whether or not it should be charged to Mill—is that of throwing out the baby of institutional and cultural history with the bathwater of doctrinal 'holism'. The psychological redescription of social facts is a very lengthy and complicated business precisely because, to use Popper's own phrase, 'psychological propensity alone'[1] explains so very little. Institutional conditions are of course describable in turn by reference to individual behaviour; but this is not at all the same as a reference to some eternal truths of human nature from which the course of history could be directly derived in any way in which Mill (influenced by Comte) may have supposed. Comte, in fact, has to be charged with two separate and even contradictory confusions: not only did he encourage the misconception that conventional historical explanation is somehow superseded by the discovery of sociology as a 'positive' science; he also encouraged the misconception that historical explanation could be ignored because the 'stages' of human history could be predicted by deduction from the innate characteristics of man. But to say that the laws which

[1] K. R. Popper, *The Poverty of Historicism*, 2nd ed. (1960), p. 154.

give the social sciences their theoretical grounding, and thus the idiographic explanations of historians, anthropologists and sociologists their
justification, are psychological laws, is neither to assert that human nature
evolves independently of its institutional by-products nor to require that
the terms of any statement about institutions be translated in practice
into extensionally equivalent psychological terms. Indeed, since psychology is itself an 'unrestricted' science, its laws will connect independent
variables of many different kinds with whatever general categories of
individual behaviour extrapolated across the range of the specialised
social sciences turn out to constitute its dependent variables.

Once given the risk of incurring a charge of 'psychologism', it might be
better to think of some alternative term to replace 'psychology' itself.
But 'ethology', which is the obvious alternative, has already two connota-
tions of which neither is quite appropriate. Mill used it to stand for the
science of the 'formation of character'; and its contemporary use is to
stand for the study of the social behaviour of animals, whose implications
for the study of human society are still largely speculative. Perhaps some
hybrid term like 'psycho-ethology' would have its uses. But whatever the
language employed, the point of substance which it should serve to bring
out is that the more general theory on which the putative laws of the
social sciences depend is an evolutionary theory of individual behaviour
as determined by the combination of genetic and environmental influences
in a manner analogous to biological speciation. This analogy, and the term
'pseudo-speciation' coined by Professor Erik Erikson, has been subjected
to a good deal of criticism. But it is in fact a perfectly respectable analogy,
as long as it is recognised as no more than such. It is also a very old one:
Tylor, in *Primitive Culture* (1871), already remarked that the ethnographer's task 'may be almost perfectly illustrated by comparing the
details of culture with the species of plants and animals as studied by the
naturalist'. It is perfectly true that the range of human behaviour for
which the concepts and methods of animal ethology are directly appropriate may be relatively small: a few redirection and displacement activities, and some non-linguistic ritualised signalling, imprinting and stereo-
typing. It is also true that, like all analogies, this one can be dangerously
misused. But this does not make it a bad analogy. The fact is that we
know almost nothing about the actual determinants of human social
behaviour although we do know quite a lot about the teleonomic selection
of genetically transmitted behaviour-organs in animals; but we can hardly
suppose that human social behaviour has no analogous determinants at
all; and it is as well to recognise that if we ask for the theoretical grounding

of the sciences of man, then it is a psycho-physiological theory including an account of the mechanisms of cultural adaptation that we are asking for. Sociologists, anthropologists and historians as well as more specialised social scientists can, and no doubt will, continue to make interesting discoveries without it. But they will never develop an autonomous 'sociological' theory which will be a substitute for it.

Someone might still want to object that 'sociological' theories do precisely set out to 'account for cultural adaptation'. Is not this what both 'structural-functionalism' and its rival 'conflict theory' (to say nothing of others) are designed to do? And is not natural selection itself such a theory whose importance for biology was, as I have allowed, recognised in advance of our present understanding of genetics? There are, however, two answers to this. The first is simply to examine the self-styled sociological theories which have in fact been put forward since Comte, Spencer and Marx and ask how far they have lived up to their predictive and explanatory claims. The second is to make clearer than I have perhaps done so far the difference between explanation and generalised description—that is, between connecting the explanandum to a specific generalisation which, within given assumptions, accounts for its occurrence and connecting it to a description of similar occurrences which is merely presumed to embody those common features whose significance an eventual explanation will elucidate and confirm.

The two answers are partly connected. If we examine the self-styled sociological theories, we shall not find in all cases that they are merely vacuous. They may be; but they may very well express the sort of half-theoretical generalisation, so to say, which summarises the evidence in such a way as to suggest not what the explanation is but rather what sort of explanation it will have to be. In this sense, the idea of natural selection can reasonably be described as 'theoretical'. But it is not, baldly stated, an explanatory theory if only because, as has often been said of it, it explains too much. In this, it is rather like sociological 'functionalism': if everything is as it is because it is 'adaptive' by definition, then nothing has been explained at all. But this does not prevent natural selection from being an important descriptive generalisation which not only is supported by an impressive range of empirical evidence but also lays down some of the principal conditions which a mature explanation has eventually to satisfy. Perhaps something of the same could (with suitable qualification) be claimed of Marxism; the parallel between Marx and Darwin, after all, was drawn not only by Engels but by Marx himself. A wide-ranging descriptive generalisation which fits the facts and has implicit theoretical content may be of substantial and even essential value in the development of an adequate theory. But it becomes so only when it becomes incorporated within a set of connected laws; and in the case of human social behaviour this will require a grounding in the specialised social sciences and through them in psychology, just as in Darwin's case it required a grounding in genetics.

It would accordingly be an exaggeration to suggest that the various schools of social theory which have at one time or another been fashionable have contributed nothing to our understanding of human behaviour. 'Functionalism' has certainly done so, even if in some of its formulations it has turned out to be merely circular. Indeed, functionalism has often been criticised more severely than it merited, particularly when it has been alleged to be incapable of accounting for 'social change'. This charge is peculiarly misplaced, because if functionalism explains anything it explains how natural selection operates among institutions and cultures in such a way that they must change in response to changes in their environment if they are to survive. But it remains true that the explanation of such changes rests on a specification of the mechanism which brings them about. By itself, functionalism cannot provide the explanation; and rather than describing it as a theory, it would be better to describe it as a set of assumptions which the successful theory, if we ever have one, will share. In this way, we are all functionalists, just as we are all structuralists[1] and all conflict theorists and all evolutionists. The merit of these 'theories' is not that they provide us either with explanations or with substitutes for explanations, but that they tell us more clearly than we might otherwise be aware what our eventual historical-cum-psychological theories will, among other things, have not to deny.

There is thus no reason why sociologists, anthropologists and historians should be inhibited from large descriptive generalisations about social systems and their constituents, whether of a synchronic or a diachronic kind. The only danger in this endeavour is that these generalisations should be allowed to stand as a tacit makeweight for the explanation of what they describe. Once this happens, there is a double risk not merely that the attempt to render them law-like will in practice render them vacuous but also that their justification will appear to depend on some autonomous 'sociological' theory whose discovery and elaboration requires a distinctive field of study for itself. There have, of course, been both anthropologists and historians who have proposed large pseudo-explanatory doctrines which claim to account for the totality of human

---

[1] Cf. chapter 2, below.

institutions. But contemporary anthropologists have become increasingly distrustful of even the most limited generalisations of a purely descriptive kind unless these are carefully restricted to a single cross-culturally comparable aspect of social organisation and behaviour; and historians, even if willing to draw comparisons both within and between different periods and cultures, are for the most part equally chary of generalisation about societies as such. It is nearly always the sociologists who have continued to imply that there must somewhere be a 'theory of social change' from which the explanation of the course of history could in principle be directly derived. But once it is recognised that sociology, anthropology and history all stand in the same relation to the underlying sciences by which their tentative explanations have in the end to be justified, it becomes at the same time clear that they have as much or as little right to descriptive generalisation as each other. Which such generalisations may turn out either to lead to or to be supported by the relatively lawlike generalisations of the specialised social sciences is then a matter to be settled by the future course of empirical research.

It is, perhaps, worth repeating in conclusion that any demarcation between the sciences is conventional, and that there are a number of other possible demarcations between the sciences of man which if only for the purposes of academic administration it may be useful to preserve. But if my argument is correct, any alternative demarcation must still recognise the relation of the sciences of man to each other within a (radically modified) Comtean hierarchy of scientific explanation. By this criterion, sociology, *pace* Comte, is not and cannot be an autonomous subject with laws of its own, however useful the particular discoveries, descriptive generalisations or idiographic explanations which may be achieved under its name.

2. What is Structuralism?*

So much has been written about 'structuralism' that to add to it may seem to call for some excuse. But it is precisely the volume and diversity of the literature[1] which prompts this paper. My purpose is not to attempt to review this literature or to criticise any one portion of it in detail, but simply to inquire at a general level how far structuralism can be said to constitute a distinctive doctrine or method in the analysis either of societies as such or of their myths and ideas.

I

Very broadly, the term 'structure' serves to mark off questions about the constituents of the object under study from questions about its workings. In sociology (or anthropology or history), therefore, questions about 'structure' can be answered in as many ways as there are held to be kinds of constituents of societies. The old-fashioned answer would be to say that societies are made up of institutions; the fashionable answer would be to say that they are made up of messages. But they can equally well be held to be made up of groups, or relationships, or classes, or roles, or exchanges, or norms and sanctions, or even shared concepts and symbols. There is always the risk of lapsing unwittingly into metaphor, as in the discredited analogy of society as an organism. But beyond this, the test of one answer as against another can only lie in its explanatory value in the context where it is employed. The only common assumption underlying all the answers is that if a society (like anything else) is to be satisfactorily explained, then the question 'what is it made of?' will have to be answered as well as, if not actually prior to, the question 'why does it do what it does?'

This, however, is to say very little—so little, in fact, as to lend support to the well-known remark of Kroeber that to invoke the word 'structure'

---

*This paper was read in an earlier draft at a staff seminar in the Department of Sociology at the University of Leicester in January 1967, and I should like to express my thanks to the members of the seminar for their comments. It was first published in its present form in the *British Journal of Sociology*, xx (1969). Since it was written, the second and third volumes of Claude Lévi-Strauss's *Mythologioues* have been published, but I have not tried to revise it in order to take account of them: for a useful and up-to-date (if rather summary) discussion by a qualified critic, see Edmund Leach, *Claude Lévi-Strauss* (London, 1970).
[1] Much of the more recent literature is in French. I have given references to English versions wherever available, but I have once or twice made slight modifications to the translation.

in the discussion of societies or cultures (or organisms, or crystals, or machines) adds nothing 'except to provoke a degree of pleasant puzzlement'.[1] But two other assumptions can be said to be built into the notion of structure apart from the assumption that the object in question is, as Kroeber puts it, 'not wholly amorphous'. The first is the assumption of a more specific interconnectedness: thus the term 'social structure' is said by Fortes, for example, to draw attention to the 'interconnection and interdependence, within a single system, of all the different classes of social relations found within a given society'.[2] The second is the assumption that form can usefully be divorced from content: Fortes, in the same passage, credits Lowie with first bringing out 'the very obvious but fundamental fact that closely similar, if not identical, forms of social relationship occur in widely separate societies and are expressed in varied custom'.[3] It is not simply, therefore, that the notion of 'structure' presupposes distinguishable elements, but that these elements constitute a system which displays a minimum persistence over time and is in principle comparable with other similarly identifiable systems. Hence social structure can be defined in such phrases as 'the assemblage of the main recurrent institutional patterns in the society, seen as complexes of roles'.[4]

But once the notion of structure is seen to overlap, or even to collapse into, the notion of system, what follows? A system is best defined simply as a set of connected variables. The term may carry the additional implication that the definitive set is the set yielding single-valued transformations; but the important emphasis is on variables as opposed to 'things'.[5] The 'structure' of a social collectivity, therefore, is a vector whose components are whatever variables the investigator has reason to regard as best able to explain how it works. Of course there underlies the notions both of structure and system the assumption that there is some ascertainable pattern which the investigator will, given sufficient patience and sagacity, lay bare. But this means simply that the inter-relations between the variables isolated are not random; and this is the assumption without

[1] A. L. Kroeber, *Anthropology* (New York, 1948), p. 325. (Contrast with this, for example, the remark of R. S. Peters, *The Concept of Motivation* (London, 1958), p. 7, that 'In explaining human actions we, like anthropologists, must all in the first place be structuralists').

[2] Meyer Fortes, 'The Structure of Unilineal Descent Groups', *American Anthropologist*, LV (1953), 22.

[3] *Loc. cit.*

[4] Dorothy Emmet, *Rules, Roles and Relations* (London, 1966), p. 145.

[5] Cf. e.g. Leach, *Rethinking Anthropology* (London, 1961), p. 7: 'Considered mathematically, society is not an assemblage of things but an assemblage of variables'.

which scientific enquiry in any field whatever would be hopeless. In this sense, there will be nothing distinctive about a 'structural' theory; in fact, any and all sociological explanations will be 'structuralist'.

Perhaps, however, it can be argued that 'structural' theories are distinguished from 'non-structural' in terms of their conception of societies as coherent and integrated wholes between whose components the internal inter-relations are particularly strong. On this view, the rival doctrine which structuralism sets out to deny is the doctrine that institutions can be explained individually and as such in non-comparative and largely historical terms. Now it is certainly true that some anthropologists who have adopted what they would be prepared to call a 'structural' approach have meant something like this by it. But it is still implausible to claim that 'structuralism' constitutes a distinctive doctrine. In the first place, its contrary is a straw man which no sociologist, anthropologist or historian would nowadays wish to defend; and in the second, 'structuralism' taken in this sense becomes in the end more or less indistinguishable from another of its presumable rivals—the functionalism of Malinowski. All theories of society presuppose some interrelation between societies' components; indeed, this is so by definition. But the strength of particular interrelations, or the priority to be accorded to particular variables, are matters for empirical study. There is little point in laying down *a priori* that the components of society are *strongly* interrelated and labelling the assumption 'structuralism'.

It is true that there is a clear distinction between structure on one side and both history and function on the other. But this does not by itself justify the escalation of a difference of emphasis into a clash of doctrines. Every historical explanation has implicit reference to structure; every structural explanation has implicit reference to origin and function. The rivalry between them is not between one theory and another but between one aspect and another of the particular theory employed.[1] It might be argued against this that the revolution in linguistics which has had so marked an influence on 'structural' anthropology was a revolution in doctrine, and that Saussure himself was insistent on the incompatibility of synchronic with historical explanation. But even in linguistics, this looks in retrospect less like a doctrine than a methodological battle-cry,[2] and as such it has been progressively modified through Troubetzkoy and

[1] Cf. G. Lautéri-Laura, 'Histoire et structure dans la connaissance de l'homme', *Annales*, XXII (1967), 796: 'Nous ne pouvons guère isoler, non plus, des champions supposés de l'une et de l'autre tendance, car, à vrai dire, la dichotomie est à l'intérieur de chacun d'eux.'

[2] Cf. Paul Ricoeur, 'La structure, le mot, l'événement', *Esprit* (May, 1967), p. 807.

Jakobsen down to Chomsky. There is no such thing as a purely synchronic sociological explanation any more than an explanation in terms of a unique and self-insulated historical sequence; and the attempt to construct one would have as little explanatory value in the one case as in the other.[1] Even Lévi-Strauss, who has made the strongest claims for structural linguistics as the paradigm of sociological explanation, is quite explicit about the simultaneous importance of diachronic analysis.[2] *Pace* Saussure, there is no justification for turning the distinction between them into an incompatibility.

The only sense in which it might be plausible to regard structuralism as a distinctive sociological doctrine is the sense in which is it assumed not merely that separate structures can be broken down into their components, but also that there is a general isomorphism *between* structures. But the use of the term is still misleading. To say that ostensibly dissimilar structures are isomorphic and that this isomorphism is not coincidental is to say no more than that the same theory explains both. It says nothing about the content of the theory. All successful theories are isomorphic to the phenomena they set out to explain. To say that structuralism is the doctrine of isomorphism between structures must, presumably, mean the belief in a *universal* isomorphism—what Merleau-Ponty describes as 'the programme of a universal code of structures, which would allow us to deduce them from one another by means of transformation-rules'.[3] But then this is no less and no more than the belief in a general theory of the social sciences. How far this belief may be well-founded, nobody is at present in a position to say. But if there is a general theory, its validity will depend on its substantive content, not on any particularly intimate connection with the notion of 'structure'. A general theory will be 'structuralist' in the sense that all socio-psychological theories are structuralist; it will be neither more nor less so if it

---

[1] Cf. e.g. F. G. Bailey, *Tribe, Caste and Nation* (Manchester, 1960), p. 9: 'I cannot think of any examples of a purely static analysis of a society'; or Fernand Braudel, 'La longue durée', *Annales*, XIII (1968), 739: 'un arrêt instantané, suspendant toutes les durées, est presque absurde toujours'; or Braudel's reference in *La Méditerrannée et le monde meditarrannéen à l'époque de Philippe II*, 2nd ed. (Paris, 1966), I, 325, to '. . . des structures sociales, donc à des mécanismeslents à s'user'.

[2] Claude Lévi-Strauss, 'Les Limites de la notion de structure en ethnologie', in R. Bastide (ed.), *Sens et usages du terme structure dans les sciences humaines et sociales* (The Hague, 1962), p. 42: 'Mais toute structure n'est-elle pas bi-dimensionelle?'; or *The Scope of Anthropology* (London, 1967), p. 23; or 'Social Structure', in *Structural Anthropology* (New York, 1963), p. 312 (with particular reference to Fortes, 'Time and Social Structure: an Ashanti Case Study', in Fortes, ed., *Social Structure : Studies Presented to A. R. Radcliffe-Brown* (Oxford, 1949), pp. 54–84).

[3] Maurice Merleau-Ponty, 'From Mauss to Claude Lévi-Strauss', in *Signs* (Northwestern University, 1964), p. 118,

turns out to be, let us say, a cybernetic theory rather than an economic one. If a commitment to 'structuralism' means only the optimistic belief that a general theory of human behaviour will one day be validated, it is hard to see why this particular term (or any other) is needed for it.

On the other hand, the fact that the term *does* often carry this implication helps to account for some of the enthusiasm and controversy which it continues to generate. In this respect, 'structure' is very like 'system'. The amount of controversy is not simply the result of an excessive concern with matters of terminology. It arises because of the strong difference of view which there has always been between those who do and those who don't believe in the possibility of a general theory of society. Much of the literature which has accumulated around the term 'system' is centred on the claim that it makes possible the formulation of hypotheses of a higher generality than could have been reached without it. But even if this claim is valid—which it may well be—the injunction 'look at it as a system' is uncomfortably like the injunction 'talk prose'. All interrelated variables constitute a system by definition, and that system has a structure by definition. For the sociologist, the two notions carry with them a substantive doctrine only if the injunction is not merely to look at society as a system, but to look at it as a system *of* something. To say merely that society is a system, and has a structure, will explain nothing at all.

It might, however, still be suggested that 'structuralism' constitutes not so much a distinctive doctrine as a distinctive method. Whatever may be said about the doctrines propounded by Saussure, it can hardly be denied that he did inaugurate a new method for the study of language which has proved outstandingly rewarding. But it remains true that the success of this method in linguistics lies in the specific demonstration that language can be broken down into components for whose analysis the method of Saussure and his successors is appropriate; and if this is 'structuralism', then what it means is, in effect, the replacement of less clear and rigorous analyses by more clear and rigorous ones. In the case of 'social' structure, it is true that to look, with Radcliffe-Brown, at actual social relations is very different from looking, with Lévi-Strauss, at formal relations between formal relations.[1] But it in no way follows that the more abstract model, even if it proves the more useful, is therefore entitled to lay exclusive claim to 'structuralist' method.

In the version of Lévi-Strauss, the essence of 'structuralist' method

---

[1] Radcliffe-Brown does, as Lévi-Strauss allows (*Structural Anthropology*, p. 303), distinguish between 'actual relations' and 'the form of the structure' (*Structure and Function in Primitive Society* (London, 1952), p. 192); but he is still insistent that 'The components of social structure are *persons*' ('Introduction', p. 4).

seems to lie in the construction of deliberately abstract models by the artificial breaking-down of the object under study and its subsequent reconstitution in terms of essentially relational properties. But isn't this true of science in general? To borrow again from Merleau-Ponty, 'the objects which science constructs ... are always bundles of relations'.[1] Nor is there anything distinctively 'structuralist' about the recognition that an explanatory model *is* a construction—that, in the phrase of Roland Barthes, it is 'l'intellect ajouté à l'objet'.[2] The only force in the injunction of structuralism as a method would seem to lie, as with it as a doctrine, in the emphasis placed on the search for isomorphism. But the success of the method, if it can be so called, will rest not on the search for isomorphism by itself but on the extent to which it leads to a valid reduction—that is, to a demonstration that one class of phenomena can be strictly identified with another. It is, of course, true that such reductions can constitute major scientific discoveries and that they are worth looking for no less in the social than the physical sciences. But the discoveries are not arrived at by means of any methodological axiom derived from the notion of 'structure'. They are arrived at by finding that the laws governing two discrete classes of phenomena are isomorphic, that the constants are identical and that the two sets of terms are empirically interchangeable.[3] It may well be that there is both an isomorphism of laws and an interchangeability of concepts between apparently discrete areas of social phenomena. But the explanatory value of the discovery will depend on the empirical identification. The value of the methodological injunction 'look for isomorphism' (or, equally, 'look for "total" phenomena') is that its implications are reductionist, not that it argues a methodological parallel between the study of language and the study of society.

In effect, the point is the same whether structuralism is put forward as a doctrine or as a method. 'Look at society as a system (or structure)' is trivial where 'look at society as a system (or structure) of information exchanges' is not. But if the suggestion that society should be looked at in cybernetic terms turns out to be useful, there will be nothing peculiarly 'structuralist' about it. On this basis it could just as well be claimed that Durkheim's dictum 'Tell me the code of domestic morality and I will tell you the social organisation' is a dictum of 'structuralism'. But this

---

[1] Maurice Merleau-Ponty, *The Structure of Behaviour* (London, 1965), p. 142.
[2] Roland Barthes, 'L'activité structuraliste' in *Essais Critiques* (Paris, 1964), p. 215.
[3] See May Brodbeck, 'Models, Meaning and Theories', in Llewellyn Gross, ed., *Symposium on Sociological Theory* (Evanston, 1959), pp. 392 ff.

means merely (as Durkheim himself makes clear) that societies develop the morality they need.[1] If this is true, it is not because of the fact that social organisation and morality are in some sense isomorphic but because there is a demonstrable causal relation between them. As a doctrine, 'societies are structures' means little more than 'societies are societies'; as a method, 'look for the structure' means little more than 'look for the right explanation', or, perhaps, 'the explanation lies deeper than you think'.

II

It may be, however, that to question the distinctive content of a 'structural' approach to societies as a whole is to misconceive its scope. Perhaps its virtue—whether methodological or doctrinal—lies not in the traditional area of 'social structure' so much as in the particular field of ritual and ideas. On this view, the merit of Lévi-Strauss is that he 'succeeds in doing for myth what Radcliffe-Brown did for social structure'—that is, he succeeds in showing that myths can only be explained in terms of their position within 'the total myth structure of the culture concerned'.[2] But once again, what exactly is distinctive about this? It is fair to say that certain forms of historical explanation of myth are more palpable rivals to Lévi-Strauss's approach than is 'non-structural' to 'structural' sociology; Lévi-Strauss is, for example, explicitly concerned to reject the explanation of myth in terms of Jungian archetypes. But the explanations which he offers in his turn must still be explanations by origin if they are to be explanations at all. There is no need to dispute the verdict of Firth that Lévi-Strauss 'has amply shown in these fields [of myth and totemism] what Freud showed elsewhere, that thought is not random but structured'.[3] No doubt, too, this demonstration depends to a significant degree on synchronic comparisons. But if it is demonstrably the case that the Oedipus myth is an attempt to reconcile the incompatible beliefs that man is autochthonous and that he is not autochthonous, or that the story of Asdiwal gives expression to the strain inherent in a system of cross-cousin marriage which is patrilocal at the same time as matrilateral, or that a myth purporting to explain the origin of clan names is in general likely to be 'demarcative rather than aetiological',[4] this does not follow simply

[1] Emile Durkheim, *Moral Education* (New York, 1961), p. 87.
[2] Nur Yalman, 'The Raw: the Cooked: Nature: Culture', in Leach, ed., *The Structural Study of Myth and Totemism* (London, 1967), p. 73.
[3] Raymond Firth, 'Twins, Birds and Vegetables', *Man*, n.s. 1 (1966), 2.
[4] Lévi-Strauss, *The Savage Mind* (London, 1966), p. 230.

from the particular rearrangement of the elements of the myth which have been selected. It can only follow from the further evidence cited to show that this rearrangement, and not any other, furnishes the clue to the original composition and subsequent preservation (with such accretions as may be) of the myth in question.

Against this, it might be said that 'structural' explanations of myth, even if they must in some sense be explanations by origin, are explanations by origin of a peculiar kind, since what is required is not the tracing of a pedigree but the deciphering of a code. Thus Leach, for example, draws an explicit parallel between the mythography of Lévi-Strauss and the decipherment of Linear B.[1] But the parallel is a dangerous one. The notion of a code presupposes the notion of an original of which the coded version is a translation. There was no doubt in anyone's mind that Linear B was a script; the question was a question of meaning, which was solved when Ventris and Chadwick effectively showed that Linear B was Greek. But it is a very different matter to speak of 'decoding' *Hamlet* or *Moby Dick*. To claim to have 'decoded' a work of art is legitimate only in such special cases as an allegorical painting or a novel *à clef*. It is still possible to argue that works of art can be explained in terms of *unconscious* symbolism (and it is, perhaps, worth remarking that Lévi-Strauss in his autobiography pays tribute to the triple influence on his intellectual development of Marxism, geology and psychoanalysis). But this too will be defensible only in terms of solving the problem of origin. It is not enough to produce a 'structural' parallel between the components of the work of art and the presumptive content of the artist's repressed impulses and fantasies. It has also to be shown that the artist *was* under the influence of these repressed impulses and that he *therefore* produced the work of art whose symbolism can be 'decoded' along these lines.

At this point, the partisans of 'structuralism' will be likely to reply that they are still not required to proffer a conventional explanation by origin, but only to show that an ostensibly haphazard complex can be accounted for by a logical reduction which is both more economical and more coherent. Thus Leach says of the kinship terminology of the Jinghpaw that it 'impressed me as highly complex, yet it must be, I argued, *from the users' point of view*, the simplest possible logical system consistent with the rules of the society'.[2] An excellent simple example is furnished by the Hanunoo system of personal pronouns, which is palpably illogical if set out in terms of the traditional categories of first, second and third

---

[1] *The Structural Study of Myth and Totemism*, p. xviii.
[2] 'Jinghpaw Kinship Terminology', in *Rethinking Anthropology*, p. 50.

persons singular and plural but which makes perfect sense in terms of the three dimensions of minimal/non-minimal membership, inclusion/exclusion of the speaker and inclusion/exclusion of the listener.[1] Here, the solution is immediately satisfying (and serves at the same time to support the view that the thought of primitive peoples is much less illogical than used to be supposed). But we are still, even in these cases, dealing with explanation by origin, for the presumption underlying the argument is that the Jinghpaw or Hanunoo or anybody else will not in fact have developed and preserved an inexplicable terminology. In other words, the question of motive is taken for granted. But where it comes to the explanation of myth, it is precisely the reason for which the myth has been composed, added to and preserved that we wish to know.

Lévi-Strauss himself is well aware of the need to rebut the charge that 'structural' explanation of myth is arbitrary. In *Le Cru et le Cuit* his rebuttal rests partly on the criteria of coherence and economy and partly on the self-denying ordinance whereby the investigator is forbidden to switch at will from logical to historical explanations of variations in the *mythe de référence*.[2] But this still leaves open the question of content. Here, Lévi-Strauss's argument appears to rest on the analogy between myth and music. But although it is evident that the musicologist can demonstrate a formal structure common to different individual compositions of which neither the listeners, the performers nor even the composer need necessarily be aware, it is less clear how far this constitutes the explanation for which the sociologist will be seeking. It is entirely legitimate to break down a myth or work of art paradeigmatically (to borrow a term from the linguists) instead of syntagmatically. Indeed, this is a commonplace of literary and artistic criticism of many different schools. But the fact that a piece of music is a fugue explains neither why Bach wrote it nor why twentieth-century Europeans still like to listen to it. Lévi-Strauss appears to reject the question of content on the grounds that structure, unlike form, doesn't *have* a content, but *is* content;[3] but this is merely (if I understand him) another way of making the point that the

---

[1] H. C. Conklin, 'Lexicographical Treatment of Folk Taxonomies', in F. W. Householder and S. Saporta, eds., *Problems in Lexicography* (Bloomington, 1962), pp. 119–41, cited by Nicholas Ruwet, 'La linguistique générale aujourd'hui', *Archives Européennes de Sociologie*, v (1964), 306–7.

[2] *Le Cru et le Cuit* (Paris, 1964), pp. 155–6.

[3] In 'L'analyse morphologique des contes russes', *Int. J. Slavic Linguistics and Poetics* (1960), quoted by J. Pauillon, 'Présentation', in *Les Temps Modernes* (November 1966), p. 782: 'la forme se définit par opposition à un contenu qui lui est extérieur; mais la structure n'a pas de contenu: elle est le contenu même, appréhendé dans une organisation logique conçue comme propriété du réel'.

'structural' view of anything is as a set of variables. If the conclusion of Lévi-Strauss's mythography is that 'Myths serve to provide an apparent resolution, or "mediation", of problems which by their very nature are incapable of any final resolution',[1] this is an explanation by origin no less than is a Freudian or Jungian explanation, or a more conventionally 'structuralist' anthropological explanation relating ritual to social organisation, or a 'genetic-epistemological' explanation in the manner of Piaget.[2] Whatever is meant by the 'structure' of myth, the components must in the end be related to the meaning and thus the structure to the content.

Thus in practice, 'structural' mythography does not deny (how could it?) that 'To study form it may be sufficient to describe it. To explain form one needs to discover and describe the processes that generate the form.'[3] For Lévi-Strauss, the matrix to be deduced from the juxtaposition and 'structural' reduction of all known myths will disclose the fundamental (and irresolvable) preoccupations of man in his relations to nature; and these will in turn be traceable to a fundamental biochemical account of the constituents of the human mind. It is a further assumption that human thought is essentially binary, and that this fact can in turn be related to the binary neurophysiological mechanisms operating in the brain; but an isomorphism of this kind is neither a necessary nor, for that matter, a very significant assumption. All psychological explanations must be compatible with at least one possible neurological model;[4] but the function of binary thinking could be performed by any number of different mechanisms, and, conversely, binary neurological mechanisms could yield any number of 'fundamental' modes of thought which need not be binary themselves. In any case, this aspect of the question is outside the scope of the present paper. I am not here concerned with what particular explanation by origin is the correct one; nor am I qualified to pass comment on any specific interpretation of a particular myth. The concern of this paper is with the question how far 'structuralism' constitutes a distinctive kind of analysis; and the answer seems to be that although the explanations of myth offered by Lévi-Strauss are substantively different from those put forward by others, and although he has

---

[1] Leach, 'The Legitimacy of Solomon', *Archives Européennes de Sociologie*, VII (1966), 80.

[2] Paiget himself is claimed as a 'structuralist' by Jean Viet, *Les Méthodes Structuralistes dans les Sciences Sociales* (The Hague, 1965), pp. 53–8; but such a wide range of authors in different fields is similarly included by Viet as in effect to support the argument that no useful theory in the social sciences will ever be *non*-structuralist.

[3] Fredrik Barth, *Models of Social Organization* (Royal Anthropological Institute, 1966), p. v.

[4] See Jerry A. Fodor, 'Explanations in Psychology', in Max Black, ed., *Philosophy in America* (London, 1965), p. 176.

been consciously influenced by post-Saussurean linguistics to a degree that others have not, there is still no clear sense in which rival explanations of myth are 'non-structuralist', or 'structuralist' explanations are not explanations by origin and content in the orthodox sense.

III

But is there yet another possible interpretation? When Firth, in 1955, announced that 'The air of enchantment which for the last two decades has surrounded the "structuralist" point of view has now begun to be dispelled',[1] he evidently did not foresee the vogue which a renovated 'structuralism' was to enjoy under the influence of Lévi-Strauss. But it might be argued that the transition from Radcliffe-Brown to Lévi-Strauss represents not so much the transition from one sociology to another as from sociology to philosophy. It is noticeable that Lévi-Strauss's 'structuralism' has attracted the attention of philosophers and literary critics to a degree that the 'structuralism' of English-speaking social anthropology has never done. Might it then be that this newer variant should be seen less as a doctrine of what societies are and how their workings are to be explained than as a fresh attempt to resolve for social science as a whole the perennial conflict between idealism and empiricism?

The brief discussion of Levi-Strauss's mythography in the preceding section suggested already that a 'structuralist' interpretation of ideas must sooner or later confront the problems of meaning as well as origin. At this point, both the ethnographer and the psychologist must give way to the epistemologist. Lévi-Strauss clearly accepts this. A philosopher by training and perhaps to some degree by temperament, he is well aware of what he is doing in proffering an explanation of culture by reference to the ultimate constituents of the human mind. Indeed, he has not only been labelled a Kantian but has accepted the label—he is only concerned to make clear that it is not a 'transcendental' Kantianism but a Kantianism transposed into the 'domaine ethnologique'.[2] Now this could be read simply as a determination to preserve, even in the search for 'Kantian' universals, a dogmatic empiricism modelled on the physical sciences. But compare the following passage, which, apart from its lack of a specific reference to ethnography, could almost have been written by Lévi-Strauss

---

[1] Raymond Firth, 'Some Principles of Social Organization', in *Essays on Social Organization and Values* (London, 1964), p. 59.

[2] 'Réponse à quelques questions', *Esprit* (November 1963), p. 631. Cf. *Le Cru et le Cuit*, p. 19.

himself: 'Philosophy is related by regular laws to the sciences, to art and society. From this relationship its tasks arise. Ours is clearly marked out for us: to follow Kant's critical path to the end, and establish an empirical science of the human mind in collaboration with workers in other fields; our task is to get to know the laws which govern social, intellectual and moral phenomena.' The author here, far from being an orthodox empiricist, is Dilthey, in his inaugural lecture at Basle;[1] and although it is in general a mistake to spend too much time tracing ideological parallels (even the method of 'binary selection' can be traced back to Plato's *Sophist*), the parallel between Lévi-Strauss and Dilthey is not, perhaps, as far-fetched as it seems.

One obvious objection to it is the physicalist basis of Lévi-Strauss's psychology. But where Piaget, for example, finds the source of the isomorphism between thought and the world, for which the central nervous system furnishes the mechanism, in the 'sociogenesis' of the human intellect, Lévi-Strauss finds it in the structural continuities of myth. Indeed, it is his explicit claim that his epistemology is ethnological instead of psychological. But by forfeiting Piaget's kind of grounds for the rejection of 'transcendentalism', he lays himself open to the same charge as the 'empirical science of the human mind' of Dilthey. For if Lévi-Strauss's 'mythography' is not, any more than Dilthey's 'hermeneutics', grounded in empirically testable psychological theory, then the perennial question of ultimate origin will be no less open (and damaging) in the one case as the other. It is not enough to base a theory of the human mind on structural ethnography plus the assumption of biochemical isomorphism, because this will still leave the investigator's own conclusions open to the charge of a regress. Piaget, at least, can claim immunity from the regress by invoking the standards of public testability for his explanation of the origins of logical thought, and thereby his own psychological theory. I am not qualified to judge how far Piaget's attempt will be held to be successful. But it is impossible to see how the theory of Lévi-Strauss could be validated in any analogous way within the framework of its own assumptions. It always remains to be asked why the mythography of Lévi-Strauss is not itself a myth; and he himself, in *Le Cru et le Cuit*, disarmingly admits of his 'third-order code' that 'on n'aura pas tort de la tenir pour un mythe; en quelque sorte, le mythe de la mythologie'.[2] We are unavoidably forced back, at the end of the structuralist exercise, to the traditional questions of origin and meaning; and

[1] H. A. Hodges, *Wilhelm Dilthey: an Introduction* (London, 1944), p. 115.
[2] *Op. cit.* p. 20.

there is nothing in Lévi-Strauss to show that the philosophical appeal of 'ethnological' Kantianism rests in the end on an epistemological foundation any less 'Kantian' than that of Kant himself.

The isomorphism of thought and the world is a familiar preoccupation of philosophy: to the Wittgenstein of the *Tractatus* just as much as to Lévi-Strauss, the fundamental categories of human thought mirror the structure of the world although not directly asserting anything about it. The role of logic in the epistemology of the early Wittgenstein is not unlike the role of myth in the epistemology of Lévi-Strauss; and in a sense, this is only to be expected, since it is part of Lévi-Strauss's purpose to show that 'the kind of logic in mythical thought is as rigorous as that of modern science'.[1] But having said that the fundamental categories of human thought, whether revealed by ethnography or by introspection, are somehow isomorphic to the world, how are we ever to demonstrate either the nature or the cause of this connection without lapsing into a regress? The same dilemma faces the Kantianism not only of Dilthey but likewise of Lévi-Strauss. Lévi-Strauss is entitled to argue that his theory is based on 'experience' in a way that Wittgenstein's or Kant's are not and do not claim to be. But to the degree that his theory is, like theirs, an epistemological theory, the search for ethnographic generalisations merely defers the problem which it is alleged to solve. The status of Lévi-Strauss's ultimate constituents is not modified by the fact that he bases them on a 'structural' reduction of universal myths rather than the 'thought-experiments' of the traditional logician.

It should be clear that to say this is not to deny the importance of the notion of isomorphic patterning (or 'structure') to epistemology as well as to communication theory—an importance of which Wittgenstein was no less aware than Lévi-Strauss or Leach.[2] But it would be unwarranted to claim for the new 'structuralism' that it resolves the philosophical difficulties which were not resolved by Dilthey or Wittgenstein or Kant himself. It is perfectly possible that philosophical discussion on these topics will be permanently influenced by the findings of 'structuralist' ethnography. Epistemology is not debated in a vacuum. The findings of psychology, for example, can drastically modify philosophers' doctrines of 'sense-data', and there is nothing inherently misconceived in the claim

---

[1] 'The Structural Study of Myth', in *Structural Anthropology*, p. 230.

[2] Compare, for example, Leach, 'Men and Machines', *The Listener* (23 November 1967), p. 663, on the transmission of isomorphism from speaker's head, voice, microphone and transmitter to listener's receiver, loudspeaker, ears and brain with Wittgenstein, *Tractatus* 4.0141 on the isomorphism between musical idea, score, sound-waves and the groove on the gramophone record.

of Lévi-Strauss to have demonstrated the mistakes both of Peirce in defining proper names as 'indices' and of Russell in putting forward demonstrative pronouns as the logical model of proper names.[1] But it is one thing to claim that the findings of ethnography can influence philosophers' doctrines; it is another to claim that they can solve either psychologists' or philosophers' problems. Not only are the epistemological difficulties of the 'ultimate constituents of the human mind' not resolved by Lévi-Strauss's mythography; they are not bypassed by it either. 'Structuralism' does not succeed in showing how the epistemological status of the 'mythe de la mythologie' can be vindicated by that mythology itself, and if the debate between empiricists and idealists will ever be settled, it will not be by appeal to it.

IV

This rapid and rather cavalier survey of a complex topic cannot suggest more than a very tentative general conclusion. But if my argument is at all well founded, it suggests that 'structuralism', whether in its Anglo-Saxon or its Gallic version, should not be claimed to constitute a novel, coherent and comprehensive paradigm for sociological and anthropological theory. Whether viewed as a doctrine or a method (and the two should in any case not be too sharply distinguished) 'structuralism' as such does not, on examination, stand for a more distinctive standpoint than a belief in the applicability of rigorous models to social behaviour; and this is equally true whether it is taken to apply to societies as a whole or only to their rituals and beliefs, or even, at a more explicitly philosophical level, to the theoretical presuppositions of social-scientific investigation itself.

At the same time, it would be altogether wrong to draw from this argument the implication that the exponents of 'structuralism' have not both made important contributions to specialist topics and also suggested ideas of wider relevance for social theory in general. Indeed, it may well be that Lévi-Strauss and his followers will extend his empirical studies beyond what is still a relatively circumspect range of societies and institutions, and that this will have valuable implications over wide areas of the social sciences. But it has not been the purpose of this paper to try to forecast the future of anthropological theory. I have merely been concerned to suggest that 'structuralist' theory may not be distinctive to quite the degree that is apt to be claimed for it.

[1] *The Savage Mind*, p. 215.

3. The Sociological Explanation of 'Religious' Beliefs[*]

The aim of this paper is methodological, not substantive. In the first section, I shall discuss the familiar problem of how 'religious' beliefs can, if at all, be usefully distinguished from beliefs of other kinds.[1] In the second, I shall try to suggest what constitutes an adequate sociological explanation of beliefs in general. In the third, I shall illustrate my argument by a direct comparison between Max Weber and Emile Durkheim.[2]

I

The usefulness of a definition of 'religious' belief must, for the social scientist's purposes, depend on how far it helps to explain the beliefs so distinguished from others. Most of the controversies over how religion should be defined, and how it should be differentiated from magic on the one hand and science on the other, have turned on the question whether religious beliefs are to be identified by their nature ('sacred' v. 'profane') or their content ('spiritual beings'). It may seem tempting to dismiss this as a purely verbal issue: commonsense distinctions between the material and the spiritual or between science and art should serve us well enough,

[*] This paper was first published in the *Archives Européennes de Sociologie* x (1969).

[1] The perennial controversies on this and related topics have been reanimated by a number of recent articles by both anthropologists and philosophers, including among others: R. Horton, 'A Definition of Religion and its Uses', *J. Royal Anth. Inst.* xc (1960), 201–26; 'Ritual Man in Africa', *Africa*, xxxiv (1964), 85–104; 'African Traditional Thought and Western Science', *Ibid.* xxxvii (1967), 50–71 and 155–87; 'Neo-Tylorianism: Sound Sense or Sinister Prejudice?', *Man*, n.s. iii (1968), 625–34; J. Goody, 'Religion and Ritual: the Definitional Problem', *Brit. J. Sociol.* xii (1961), 142–64; E. Gellner, 'Concepts and Society', *Trans. Vth World Congress of Sociology, 1962*, i, 153–83; P. Winch, 'Understanding a Primitive Society', *Amer. Philos. Quart.* I (1964), 307–24; M. E. Spiro, 'Religion: Problems of Definition and Explanation', in M. Banton, ed. *Anthropological Approaches to the Study of Religion* (London, Tavistock, 1966), pp. 85–126; J. Beattie, 'Ritual and Social Change', *Man*, n.s. i (1966), 60–74; I. C. Jarvie and J. Agassi, 'The Rationality of Magic', *Brit. J. Sociol.* xviii (1967), 55–74; S. Lukes, 'Some Problems about Rationality', *Arch. Eur. Sociol.* viii (1967), 247–64; M. Hollis, 'Reason and Ritual', *Philosophy* xliii (1968), 231–47; J.D.Y. Peel, 'Understanding Alien Belief-Systems', *Brit. J. Sociol.* xx (1969), 69–84.

[2] I have used the first edition of Durkheim's *Les Formes Elémentaires de la Vie Religieuse* (Paris, Alcan, 1912), but the fourth of Weber's *Wirtschaft und Gesellschaft* (Tübingen, Mohr, 1956) in which the section 'Typen religioser Vergemeinschaftung (Religionssoziologie)' appears as i, 245–381. All references to Durkheim and Weber are to these except where otherwise specified.

and it is in any case a sensible methodological maxim to be flexible in matters of definition. But this is not by itself a justification for giving up at the outset and falling back on 'facts that admittedly are religious' (Jane Harrison),[1] or 'feeling our way towards the meaning it should have in given circumstances' (Nadel).[2] If we wish to explain the beliefs which historians and ethnographers have inclined to label 'religious', do we or do we not need the distinctions which their use of this label implies?

To clear the ground a little, it may be as well to anticipate a part of my argument. Although beliefs of any sort may be legitimately *explained* in categories foreign to the subjects themselves, they can only be *identified* in the subjects' own terms. It is for this reason that it is so dangerous for the observer to impose any descriptive terms of his own which are not directly derived from his documentary evidence or fieldwork. This applies particularly to the terms 'rational' and 'irrational' where they are used to distinguish the subjects' categories from the observer's. Sometimes, of course, 'rational' is used to convey a more or less overt value-judgement. Sometimes it is used to mark a distinction which the subject himself already recognises, as when actions done from an avowed practical purpose are distinguished from actions done for some other reason (Weber's distinction between *Zweckrationalität* and *Wertrationalität* and the distinction derived from it in English between 'instrumental' and 'expressive' action). But where beliefs, and not actions, are under discussion, it is at best gratuitous, and at worst misleading; and although I shall later be arguing in favour of a viewpoint which I attribute to Max Weber, I shall not attempt to defend him from the charge that his use of 'rational' and its cognates is 'irredeemably opaque and shifting'.[3] In fact, I shall avoid using 'rational' altogether in distinguishing between categories of belief, whether 'religious' or otherwise.

It is also as well to emphasise at the outset that the explanation of putatively 'religious' *actions* raises problems which are quite separate from those of explaining *beliefs*. Admittedly, the question of ritual is at many points intimately bound up with that of belief, and the distinction between *Zweckrationalität* and *Wertrationalität* is central to it. But an answer to the question why people hold the beliefs that they do does not depend on answering the question why they perform the actions that they do. It is, if anything, the other way round: ritual furnishes clues which help the observer to establish what the performers *do* believe, but

[1] J. E. Harrison, *Themis* (Cambridge University Press, 1912), p. 29, quoted by Goody *op. cit.* p. 142.
[2] S. F. Nadel, *Nupe Religion* (London, Routledge, 1954), p. 7.
[3] Lukes, *op. cit.* p. 259 n. 57.

it will not tell him *why* they believe it. Moreover, ritual actions are often related, on any plausible interpretation, not to beliefs at all but to desires. This assertion does not depend either on debatable psychoanalytic pre-suppositions or on ethnological generalisation about 'magic': to take just one trivial example from our own culture, a person who has pressed the button to call the elevator in a multi-storey block may sometimes be observed to press it once or twice more while he is waiting, not because he expects it to bring the elevator sooner (he knows quite well that it will not) but as a consciously symbolic gesture giving vent to his impatience. In practice, it is often difficult to tell whether a 'ritual' action is in fact of this kind or whether the performer does hold to a belief of some sort about the effects which his action will bring about: this is indeed the crux of many of the longstanding controversies about magic to which I shall have briefly to refer again later. But the explanation of beliefs involves the explanation of ritual only to the extent that an established ritual practice may furnish evidence that a belief, or set of beliefs, implied by it is in fact more or less widely held.

The question which needs first to be answered, therefore, is what exactly people *do* believe. Only then is it worth trying to decide whether one category of beliefs can usefully be labelled 'religious'. There is nothing, of course, to prevent those who so wish from continuing not only to use 'religious' but also to define it in terms of either the sacred or the supernatural. But these two rivals, influential though they have been, have failed not only to lead to convincing theories by which religion could be claimed to have been explained but even to be capable of formulation in such a way as to cope with damaging borderline cases. Tylor's criterion of the supernatural, intuitively appealing though it is, has never been stated in a way which yields a satisfactory boundary between the supernatural and the natural. Durkheim's criterion of the sacred, though tied to an original and ingenious theory of religion, turns out similarly to afford no means except the observer's own categories of showing where 'des choses sacrées, c'est à dire séparées, interdites' begin and end. Dissatisfaction with Durkheim's definition of religion, both on this ground and because of its specific reference to a church,[1] has led to a revival of

---

[1] See W. Lloyd Warner, *A Black Civilization* (New York, Harper, 1937), pp. 229 ff. for a criticism based on Australian fieldwork. For a criticism which seems to be directed against Durkheim, although not by name, see Weber, pp. 259–60: 'Oder aber man behandelt als entscheidend für den Priesterbegriff: dass die Funktionäre, sei es erblich oder individuell angestellt, im Dienst eines vergesellschafteten sozialen Verbandes, welcher Art immer er sei, tätig werden, also als dessen Angestellte oder Organe und lediglich im Interesse seiner Mitglieder, nicht wie die Zauberer, welche

Tylor's usage, which has at least the merit of seeming more immediately suited to the practising anthropologist's needs.[1] But its revival is more for want of a better than for any newly discovered merits of its own. Anthropologists are understandably reluctant simply to abandon the long-established distinction between religion, magic and science, and so the problem continues to be posed in such a way as to imply that there must be *some* definition which will preserve as much of the common-sense distinction as is valuable.

I shall not attempt to summarise the arguments for and against either Tylor's or Durkheim's definitions or such modifications of them as have been proposed. But it may be useful to set out in very brief summary the four main alternative views of the relations between 'religion', 'magic' and 'science'. I have labelled them the Durkheimian, Frazerian, neo-Durkheimian and neo-Frazerian views, but these are labels of convenience only; I shall not attempt to justify them by textual citation.

1. *The Durkheimian view*: There is no significant distinction between magic and religion.[2] 'Magico-religious' beliefs are characterised by their position on the sacred side of the sacred/secular division, and the explanation of them is to be sought in the form and nature of social organisation and the sentiments inspired by society itself. At the same time, however, the line between magico-religious and scientific beliefs should not be too strongly drawn, since scientific beliefs can likewise be explained by reference to social conditions and perform an analogous function for the believer.

2. *The Frazerian view*: Magical, religious and scientific beliefs are characteristic of three successive stages of intellectual and cultural development. Religious beliefs, i.e. beliefs in supernatural beings, replace magical

einen freien Beruf ausüben. Auch dieser begrifflich klare Gegensatz ist natürlich in der Realität flussig. Die Zauberer sind nicht selten zu einer festen Zunft, unter Umständen zu einer erblichen Kaste, zusammengeschlossen, und diese kann innerhalb bestimmts Gemeinschaften das Monopol der Magie haben. Auch der katholische Priester ist nicht immer "angestellt", sondern z. b. in Rom nicht selten ein armer Vagrant, der von der Hand in dem Mund von dem einzelnen Messen lebt, deren Wahrnehmung er nachgeht.'

[1] Horton, 'Ritual Man . . .', p. 95, claims that 'few anthropological fieldworkers suffer from much doubt as to which of the behaviour they deal with is religious and which is not. And most of them tend to accept as a working definition the proposition that religion includes a belief in one or more spiritual beings'.

[2] This statement does, perhaps, call for a note in view of the distinctions which Durkheim explicitly makes. Not only does he claim that magic has no church; he also claims that 'il n'y a pas de péché magique' (p. 430). But it also follows from his theory that 'les forces magiques ne sont, croyons-nous, qu'une forme particulière des forces religieuses' (p. 320, n. 1; cf. p. 463, n. 1) and 'la foi qu'inspire la magie n'est qu'un cas particulier de la foi religieuse en général' (p. 577).

beliefs when magical beliefs are seen to be false, and in the same way, they are replaced in turn by the objectively validated results of science. Thus magic is merely bad science, and religion is merely substitute science.

3. *The neo-Durkheimian view* : Magical and religious beliefs differ from scientific beliefs in that they should not be taken literally in the first place. Just as ritual actions must be understood in terms of the social values which they symbolise and not what appears to be their ostensible purpose, so must magico-religious beliefs be understood in terms of what they symbolise and not what they literally say. They should be explained in the way that we explain myth and drama, not in the way that we explain manuals of technology.

4. *The neo-Frazerian view* : Magical beliefs should, as Frazer recognised, be bracketed with scientific and distinguished from religious, since both are empirically derived from observation of the world. Frazer's own theory is, of course, historically false. But if a people believes that certain actions produce certain consequences, the anthropologist should not consign these beliefs to the category of religion, or non-science, simply because he has good grounds of his own for believing them to be wrong. He is entitled only to conclude that the people in question lacks strict standards of verification.

Now perhaps the first observation to be made after comparing these four views is that they are by no means entirely irreconcilable, particularly the 'Frazerian' and 'Durkheimian'. However mistaken Frazer's conjectural history or Durkheim's dismissal of the significance of belief in gods,[1] they are agreed on two important and related issues. First, both are evolutionists, Durkheim no less than Frazer; second, both recognise (unlike some neo-Durkheimians) that 'primitive' cosmologies may well be attempting the same task as modern science.[2] In other words, wherever the 'supernatural' does or doesn't come into it, every people's beliefs are an attempt of a kind to make sense of the world as they find it: in

---

[1] See, e.g. Spiro, *op. cit.* pp. 92–4 for factual (quite apart from methodological) criticism of Durkheim's view of Buddhism.

[2] For Durkheim's views cf. p. 35: 'Pour lui (le primitif), il n'y a rien d'étrange à ce que l'on puisse, de la voix ou du geste, commander aux éléments, arrêter ou précipiter le cours des astres, susciter la pluie ou la suspendre, etc. Les rites qu'il emploie pour assurer la fertilité du sol ou la fécondité des éspèces animales dont il se nourrit ne sont pas, à ses yeux, plus irrationels que ne le sont, aux nôtres, les procédés techniques dont nos agronomes se servent pour le même objet'; p. 290: 'Le wakan, en effet, joue dans le monde, tel que se le représentent les Sioux, le même rôle que les forces par lesquelles la science explique les diverses phénomènes de la nature'; pp. 341–2: 'Les explications de la science contemporaine . . . ne diffèrent pas en nature de celles qui satisfont la pensée primitive.'

Durkheim's words, 'toute religion est une sorte de technique qui permet à l'homme d'affronter le monde avec plus de confiance';[1] and in the natural course of cultural evolution, some such attempts give way to others. At the outset, Frazer could agree with Durkheim, the tripartite distinction is largely irrelevant: only much later does the success of science differentiate it in the eyes of its practitioners from 'primitive' science, i.e. magic, and 'non'-science, i.e. religion.[2] At what stage these distinctions are formulated, and how far even those people who make them retain a system of 'sacred' beliefs and/or rituals, are matters which can then be decided by historical and ethnographic research.

That Frazer and Durkheim can be reconciled more closely still could, indeed, be argued by reference to Malinowski, who explicitly tries to retain both Durkheim's twofold distinction between sacred and secular and Frazer's threefold distinction between magic, science and religion. But the attempt is not, in the event, successful and Malinowski's analysis, however valuable his descriptive observations of Trobriand beliefs and practices, slides uneasily between the categories of the observer and categories imputed to the participants. It is more revealing to compare the neo-Durkheimian and neo-Frazerian views, whose exponents have tended to emphasise their differences rather than seek to compose them. To the neo-Durkheimians, the neo-Frazerians are guilty, with Frazer, of distorting 'primitive' beliefs by imposing the observer's categories on them where they have no place; to the neo-Frazerians, the neo-Durkheimians fall over so far backwards to avoid Frazer's error that they fail to recognise empirical beliefs when they are staring them in the face—when, that is, their informants have quite explicitly avowed their conviction that certain causes lead to certain effects.

[1] P. 272; cf. e.g. p. 32: 'Les nécessités de l'existence nous obligent tous, croyants et incrédules, à nous représenter de quelque manière ces choses au milieu desquelles nous vivons, sur lesquelles nous avons sans cesse des jugements à porter et dont il nous faut tenir compte dans notre conduite.'

[2] Similarly Weber, 'Die Wirtschaftsethik der Weltreligionen: Einleitung', *Ges. Aufs. zur Religionssoziologie* (Tübingen, Mohr, 1922, cited hereafter as *GAzR*), I, 254: 'Die Einheitlichkeit des primitives Weltbild, in welchem alles konkrete Magie war, zeigt dann die Tendenz zur Spaltung in ein rationales Erkennen und eine rationale Beherrschung der Natur einerseits, und anderseits "mystische" Erlebnisse, deren unaussagbare Inhalte als einziges neben dem entgotteten Mechanismus der Welt noch mögliches Jenseits: in Wahrheit als ein ungreifbares, hinterweltliches Reich gottinigen, individuellen Heilsbesitzes, übrig bleiben.' Cf. the remark made by Jarvie and Agassi, *op. cit.* p. 57, that 'few people these days bother to claim that religion is rational in either the weak or the strong senses', or Horton, 'Ritual Man . . .', p. 96: 'the primary intention of much African religious thought seems to be just that mapping of connexions between space-time phenomena which Christian thought feels is beyond its proper domain.'

There is no doubt that the disagreements between the neo-Durk-heimians and neo-Frazerians are genuine and strongly entrenched, as a reading of the articles which I cited at the beginning of this paper will make clear. But how far are they disagreements between the adherents of rival explanatory theories? For the purposes of this paper, the point to be emphasised is how much of the disagreement is not over the *explanation* of beliefs (where it is beliefs as opposed to rituals whose interpretation is at issue), but over their *identification*. What *do* the Azande, Nupe, Dinka, Kalabari, Lugbara, etc., believe? It is often difficult to tell. But it would be equally implausible to suppose that *everything* which they say or do of a 'magico-religious' kind must be interpreted in *either* a neo-Durk-heimian *or* a neo-Frazerian fashion. To see this, it is enough to consider two well-known examples from Evans-Pritchard: belief in witchcraft among the Azande and the belief that 'twins are birds' among the Nuer. Why, in the first case, should we question that a Zande believes what he says when he attributes the cause of a person's death to witchcraft? As Evans-Pritchard says elsewhere himself, 'many peoples are convinced that deaths are caused by witchcraft. To speak of witchcraft being for these peoples a supernatural agency hardly reflects their own view of the matter, since from their point of view nothing could be more natural. They experience it through the senses in deaths and other misfortunes, and the witches are their neighbours.'[1] What is more, it is difficult to see why anyone should wish to suggest that the belief ought not to be taken literally, but translated as a symbolic expression of some other belief or value-judgement about the social order. As Hollis comments, 'A Zande who believes he has been bewitched surely does not believe that he has offended some social authority or other. If he did, he could perfectly well say so.'[2] And if we ask the rather different question how it is that the Azande fail to see that their beliefs about witchcraft are false, then the answer is adequately provided by the full and convincing account which Evans-Pritchard has given of the self-confirming nature of these beliefs.[3]

On the other hand, there is equally little ground for assuming, when

---

[1] E. E. Evans-Pritchard, *Theories of Primitive Religion* (Oxford, Clarendon Press, 1965), p. 110.

[2] *Op. cit.* p. 235. Cf. the comments of Spiro, *op. cit.* pp. 105–6 on the 'extraordinary statement' of E. R. Leach, *Political Systems of Highland Burma* (London, Bell, 1954), p. 182, that 'the various sorts of Kachin religious ideology are, in the last analysis, nothing more than ways of describing the formal relationships that exist between real persons and real groups in ordinary Kachin society'.

[3] E. E. Evans-Pritchard, *Witchcraft, Oracles and Magic among the Azande* (Oxford, Clarendon Press, 1937), *passim*.

a Nuer asserts that 'twins are birds', that he *should* be understood literally. To say that a twin is a bird in the sense that a sparrow is a bird would no doubt be as strange to the Nuer as to the anthropologist observing them;[1] as the anthropologist duly learns, if he does his fieldwork properly, 'twins and birds, though for different reasons, are both associated with spirit, and this makes twins, like birds, "people of the above" and "children of God" '.[2] To claim to understand a culture, whether an alien culture or the investigator's own, is to claim among other things to know what should and what should not be taken literally in it.[3] The disputes between neo-Frazerians and neo–Durkheimians arise not because we have to commit ourselves to taking literally either everything or nothing but because in the case of *some* ostensible beliefs asserted by members of unfamiliar cultures, it is very hard to tell which sort of interpretation is right.[4] If a man is observed always to chant spells when he plants his crops, it may be that he believes that this will help his crops to grow; it may be that he attributes no causal efficacy to it whatever, but that it expresses his interest in what he is doing, like a sea-shanty; it may be that it not merely expresses his interest in what he is doing but helps him, in his view, to do it more carefully.[5] The anthropologist has first to decide which interpretation is correct. Only then is he in a position to try to *explain* the

---

[1] Cf. Leach, *op. cit.* p. 14: 'It is nonsense to ask such questions as: "Do nats have legs? Do they eat flesh? Do they live in the sky?" ' In this case, however, Leach is giving his own view rather than that of a native informant, and it would need further evidence to establish that a representative sample of Kachins would regard 'Do nats eat flesh?' as a meaningless question. Leach's own evidence suggests that they might rather regard the assertion that nats eat flesh as meaningful but false, since at sacrifices nats are held to take only the 'breath' (*nsa*) and leave the carcase to be eaten by human beings (p. 173).

[2] Evans-Pritchard, *Nuer Religion* (Oxford, Clarendon Press, 1956), p. 132.

[3] It is sometimes implied in the (neo-Durkheimian) anthropological literature that it is ethnocentric and patronising to take alien beliefs too literally. This may or may not be so in the particular case. But the imputation can work both ways. Compare, for example, Marc Bloch, *Feudal Society* (trans. Manyon; London, Routledge, 1961), pp. 83–4: 'Though the instinctive reactions of a vigorous realism were never lacking, a Robert the Pious or an Otto III could nevertheless attach as much importance to a pilgrimage as to a battle or a law, and historians who are either scandalized by this fact or who persist in discovering subtle political manoeuvres in these pious journeys merely prove thereby their inability to lay aside the spectacles of men of the nineteenth and twentieth centuries.'

[4] See, for example, Spiro, 'Virgin Birth, Parthenogenesis and Physiological Paternity: an Essay in Cultural Interpretation', *Man*, n.s. III (1968), pp. 242–61, and the exchange of letters *ibid.*, pp. 651–6, for argument on a representative topic which goes back at least as far as the observations of Carl Strehlow (Durkheim, p. 358 n. 2).

[5] This variant of the 'neo-Durkheimian' view was already being argued by Collingwood against Frazer in 1937: see R. G. Collingwood, *The Principles of Art* (Oxford, Clarendon Press, 1938), pp. 57–69.

belief, if indeed there is one there to explain at all, and to decide what is gained by labelling it 'religious' or 'magical'.

For that matter, it is to be expected that all three interpretations may apply not merely to different rituals in the same society but to the same ritual in the minds of different people in the same society. Consider the beliefs that are held in our own society about prayer. Some people believe in its efficacy; others have no belief in it whatever, but enjoy it on occasions for its aesthetic merits; others believe that although its ostensible content is wholly erroneous it can still help to make people feel braver, more penitent or whatever is appropriate than they would feel without it. Furthermore, social symbolism may be quite overt in 'magico-religious' rituals even of 'primitive' peoples, and such peoples may be quite well aware of what the anthropologist is likely to call its 'latent function'. Lienhardt, for example, in his account of the religion of the Dinka, describes how the division of sacrificial meat when a bull or an ox is killed is deliberately done in a fashion symbolic of the relationships of the members of the sacrificing group;[1] and Horton, having described how it sometimes happens among the Kalabari that 'Christian observances become symbols of factional allegiance', goes on to emphasise that in such cases Kalabari themselves say that these people are not believing Christians.[2] This is not to deny that in all cultures some of what people say and do may be said and done because of its *unrecognised* symbolism, and has, therefore, to be explained at least in part by reference to psychological theory. But again, this is a matter for the appropriate empirical research. It may well hold true of a great deal of art, and thereby of a great deal of what is usually meant by 'religion'. But even if it is successfully demonstrated over an extensive area, it will certainly not follow that *all* 'religious' or 'magical' ritual is to be explained along similar lines.

To decide the question, therefore, whether it is useful to try to isolate a distinctive category of 'religious' beliefs, we have first to have distinguished apparent beliefs from real ones; and it is the difficulty in this, just as much if not more than the difficulty in *explaining* beliefs, that has generated so much controversy about both 'magic' and 'religion'. The identification of beliefs is difficult, moreover, not merely because of what may be involved in learning the language and ritual of an alien culture, but also because belief itself is not a yes-or-no affair. This is so in two ways: first, it is possible in both 'secular' and 'religious' matters for a

---

[1] Godfrey Lienhardt, *Divinity and Experience* (Oxford, Clarendon Press, 1961), pp. 23–4; cf. p. 234.
[2] Horton, 'A Definition . . .', p. 203.

person neither wholly to believe nor wholly to disbelieve something; second, it is possible for different people to have different standards by which the validity of a belief may be assessed.

What evidence entitles us to assert or deny that an Anglican clergyman subscribes to the 39 Articles, or that a soldier going into battle believes that his talisman will bring him luck, or that a little girl knows that her doll is not a person? It may not be at all easy to say. Perhaps the clergyman is going through a recurring cycle of faith and doubt; perhaps the soldier, though not in general superstitious, feels that nothing is lost by keeping an object which might, who knows, have some such property as the anecdotes of his fellows attribute to it;[1] perhaps the child is only halfway to distinguishing the inanimate and animate from each other. This last example raises particular difficulties of its own. But I cite it because it is specifically invoked not only by Durkheim but also by E. R. Dodds in *The Greeks and the Irrational*, and it is, I think, instructive in this context to quote them directly.

Here, first of all, is Dodds: 'If we may judge by the furniture of their tombs, the inhabitants of the Aegean region had felt since Neolithic times that man's need for food, drink and clothing, and his desire for service and entertainment, did not cease with death. I say advisedly "felt", rather than "believed"; for such acts as feeding the dead look like a direct response to emotional drives, not necessarily mediated by any theory. Man, I take it, feeds his dead for the same sort of reason as a little girl feeds her doll; and like the little girl, he refrains from killing his phantasy by applying reality-standards. When the archaic Greek poured liquids down a feeding-tube into the livid jaws of a mouldering corpse, all that we can say is that he abstained, for good reasons, from knowing what he was doing; or, to put it more abstractly, that he ignored the distinction between corpse and ghost—he treated them as "consubstantial".'[2]

And here is Durkheim (pp. 93–4): 'Quand nous entendons un enfant apostropher avec colère un objet qui l'a heurté, nous en concluons qu'il y voit un être conscient comme lui; mais c'est mal interpréter ses paroles et ses gestes. En réalité, il est étranger au raisonnement très compliqué qu'on lui attribue. S'il en prend à la table qui lui a fait du mal, ce n'est

---

[1] Cf. the observation of Malinowski, *Magic, Science and Religion and Other Essays* (Glencoe, Free Press, 1948), p. 14, that 'It is most significant that in lagoon fishing, where man can rely completely on his knowledge and skill, magic does not exist, while in the open-sea fishing, full of danger and uncertainty, there is extensive magical ritual to ensure safety and good results'.

[2] E. R. Dodds, *The Greeks and the Irrational* (University of California, 1951), p. 136, citing among others (n. 6) Lévy-Bruhl and Malinowski.

pas qu'il la suppose animée et intelligente, mais c'est qu'elle lui a fait du mal . . .Il y a si peu confusion que, quand l'émotion de l'enfant est calmée, il sait très bien distinguer une chaise d'une personne: il ne se comporte pas avec l'une comme avec l'autre. C'est une raison analogue qui explique sa tendance à traiter ses jouets comme s'ils étaient des êtres vivants. C'est le besoin de jouer, si intense chez lui, qui se crée une matière appropriée, comme, dans les cas précédent, les sentiments violents que la souffrance avait déchaînés se créaient la leur de toutes pièces. Pour pouvoir jouer consciencieusement avec sa policinelle, il imagine donc d'y voir une personne vivante. L'illusion lui est, d'ailleurs, d'autant plus facile que, chez lui, l'imagination est souveraine maîtresse; il ne pense guère que par images et on sait combien les images sont choses souples qui se plient docilement à toutes les exigences du désir. Mais il est si peu dupe de sa propre fiction qu'il serait le premier étonné si, tout à coup, elle devenait une réalité et si son pantin le mordait.'

These two accounts differ only, it may be said, in degree: what to Durkheim is almost conscious pretence on the part of the child is to Dodds rather a repression of disbelief. But the example shows fully the difficulties of identification characteristic of the investigation of any but the most common sense beliefs. How is the anthropologist or historian ever to give an uncontroversial account of states of mind which lie somewhere between the point at which literal faith gives way to 'believing what you know to be untrue' and the point at which the acting out of unconscious symbolism gives way to the deliberate manipulation of fiction?

The analogy between the development of a child and the development of a 'primitive' culture is notoriously discredited, but in this instance, however Tylor or Lévy-Bruhl may have misused it, it is appropriate. Just as a child learns that terms which it has first taken literally are to be construed as metaphor or fantasy, so does a language itself change with a culture's development, and terms become metaphorical which were once employed literally within a now discarded system of beliefs. In the sixth edition of *Notes and Queries on Anthropology*, the following is given among other examples of 'Religious Beliefs concerning Man': 'The soul may be thought of as an insubstantial replica or wraith, or as a formless emanation, it may be likened to the shadow, breath or reflection, various parts of the body may be conceived of as the seat of the soul—head, heart, liver, etc.'[1] But if I use 'breath' or 'spirit' as a metaphor for 'life',

---

[1] Royal Anthropological Institution, *Notes and Queries on Anthropology*, 6th ed. (London, 1951), p. 176.

I am certainly not giving expression to a religious belief (whatever 'religion' is supposed to mean in this context), any more than if I used a metaphor like 'hot-headed' or 'good-humoured' which once had, but has long since lost, a literal ('scientific'? 'magical'?) meaning. And if our own term 'soul' is nowadays predominantly, though by no means exclusively, used metaphorically, what about 'mind'? Does its use imply a quasi-scientific belief about brain-states, a metaphysical belief in Cartesian dualism, or is it merely a dispositional metaphor, the 'ghost in the machine' exorcised by Professor Ryle? Or compare, to take an alien culture which is happily well-documented, the shifting beliefs of the Greeks between the Archaic and Classical periods about the mind: the three terms ψυχή, θυμός and νοος (νοῦς) are all in Plato's vocabulary just as they are in Homer's, but to Homer the three meant something radically different. They were not identical to Plato any more than to Homer, but to Homer they were 'separate organs, each having its own particular function'.[1] This sort of cultural shift is characteristic not merely of the beliefs implicit in the use of particular terms but in the use of myths as such. At the outset their authenticity may be unquestioned; but by a gradual progression they give way to self-conscious history on the one hand (Herodotus)[2] and self-conscious fairy-tales on the other (Ovid: 'Prodigiosa loquor veterum mendacia vatum'). The problem is equally troublesome whether we are dealing merely with individual concepts or with a whole system of related myths. Between the stage of literal belief and the stage at which 'myth' in our present sense takes on that meaning, there is a broad, shifting, indeterminate area in which the question 'what *exactly* do they believe?' seems to be unanswerable.

This leads on to the second difficulty. It is not only beliefs and thereby meanings which change, but criteria of truth and falsehood. One man's myth may be another man's logic. If ethnography has taught us anything, it might be claimed, it is that we should not be parochial about our philosophy any more than our Victorian forebears should have been parochial about their religion. It may be conceded that some minimal formal requirement of consistency is necessary for any statement of belief to be intelligible at all. But may it not still be objected, as it is by Winch, that 'these formal requirements tell us nothing about what in particular is to *count* as consistency, just as the rules of the propositional

---

[1] Bruno Snell, *The Discovery of the Mind* (trans. Rosenmayer; New York, Harper, 1960), p. 14.
[2] On the absence of a hard-and-fast distinction between myth and history, see M. I. Finley, 'Myth, Memory and History', *History and Theory* IV (1965), 281–302.

calculus limit, but do not themselves determine, what are to be proper values of p, q, etc.'?[1] Perhaps, therefore, it is not enough for the anthropologist to express their beliefs in their own terms, for he may still, in reporting them as their beliefs, be imprisoned in his own preconception about what can be said to constitute a belief at all: his assertion 'they believe X' is then not, as it appears to be, a statement of empirical fact but the imposition of an observer's category where it may be entirely out of place.

These two difficulties are both serious. But they are still only practical difficulties. They should not be exaggerated into impossibilities in principle, and they are not a basis for either asserting or denying that beliefs should be explained in one way rather than another. Admittedly, there are bound to be borderline cases in matters of belief where neo-Frazerians and neo-Durkheimians are likely to take different sides. Admittedly also, there is a point at which empirical questions about people's beliefs are bound to give way to philosophical questions, and this will arise in a manner, or at a point, to which there is not an equivalent in the sciences of nature. But it would be a mistake to conclude from this that either the identification or the explanation of beliefs is rendered either unattainable or arbitrary; if anything follows from the recognition of these difficulties, it is that the category of 'religious' beliefs is even less useful than it has appeared already. In any case, these problems are not, as I have already hinted, in any way peculiar to the investigation of cultures other than the observer's own. There are in our own culture just as much as in the cultures documented in the ethnographic literature not only beliefs of which it is difficult to say whether particular persons or groups do or don't hold them but also different and incompatible criteria of what can properly be said to constitute belief. If, therefore, it is seriously suggested that these difficulties make beliefs, however extravagantly 'religious', somehow mutually inaccessible between cultures, it will follow that I cannot claim to assert what is believed by anyone at all who either isn't wholly clear in his own mind or has different criteria of belief from my own. But this is palpably false. In either my own culture or any other with which I may make myself sufficiently familiar, I can perfectly well answer the question 'does X believe . . . ?' with 'he isn't sure'; and I can also perfectly well report his belief that, let us say, 'God is both Three and One' while myself remaining convinced that this assertion is meaningless or self-contradictory. There is no vicious regress lurking inside the notion of beliefs about the criteria of assessment of beliefs. Whether I

[1] *Op. cit.* p. 318.

share someone else's criteria or not, I can report quite impartially on his stock of what *he* holds as his beliefs; and although criteria of belief may be both inter-culturally and intra-culturally variable, the notion of belief itself is not. To say this is not in some underhand way to commit primitive people or small children to a capacity to understand the truth-tables of Wittgenstein's *Tractatus*, any more than it is to deny that some people's views about the existence of gods, or God, are diametrically opposed to others'. It is merely to make the obvious point that without a notion of negation, and with it a notion of *some* kind of truth and falsehood, there could not be, in any culture, a system of beliefs or even a language at all.

In a similar way, a spurious philosophical difficulty about language itself is sometimes constructed from an argument based on the difficulties of translation. Once again, it hardly needs to be conceded that translation of 'religious' idiom *is* difficult, as Evans-Pritchard effectively brings out: 'I have read somewhere of the predicament of missionaries to the Eskimoes in trying to render into their tongue the word "lamb" as in the sentence "Feed my lambs". You can, of course, render it by reference to some animal with which the Eskimoes are acquainted, by saying, for instance, "Feed my seals", but clearly if you do so you replace the representation of what a lamb was for a Hebrew shepherd by that of what a seal may be to an Eskimo. How is one to convey the meaning of the statement that the horses of the Egyptians are "flesh and not spirit" to a people which has never seen a horse or anything like one, and may also have no concept corresponding to the Hebrew conception of spirit? . . . Or how do you render into Amerindian language "In the beginning was the Word"?'[1]

That the pedagogic difficulties of Christian missionaries are formidable can hardly be denied. It is also quite true that there seems something unsatisfying about the need to resort to explication and periphrasis in a highly-charged 'religious' context. As it is put by a recent author on the philosophical theory of meaning, 'when we have to describe the sentence's causes, effects or purposes in a roundabout way—"They utter this in order to placate the rain deity"—because we know of no familiar equivalent, it seems a poor second best; the sentence's vital spark has been put out.'[2] But it would, as the same author makes clear, be quite wrong to

---

[1] *Theories of Primitive Religion*, pp. 13–14. Cf. e.g. his Foreword to Lucien Lévy-Bruhl, *The 'Soul' of the Primitive* (tr. Clare; London, Unwin, 1965), p. 6.

[2] L. Jonathan Cohen, *The Diversity of Meaning*, 2nd ed. (London, Methuen, 1966), p. 68.

conclude from this that 'religious' or any other vocabulary is somehow incomprehensible between cultures, or even to talk like Malinowski about 'quite untranslatable' particles.[1] If this were so, it would follow that language learning would be impossible altogether, which is of course absurd. What is more, the notion of incomprehensibility between cultures is self-defeating, since it would mean that the anthropologist could not express, and therefore could not discover in the first place, what *is* the untranslatable belief which he claims the members of the alien culture to hold.[2] It would be truer to say that the understanding of alien beliefs may require the learning, at least in part, of the alien language. But it would be ridiculous to suggest that this is in any sense impossible in principle; in fact, it is already going on within the culture in question wherever instruction is being transmitted from initiates to novices whether about the 'supernatural' or anything else. There is nothing more incomprehensible in principle to an English anthropologist about the Nuer belief in Kwoth than about the Anglican catechism or the multiplication table or the official history of the Second World War.

There is accordingly no warrant for arguing that other people's beliefs cannot be identified, or that they cannot be translated, or that they cannot be understood (unless, of course, 'understanding' is defined in some special sense whereby to understand a belief is made to entail, or be synonymous with, sharing it). It is true that beliefs of the kind commonly labelled 'religious' are often difficult to identify; that they may not be categorically held or categorically rejected or even fully understood by the presumed believers themselves; that they change their meaning over time; that they can seldom be translated from one language to another without circumlocution; and that the anthropologist can never be absolutely certain that he has properly identified them, since further fieldwork might always disclose some further nuance of phrasing or context which

---

[1] *Op. cit.* p. 231.

[2] Cf. Cohen, *op. cit.* pp. 85–87; or W. Haas, 'The Theory of Translation', in G. H. R. Parkinson, ed., *The Theory of Meaning* (Oxford University Press, 1968), p. 107: 'In the Kikuyu Bible, for instance, "the Holy Ghost" is rendered by words which, if they were matched with English words, would correspond to something like "white liver." But they are *not* so matched. There is no bilingual dictionary of metaphors. If the powers of combination and contrast of the Kikuyu metaphor, in its Kikuyu context, are parallel to those of the English expression "the Holy Ghost", in its place amongst other English expressions, then the internal difficulty of the corresponding Kikuyu phrase stands to be resolved in the required way by those who hear it. The language will have been *made* to provide the required correspondences, as English once was, when missionaries introduced the strange expression "haleg gast" into their sentences.' For the general 'principle of expressibility', see John R. Searle, *Speech Acts* (Cambridge University Press, 1969), pp. 18–19.

had escaped his notice. But this is very different from any suggestion either that 'religious' beliefs cannot be beliefs at all or that they cannot be the subject of scientific inquiry just as much as any other area of human behaviour.

Once, therefore, the problems of identifying beliefs have been resolved, and with them much of the argument between neo-Frazerians and neo-Durkheimians about both 'magic' and 'religion', what can be said about the need to distinguish 'religious' beliefs from others? The moral which I wish to draw from these introductory remarks, and to support further in the following section, is that for the sociologist's purposes there is then no need at all. It is not a question of giving up because it is too difficult— of continuing, that is, to employ the term while admitting, like Nadel, that it is being used imprecisely. If some commonsense distinction like Tylor's *had* turned out to lead to a validated explanatory theory, then there would be good reason to retain 'religious' in precisely the sense in which the successful theory (in Tylor's case, animism) had used it. But the arguments which *are* properly speaking about explanation continue because the theory was *not* successful, any more than Durkheim's which succeeded it; and this lends strong presumption to the view that no other version of the common-sense distinction between 'religious' and 'scientific' (let alone 'magical') beliefs is going to furnish a significantly rewarding theoretical category. It remains, of course, true that distinctions of *some* kind will have to be made among beliefs if any of them, including those traditionally labelled 'religious', are going to be explained at all. But the categorisation religious/magical/scientific has, for all the dispute is has engendered, achieved little beyond helping to perpetuate the confusion between explaining beliefs and identifying them, and there seems no reason to suppose that some new and subtler version of it will turn out to be what sociologists (as opposed to theologians) should after all be looking for. When the investigator is confronted by 'magico-religious' beliefs and practices, what matters is not whether he can fit them to one or other of the textbook definitions of 'religion' or 'magic' but whether there *is* a belief to be explained and what specification of antecedent conditions will (at least provisionally) serve to explain it. It is possible that some version of either or both the sacred and/or the supernatural may still turn out to be indispensable categories for the purpose. But by now the onus is on those who wish to argue in their favour.[1]

---

[1] Those who *do* wish to retain 'religious' in a putatively explanatory sense might do well to clarify their proposed use of it by a Venn diagram, as is done by Samuel Z. Klausner, 'Kommentar zu: *Cohn*, Ist Religion Universal?', *Int. Jahrb. f. Religionssoziologie*, II (1966), 214.

In any case, a number of the distinctions between beliefs which do seem to be of explanatory value either lie within the traditional distinctions or cut across them altogether. For example, the distinction expressed by Weber in the terms *Gotteszwang* and *Gottesdienst* continues to be recognised as useful, whether or not it is original to Weber or its importance in the evolution of priesthood, prophecy and in due course European Protestant 'rationality' is as he suggested. The idea of a transition from 'shame-culture' to 'guilt-culture' is at least suggestive in a variety of contexts, even if no stronger claims can be sustained for it than that. But these two different forms of relationship between suppliant and deity may *both* be 'religious' rather than 'magical', unless the definition of 'magical' is so restricted as necessarily to coincide with *Gotteszwang*. If, on the other hand, a distinction is made in terms of the kind of supernatural power to which *either* manipulatory *or* propitiatory supplication is addressed, then this too will produce a distinction equivalent to religion/magic only by fiat, and precision will have been artificially gained at the expense of the previous distinction between manipulation and propitiation themselves which appeared at first to be the decisive one. In any case, as the earlier discussion has already suggested, 'magic' leads to as many difficulties of its own as 'religious', since if 'magic' is marked off from 'religion' by some criterion of quasi-empirical content, it becomes increasingly hard to distinguish in its turn from 'science'. The mistake is to try to force the various distinctions which suggest themselves into either a religious/magical/scientific or a magico-religious/secular-profane or a supernatural/natural straitjacket. Once beliefs are successfully distinguished from non-beliefs, the categories into which beliefs are assigned must be framed in such a way as will best explain why those who hold them hold them; and once 'religious' has turned out to create more difficulties than it solves, then for explanatory purposes, at any rate, it is better abandoned.

But surely (someone may still ask) the term 'religion' cannot be discarded altogether? Certainly not. But where it is most useful, I suggest, is when it is used in the sense where 'ideology' would do almost as well—that is, in denoting those distinctive combinations of factual with ethical beliefs which constitute the 'religion' of the Nuer, Dinka, Tokugawa Japanese, Homeric Greeks, Roman Catholics, Benthamite Utilitarians, Jews, Muslims, Anarchists, Narodniks, Christian Scientists, Dialectical Materialists and all the rest.[1] In other words, if there is a general

---

[1] A broad definition along these lines is to some extent sanctioned by common usage, but often with the implication that talk of *atheistic* religion is a joke, or at least a

distinction to be retained between 'non-religious' and 'religious' beliefs, it is merely a distinction between what may be loosely called 'matter-of-fact' beliefs on one side and beliefs about the conduct of life on the other. The latter may stand in many different sorts of relation to the matter-of-fact beliefs about the cosmos which the people in question also hold. But they are a universal and unambiguous category—all cultures have *some* beliefs about *Lebenspraxis*—and they are normally the beliefs in which the sociologist, anthropologist or historian is particularly interested. How they are to be explained is still, of course, a matter for empirical research to decide. But to use 'religion' (or 'ideology') in this sense is at any rate unlikely to make the task of explanation any *more* difficult than otherwise, as long as it is made quite clear that this is all that is meant by it.

I I

But what does it mean to talk about 'explanation' of beliefs? This is not a paper in the philosophy of science, and I have neither the wish nor the space to explore the controversies by which that term is surrounded. It is, however, necessary to make clear that I take explanation to be causal in the broad sense, and to consist in more than a conceptual elucidation of logically connected beliefs or an incidental description of such concomitants of the beliefs as may help to make them more 'reasonable' than they would otherwise appear. Both these ancillary themes are often to be found in anthropological or historical accounts of systems of belief, but they are relevant to their explanation only if they help to establish the necessary and sufficient conditions which, if satisfied, will make it possible to predict that persons of the attributes and in the circumstances specified will (or would have, or did) come to hold these beliefs. (Hypotheses of this kind may, of course, be statistical rather than individual in form, as is often the case in both the social and the physical sciences.) To put the problem in this way may seem already to brush aside the arguments of those who hold the explanation of human actions and beliefs to rest on the imputation of reasons as opposed to causes. But for the purposes of the social scientist, reasons can be accommodated comfortably enough within the framework of necessary and sufficient conditions under which these reasons, whatever they may be, are considered adequate by the people in question and the beliefs which they entail are accordingly

metaphor. This uncertainty is nicely brought out by Weber in a passage where he refers to Confucianism as 'Die religiöse (oder wenn man will: irreligiöse) Standesethik dieser Schicht . . .' (*GAzR*, I, 239).

adopted and retained. Besides, not even the most committed partisans of free will can maintain that we believe what we do because we have *decided* to.

One other preliminary point about explanation does, however, need to be made. What counts as an explanation depends upon the context in which the request for one is made; and it accordingly depends on what is sometimes called the 'contrast class' in which the explanandum does *not* occur. In other words, where any belief or practice is being provisionally accounted for, there must be in the investigator's mind some reason to suppose that something is present (or missing) which serves to bring about *this* belief or practice among *these* people. It would be ridiculous to point to the performance of some customary ceremony and to say merely to the investigator 'explain it!', or even, with a little more sophistication, 'what are the necessary and sufficient conditions of that?' The antecedent conditions are numberless: it all depends what sort of story you want to be told. To take again the example of the Azande as studied by Evans-Pritchard, let us suppose that we wish to ask for an explanation of the dances of Zande witch-doctors. This may be a historical question about Zande culture, distinguishing between indigenous and foreign influences; it may be a psychological question about the circumstances under which specified emotions will or will not find expression in dancing; it may be a socio-cultural question about Zande beliefs about the appropriateness or efficacy of performing the dances on certain occasions; or it may be a more detailed question about why the dances are public (because of the prestige accruing to the person for whom they are performed) or why the dancers' movements are so exaggerated (because of the symbolism of the gestures). If there is some sort of theory of which the occurrence of the dances at all furnish a decisive test, then the contrast class will be precisely defined in terms of it and there will be evidence of an antecedently specified kind which will either invalidate or support it. But even then it would be misleading to suggest that there is something which could be designated *the* explanation of even a single ceremony or a single one of the beliefs underlying it. It is rather that the investigator is looking for one or more specifiable conditions which can be shown, once given a general background of conditions known to be necessary, to be 'contingently sufficient' for the case under study.[1]

---

[1] For fuller discussion of this notion, and of the model of explanation implied by it, see various papers by Michael Scriven, such as: 'Truisms as the Grounds for Historical Explanations', in Patrick Gardiner, ed., *Theories of History* (Glencoe, Free Press, 1959), pp. 443–75; 'Explanations, Predictions and Laws', *Minnesota Studies in the*

This said, however, it is possible to distinguish three subordinate questions which may underlie a request for the explanation of 'religious' or any other beliefs: first, what is the origin of the belief, second, how did it come to be generally adopted, and third, why does it continue to be held? Now if there is a fully-fledged theory of some kind which claims to account for the belief in question, it might conceivably answer all three of these questions, and resolve all of the hitherto puzzling differences from the contrasted cases, at one blow. Perhaps there will then be nothing more that seems to call for explanation at this level. I have already remarked that Tylor's animism is a perfectly respectable candidate for a theory which, if it were successful, would not only account for what ethnographers found puzzling about the beliefs which they appeared to have identified but would also have justified the retention of 'religious' as a distinctive category of beliefs about man and his place in the cosmic order. If Tylor had been right, we would have a plausible account both of how this distinguishable category of beliefs came to be generally adopted at a specified stage of cultural evolution and also how such beliefs might be predicted to give way to others in their turn. Similarly, if Durkheim had been right, we would see in central Australian totemism the origin of a (different, but equally distinguishable) category of beliefs and would understand why they are universal in human societies, albeit in widely differing forms. But since neither theory is successful, and no subsequent theory has been put forward which has succeeded any better at so ambitious a level, it is at least possible that attempts like these may be misconceived, and that we should do better to try to answer the questions about origin, acceptance and persistence in altogether less sweeping terms.

In practice, questions about origin and acceptance often turn out to be unanswerable, simply because in societies without documentary records the historical evidence is not and never will be available. The anthropologist is very seldom able to do more than identify some recent cultural contact by which new doctrines may first have been brought to the notice of the people he is studying and to sift out from the accretion of spurious

Philosophy of Science III (1962), 170–230; 'Review of Ernest Nagel, *The Structure of Science*', *Review of Metaphysics* XVII (1964), 403–24, and 'Causes and Connections in History', in William H. Dray, ed., *Philosophical Analysis and History* (New York, Harper, 1966), pp. 238–64. I should make clear, however, having once cited Scriven, that I do not agree either with his critique of the 'deductive-nomological' model of explanation and qualified endorsement of the so-called 'rational' model where human behaviour is in question, or with his extravagantly broad use of the term 'explanation' itself (on which see e.g. the remarks of May Brodbeck in *Minnesota Studies*, III, 240).

legend a small kernel of historical truth about some individual leader or prophet who has directly transformed the pattern of traditional belief. Indeed, there is a sense in which questions of origin are unanswerable even for literate and sophisticated cultures, since it seems reasonable to assume that 'religious' and/or 'scientific' beliefs of some kind—attempts, that is, of some sort to make sense of the world beyond the brute facts of immediate experience—are evolved prior to the development of literacy. It accordingly follows that unless we can, after all, accept some Durkheimian-cum-Tylorian evolutionary theory which enables us to see in the most primitive cultures still extant our own culture's previous condition, there can never be evidence for any people in the world which would show how their very first beliefs were developed in the irrecoverable prehistoric past. But this does not make any and all attempts at explanation by origin pointless. In the first place, it may well be enough to be able to show, by sufficiently thorough cross-cultural comparisons, the circumstances under which *someone or other* will *sooner or later* be bound to elaborate or codify a system of beliefs of a fairly precisely specified kind. There are a great many beliefs and practices whose coincidences in widely separated cultures are (to echo, this time, a phrase from *The Golden Bough*) too close and too numerous to be accidental.[1] If, taking a Weberian example, we are interested in particular in the taboo on usury, the explanation we are seeking need not depend at all on identifying the first spokesman to enunciate it; it may be enough, simply by a comparison of what we know from Reformation Europe, Rome after the Punic Wars, and a sufficient number of other instances, to relate the predictable occurrence of the taboo to specified economic and social conditions on one side and a psychological theory about attitudes to wealth and property on the other. In the second place, it is possible, without accepting the sort of assumption made by Durkheim, to find in the history of cultures for which documentary records are available evidence which will furnish at least a partial test of a hypothesis linking specified antecedents with specified consequences. That even the most meticulous study of the best-documented culture will by itself furnish a decisive test for a theory as

---

[1] The ethnographic literature is full of such parallels between cultures so far separated that a diffusionist explanation seems out of the question. What social-cum-psychological explanation will account, for example, for such a specific coincidence as that of the eating of raw flesh before sunrise both at Saracen sacrifices reported by Robertson Smith and Dinka sacrifices reported by Lienhardt (*op. cit.* p. 143 n. 2)? It is surely a sensible presumption that there is *some* common explanation of the two, even though we may be unable to say (*pace* bk. III, ch. II of *The Elementary Forms*) why sacrifice is practised at all in the first place.

ambitious as Durkheim's may indeed be impossible. But it would be equally foolish to go to the other extreme and deny that any one established historical sequence can ever tell the investigator anything at all about any other. An explanation incapable of generalisation is, after all, not an explanation at all: without the assumption of replicability there can be no warrant to suggest the connection between *post hoc* and *propter hoc* which has been postulated in the particular instance.

It may be useful to offer an illustration taken from a different but not wholly dissimilar area of study—the evolution not of beliefs but of art-forms. Consider the case of oral epic poetry which has been intensively studied in the last few decades and about which some generalisations seem now able to be fairly confidently made. How do we set about explaining the origin, acceptance and persistence of the oral epic? Since the contrast classes are in practice fairly clearly defined, we are in a position to specify the contingently sufficient causes which, *in given historical circumstances*, may enable us to predict its rise, spread and decline. We start from the striking coincidence of long heroic narrative poems being composed and recited in very different areas and cultures from Homer's Greece to Beowolf's Denmark to twelfth-century France to Serbo-Croatia under the occupation of the Turks. We are well aware that such poetry is by no means universal in European and Near Eastern cultures, so that the search for contingently sufficient conditions is conducted within already fairly restricted limits. At the same time there is no question of attempting to account completely for every detail of individual poems; it may be possible to trace many features of narrative and symbolism to their earlier sources within the local tradition, but it is no more possible to explain every line of Homer than every verse of the New Testament or every bar of Beethoven.[1] But an adequate theory of the oral epic will be concerned rather to demonstrate how the common features of the poetry of different cultures arise from common origins—how, that is, each long oral narrative poem that has come down to us derives from a similar 'heroic age' and what are the characteristic features of such ages which account for poetry of this kind. Briefly, the answer seems to be that 'The main components of such an age, which tend to occur in the development of many different nations, are a taste for warfare and adventure, a powerful nobility, and a simple but temporarily adequate

[1] Thus Karl Popper, *The Open Society and its Enemies*, 3rd ed. (London, Routledge, 1957), II, 210: 'I don't wish to quarrel with the metaphysical determinist who would insist that every bar of Beethoven's work was determined by some combination of hereditary or environmental influences. Such an assertion is empirically insignificant, since no one could actually explain a single bar of his writing in this way.'

material culture devoid of much aesthetic refinement. In such conditions the heroic virtues of honour and martial courage dominate all others, ultimately with depressive effects on the stability and prosperity of the society. It is usually during the consequent period of decline that the poetical elaboration of glorious deeds, deeds that now lie in the past, reaches its climax.'[1] The contrast classes are clearly implicit in the list of 'components'. This, no doubt, is still an incomplete account which further research may elaborate or amend. But meanwhile, the cultures in which oral heroic poetry is found are to be contrasted with those which (for whatever causes in their turn) are not warlike, do not have a social hierarchy topped by a powerful nobility or even a nobility at all, are either too well or too badly endowed with material wealth and have either no aesthetic tradition of any kind or a tradition which has already passed into the stage of printed books, prose history, and largely lyric or perhaps dramatic poetry.

What does this example show? It shows, I suggest, the way in which the successful explanation of collective beliefs and practices, wherever they are to be placed along the continuum from science to art, must in practice be idiographic explanation. All idiographic explanation presupposes some implicit reference to general laws, and, as I have already remarked, it may on occasion furnish a decisive test for a theory (by which I mean a systematically related set of lawlike, disconfirmable generalisations). But it is not necessary, for such explanation, that the anthropologist or historian should be able to state the laws. Nor is it to be expected that the laws, if they ever *are* stated, will link social circumstances to categories of belief as broad as 'religious' (whether 'sacred' or 'supernatural') in one-to-one correspondence. Collective beliefs and practices are to be explained in terms of particular concatenations of contingently sufficient conditions. To put forward such explanations is not to say that the conditions specified in this instance are always linked to these particular beliefs in a lawlike way, but only that subject to certain other (not necessarily stated) antecedent conditions they can be, and in this instance demonstrably have been, the decisive influence not present in the contrast class. Among the unformulated laws to which the explanation implicitly appeals some will, of course, be psychological, since to ask how it is that the specified conditions can operate as causes at all is to ask what it is about individual human beings which furnishes the link between particular historical circumstances and the beliefs and practices which these circumstances are alleged to induce. It will depend on the context of the

[1] G. S. Kirk, *Homer and the Epic* (Cambridge University Press, 1965), p. 2.

enquiry which kind of condition is cited as either necessary or contingently sufficient.[1] But in the end, it is perfectly reasonable to hope that the accumulated evidence will enable us to establish precise and wide-ranging empirical generalisations, and from these in turn to produce a 'theory' of whatever designated category of beliefs and/or practices can be predicted (or 'inversely deduced') by reference to a designated set of both psychological and social variables.

At this point, somebody may want to object that I have lumped historical, sociological and anthropological explanations together. I have, however, done so deliberately, since I can see no distinction which is of any methodological significance whatever between the three. There is, as I have already implied, a distinction between these three on the one hand and psychological explanations on the other, since there is clearly a line to be drawn between that part of a complete explanation which accounts for the workings of the human mind as such and that part which has perforce to take these as given.[2] But aside from purely conventional occupational distinctions based on participant observation as opposed to documentary research, or specialisation in small pre-industrial as opposed to large industrial societies, there is no distinction relevant to the concerns of this paper. Nor are 'religious' beliefs or practices, however 'religious' is defined, the proprietary subject-matter of sociologists more than anthropologists or anthropologists than historians, whatever may be their views of the ostensible difference between their three specialisms. A theory of the origin, acceptance and persistence of 'religious' beliefs, whatever that turns out to include, will not be distinctively historical, sociological or anthropological, any more than a theory of non-'religious' beliefs, or crime, or birth-rates, or voting behaviour; it

---

[1] It is perfectly possible that the satisfactory explanation of belief does, in fact, depend more on psychological than social variables, once given a certain minimum of necessary social conditions. That this is true of religious beliefs is explicitly argued by Spiro, *op. cit.* pp. 109 ff. in terms of the question 'What desires are satisfied by religion?' (which Spiro wishes to define in such a way as requires a belief in 'superhuman beings'). It is, however, a matter to be settled by empirical research, and it is pointless to try to dogmatise about it in advance.

[2] Some such division is often made explicit in the writings of sociologists of religion: thus, for example, J. Milton Yinger, *Religion in the Struggle for Power* (New York, Russell, 1961), p. 3: 'Sociology's general interest in religion concerns its relation with interhuman behaviour patterns'; or Wilhelm E. Mühlmann, 'Elementare Fragen einer Soziologie der Religion', in D. Goldschmidt and J. Matthes, eds., *Probleme der Religionssoziologie* (Köln. Zeits. f. Soziol. und Sozialpsychol., Sonderheft 6, 1962), p. 52: 'Die Aufgabe der Religionssoziologie ist vielmehr, die Fäden blosszulegen, die das Religiöse mit den weltlichen Bedingungen seiner Entstehung und seiner Existenz verbinden.'

will simply set out the several causes, psychological and social, which jointly account for the origin, acceptance or persistence of the beliefs identified as a dependent variable and categorised as the common explanation of ostensibly different beliefs may dictate.[1]

But what, it might still be asked, about the claims which have been made on behalf of distinctive schools of anthropological theory? This again raises wider questions than I can try to answer here. But in terms of what would, in the given context, constitute an adequate explanation of the origin, acceptance and persistence of any system of beliefs, talk of 'structural' as distinct from 'functional' or 'historical' theory, and so forth, serves merely to highlight one rather than another subset of the relevant antecedent necessary and contingently sufficient conditions. To say this is not to deny that a distinctive explanation of a 'structuralist' kind in the manner of Lévi-Strauss might turn out to be appropriate over a wide range of 'religious' belief. But if so, its distinctiveness will reside in the substantial content of the particular answer given to the question of origin, acceptance and persistence (and, perhaps, the prior question of identification as well). It will not reside in the replacement of questions about antecedent necessary and contingently sufficient conditions with questions exclusively about 'structure'. A satisfactory explanation in terms of the contrast classes specified cannot but have implicit reference not only to structure and the synchronic interrelation of components but also to history and function.[2]

The same applies equally to the claim that 'functionalism' is a distinctive anthropological (or sociological) theory by which systems of belief might best be explained. 'Functionalism' may, as may 'structuralism', be used to stand for a distinctive doctrine—in this case, presumably, some hypothesis about the way in which environmental pressures produce

---

[1] That the contributions of many different disciplines may be necessary to the satisfactory explanation of religion is said often enough: thus, for example, Raymond Firth, 'Problem and Assumption in an Anthropological Study of Religion', *J. Roy. Anthrop. Inst.* LXXXIX (1959), 136: 'We can no longer afford to neglect the more professional theoretical analyses of religion not only by sociologists, with whom we have kept in comparative general touch, but also by psychologists, historians, philosophers, theologians and other students of comparative religion, some of whom have displayed a growing sociological awareness.' But this way of putting it assumes a collaboration between specialised disciplines rather than specialisation in some defined category of beliefs and practices as such (quite apart from the condescension implicit in the concluding phrase). Of course, it is true that 'religious' beliefs and practices, or any other designated category, can be studied from a variety of different aspects; but this does not amount to a vindication of the view that 'historical', 'sociological' or 'anthropological' explanation is somehow distinctive from, let alone superior to, the others.

[2] For a fuller development of this argument, see chapter 2, above.

adaptive changes in beliefs through the workings of specified social and psychological mechanisms. But once again, few sociologists are likely to deny that the consequences of environmental pressures will play *some* part in *any* satisfactory account of how beliefs originate, are more or less widely accepted, and either persist or are replaced by others in their turn. This aspect of a proposed explanation must not, of course, be taken to the point where it becomes circular, like the 'functionalism' of Malinowski: it is not enough to say that a belief is held because of the 'adaptive' consequences to which it can be shown to lead unless it can also be shown how and in what way it would be modified if it did not lead to these consequences,[1] and this claim must depend in turn on some implicit psychological generalisation. But it is perfectly reasonable to hypothesise that need-fulfilment of some kind accounts for the retention of a belief in a situation where there are grounds for supposing that the believers in question would otherwise have abandoned it. It is, like every idiographic historical-cum-psychological explanation, a matter of collecting adequate empirical evidence to account for the given case.

Examples to illustrate this are not very easy to find in a rough-and-ready sampling of the ethnographic literature, if only because anthropologists seem often to be concerned with something other than explanation. Their principal concern may well be no more than the accurate and comprehensive description of the 'magico-religious' beliefs of the people with which they are concerned and of the ritual practices which are bound up with these beliefs. Such description may at the same time involve some elucidation and justification: the systematic fieldworker will

---

[1] Spiro, *op. cit.* p. 114, questions the appeal to 'unintended social functions' on the ground that it implies the claim that if the efficacies of Hopi rain ceremonies, the Catholic Mass and the like 'for the attainment of these designated ends were to be disbelieved, they would nevertheless be performed so that their solidarious functions might be served'. This, however, is too extreme. As I suggested above, there are people who see an aesthetic value in such ceremonies even after they are no longer taken literally, and their retention for this quite different reason may equally well serve the 'solidarious functions'. In such a situation, we could say that a 'neo-Frazerian' situation has given way to a 'neo-Durkheimian' one. However, it remains true that if the literal belief is what appears to sustain the ceremony in question, the observer will need always to be able to show that it really is held. Thus, for example, Meyer Fortes, *Oedipus and Job in West African Religion* (Cambridge University Press, 1959), p. 61: 'What ancestor-worship provides is an institutionalized scheme of beliefs and practices by means of which men can accept some kind of responsibility for what happens to them and yet feel free of blame for failure to control the vicissitudes of life.' This is a perfectly respectable 'functional' argument. But it depends on the ancillary argument that the customary rituals of placation and expiation are 'effective simply because the ancestors *are believed* [my italics] not only to exact punishment for wrong conduct but also to behave justly and benevolently in the long run.'

want not only to present the system of beliefs and practices as an integrated whole but also to show how they come to seem natural and thus
reasonable in their own ecological and cultural context. But this is not to
explain them; and if the argument is taken beyond the level of description,
it is often only for the purpose of helping to establish some empirical
generalisation of an implicitly causal kind about the *effects* of the system
of beliefs and practices on other areas of the total social system.[1] This
further argument may, to be sure, have 'functional' implications which
will help to account for the persistence of at any rate some aspect of the
system of beliefs and practices in the sort of way I have just discussed.
But it is seldom if ever that such an argument is spelt out in sufficient
detail for it to be clear just what evidence would falsify it.

One good example for my purpose is, however, furnished by Nadel's
Nupe Religion in the chapter which discusses the adoption by the Nupe
of some, but not other, originally alien beliefs and practices. Nadel is
suitably cautious about his argument: 'It must be admitted that in the
anthropological field the prerequisite evidence is not easy to procure and
that even the first step, the mere discovery of the alien elements, may be
difficult or uncertain'.[2] But the evidence is at any rate sufficient for Nadel
to be able to list seven different alien observances whose provenance is
well known. Four of these were adopted by the Nupe and three rejected;
and after comparing them in terms of a number of variables which might
be supposed to be significantly relevant, Nadel offers an explanation based
chiefly on the extent to which they did or did not answer to a pre-existing
need. Thus, for example, 'The *Sogba* cult seems to exemplify this
balance between interest and congeniality even more clearly. For the
Nupe adopted only that aspect of it which corresponds to a strongly
pronounced and in a sense inexhaustible interest (in fecundity), while
rejecting both the annual ceremonial, whose aims seem redundant, and
the *sogba* ordeal, which was altogether alien to the pre-existing aims or
interests.'[3] This explanation cannot, to be sure, be definitive, and it risks
circularity if pre-existing interests are invoked *post hoc* without supporting
evidence. But it illustrates very well the context within which contingently sufficient conditions for such observances can effectively be posited.
Nadel starts from a pre-existing background of traditional Nupe beliefs
and practices which are adequately identified; he then identifies and
locates the alien observances with which the Nupe are known to have come

---

[1] Thus Spiro, *op. cit.* p. 122: 'Many studies of religion, however, are concerned not
with the explanation of religion, but with the role of religion in the explanation of
society.'

[2] *Op. cit.* p. 207.   [3] *Ibid.* p. 222.

into contact; he describes the significant features of those accepted and those rejected; he suggests which of these features appear decisive on the basis of cross-comparison; and he invokes such common-sense psychological generalisations as are necessary to make the connection between the apparently decisive features and the adoption by individual Nupe of the observances. Thus all the characteristic features of sociological-anthropological-historical explanation are present: the assumed necessary conditions, the specified contrast class, the hypothesis of contingently sufficient conditions and the implicit appeal to unstated psychological laws. However tentative (and, for all I know, mistaken), it is an authentic candidate for explanation of certain designated Nupe rituals and beliefs.

This example, however, is still very limited in scope and application. Where the explanation sought has been restricted from the outset to the absorption of some, but not other, observances into an already well-established system of practices and beliefs, the problem of explaining a class of beliefs as such has in effect been bypassed. How is the model of explanation which I am advocating to be generalised? And what, within such explanations, will be the sort of classificatory terms which I have suggested will be more useful than 'religious' has been?

The best example with which to offer an answer to these questions is, I think, that of the Melanesian cargo cults and of millenarism in general.[1] Both have received steadily increasing attention in recent years, not only for their intrinsic interest but also for their possible implications for social-scientific methodology. One commentator, indeed, has gone so far as to claim that 'cargo cults create a crisis within structural-functional anthropology'.[2] This is a little extreme: unless 'structural-functionalism' is held to be all-embracing, there is no reason why an explanation appropriate to the Trobriand *kula* should have to be appropriate also to Melanesian millenarism. What is more, if functionalism is defined as a theory of teleonomic adaptation to environmental change then it can quite well be fitted to the cargo cults, even if at a level rather too general to be very satisfying. As always, it depends how the problem has been initially

---

[1] On millenarism in general, see particularly Norman Cohn, *The Pursuit of the Millennium*, 2nd ed. (New York, Harper, 1961); Sylvia L. Thrupp, ed., *Millennial Dreams in Action* (Comp. Studies in Society and History suppl. vol. II, 1962); and Yonina Talmon, 'Millenarian Movements', *Arch Eur. Sociol.* VII (1966), 159–200. On cargo cults, see particularly Peter Worsley, *The Trumpet Shall Sound* (London, MacGibbon, 1957); Kenelm Burridge, *Mambu* (London, Methuen, 1960); and Peter Lawrence, *Road Belong Cargo* (Manchester University Press, 1965).

[2] I. C. Jarvie, 'On the Explanation of Cargo Cults', *Arch. Eur. Sociol.* VII (1966), 300, crediting the suggestion initially to W. E. H. Stanner, *The South Seas in Transition* (Sydney, 1953).

defined. A more useful moral to draw is that 'the study of millenarism has brought about a veritable rapprochement between history, sociology and anthropology'[1]—as, according to the arguments of the present paper, one would expect. It is true that much of the work done on millenarism has been concerned with purposes which I have already distinguished from explanation: the investigators are often more concerned either with a descriptive presentation of the beliefs and their context or with an analysis of their results, and particularly of the social and political functions which they may serve. But where explanation *is* put forward, it serves very well to illustrate the thesis I am advancing here.

The model of explanation adopted by particular investigators is, as a rule, left largely implicit. Cohn, however, in the concluding section of a paper on the comparative study of millenarian movements,[2] suggests in outline a set of circumstances favourable to the rise of millenarian movements which, although he explicitly disclaims for it any predictive value whatever, nevertheless furnishes a useful sketch of the way in which necessary background conditions, specified contrast classes, conditions hypothesised as contingently sufficient and implicit psychological laws are all necessary to any putative sociological-historical-anthropological explanation. How far those suggested by Cohn or others are in fact the right ones can only be decided by the results of specialist research. But the sort of candidates which Cohn suggests as appropriate are, for example: as necessary background conditions, a traditional world view containing somewhere the promise of a future age of bliss, a collective experience of severe mortification such as can be supposed to result from the defection or failure of traditional authority, and a prophet endowed with the necessary personal gifts (who is not, of course, strictly a 'background' condition, but who does seem to be a necessary, and not merely a contingently sufficient one); as contrast classes, either societies such as traditional India or ancient Greece, or more specifically, groups within medieval Europe or post-Columbian Latin America or colonial Melanesia, where millenarian movements did *not* occur; as hypothesised contingently sufficient conditions, particular mythologies, or the persecution of a designated class or sect, or the emotional frustrations of, say, women of means and leisure for whom no institutional outlet has been provided; as implicit psychological laws, whatever stricter generalisations will properly

[1] Yonina Talmon, 'Pursuit of the Millennium: the Relation between Religious and Social Change', *Arch. Eur. Sociol.* III (1962), 126.
[2] 'Medieval Millenarism: its Bearing on the Comparative Study of Millenarian Movements', in Thrupp, *op. cit.* pp. 40–3.

account for such observations as that 'where a particular frustration or anxiety or humiliation of this nature is experienced at the same time and in the same area by a number of individuals, the result is a collective emotional agitation which is peculiar not only in its intensity but also in the boundlessness of its aims'.[1] It is clear that an explanation along these lines will, like all sociological explanations of beliefs and/or the collective action stemming from them, be idiographic; but, as I have suggested, it will, like all idiographic explanations, have implicit reference to general laws, whether or not these are, or can be, specified. It follows from this that some classification of beliefs, once they have been successfully identified, is a necessary prerequisite of their explanation. But if the example of millenarism can serve as a guide, the classification which furnishes a common framework of explanation will cut across any of the definitions commonly offered of 'religious' and 'non-religious'. It is always possible that *within* the category of millenarian beliefs, a distinction between 'religious' and 'secular' may be useful, depending on what more detailed contrasts the investigator finds puzzling;[2] but this is a separate matter from its usefulness in explaining millenarian beliefs as such.

Among millenarian movements, the cargo cults serve particularly well to show both how the explanations which appear to have been most successful follow the model of explanation which I have outlined, and also how irrelevant to it is the category of 'religious' as distinct from 'historical', 'philosophical' or 'scientific' beliefs. It seems now broadly agreed that the cargo cults are to be seen as 'a typical kind of millenarism *and* a typical Melanesian religion'.[3] Lawrence, in particular, brings out just how the necessary sense of deprivation and resentment was brought about by the history of contact with Europeans and how, given the necessary prophet at the appropriate time, the particular mythology of the traditional culture served to rationalise these feelings in a millenarian form. As he

---

[1] *Ibid.* p. 42.

[2] Thus Worsley, *op. cit.* p. 237, suggests that a 'religious' element can be due to the need of a political leader to avoid identification with any particular section of society. I do not know how far this may be plausible in any given instance. But a secular millenarian doctrine need not necessarily be sectional (though they often are); and in any case, the usefulness of a theistic ideology to a political leader is not an explanation but a specification of function.

[3] Jarvie, *op. cit.* p. 310; cf. Burridge, *op. cit.* p. 274: 'They are typical millenarian movements acted out in terms of a particular cultural idiom', or Mircea Eliade, in Thrupp, *op. cit.* p. 139: 'It is impossible either to grasp the full significance of "cargo-cults" or to appreciate their extraordinary success without taking into account a mythical-ritual theme which plays a fundamental role in Melanesian religions: the annual return of the dead and the cosmic regeneration which this implies.'

puts it, 'The natives believed that they could obtain cargo largely by ritual because, for reasons already given, their assumptions about the nature and dynamics of the cosmic order were virtually unchanged. . . . It was impossible to regard cargo as the product of human endeavour or skill. Thus the means devised to solve the technical problems of explaining its source and exploiting it to the natives' advantage were of exactly the same kind as those used in the case of the traditional material culture.'[1] Now of course the traditional mythology which, together with the history of Melanesian contacts with Europeans and the appearance of suitable prophets, constitutes the outline of an explanation of the cargo cults is a 'religious' mythology as the term is conventionally used. But this is of no explanatory value whatever in itself. It would not matter if the Melanesians' traditional beliefs about the creation of the material world, the nature of historical time, and so forth were such as visiting anthropologists might more naturally label 'scientific'. What matters in the explanation of cargo cults is that certain traditional Melanesian beliefs (which have, as always, to be accurately identified by the qualified observer) are peculiarly compatible with millenarism and therefore play the role in the explanation of cargo-cult beliefs which I have outlined. Insofar as the cargo cult is a coherent blend of cosmology and ethics then it may be labelled a religion in the sense I have admitted to be innocuous enough. But in attempting to explain these beliefs, it is fruitless to argue whether they are to be labelled 'religious', 'magical' or 'scientific' (let alone 'rational').

So brief a discussion as this cannot attempt to answer all the questions which might be raised by the model of explanation I have put forward. But the example I have used is, I think, sufficient to show that in accounting for collective beliefs there is no valid distinction between 'sociological', 'anthropological' and 'historical' explanation; that the requisite explanation need not be dependent at any point on a definition of 'religious' beliefs as distinguished from others; and that although it must have implicit reference to the psychological laws presumed to account for the link between social circumstances and beliefs, these laws need not be framed explicitly if the sociologist-anthropologist-historian is to be able to formulate the list of necessary and contingently sufficient social conditions which will resolve his puzzlement.[2] It might be said that this

---

[1] *Op. cit.* p. 235.

[2] Another recent discussion to which the model might equally well be fitted is Michael Walzer, *The Revolution of the Saints* (London, Weidenfeld, 1966). Walzer is concerned, once again, with the function of Puritanism as an ideology of transition as much as with its origins. But once given that Puritanism is 'one possible way of perceiving and

division of labour is itself as much a matter of academic convention as that between sociologists and anthropologists: certainly, there is nothing to prevent the same investigator from exploring both the workings of individual psychology and the relation of social circumstances to systems of collective doctrine and ritual.[1] But I hope I have said enough to make clear that there is a difference of kind between psychological theory and sociological (and therefore idiographic) explanation which there is not between explanations conventionally labelled 'sociological' and explanations conventionally labelled 'anthropological' or 'historical'. In other words, this is a division of labour which seems not merely conventional but justified; and it is for this reason that in the title of this paper the term 'sociological' is not in inverted commas although the term 'religious' is.

Rather than try to illustrate my argument from further examples drawn from contemporary historical or ethnographic research I have chosen to devote a concluding section to Weber and Durkheim. This is for two reasons: first, the examples which they furnish serve to reinforce my argument at least as well as contemporary examples would do; second, both still exercise an influence on the subject which, in my view, is in the wrong proportion to their deserts. In what follows, I shall not try to assess their writings by detailed reference to the model of explanation I have put forward. I would, however, claim that reference to the model highlights both the merits of the one and the demerits of the other.

III

I do not propose to attempt a synopsis of the religious sociology of either Weber or Durkheim. But their respective influence, and the relative standing of their writings on religion in the eyes of many commentators, are aptly summarised in the following extract from a recent review of Weber: 'It is notable that there has been no systematic development of Weber's approach to religion, while Durkheim's influence by contrast

responding to a set of experiences that other men than the saints might have viewed in other terms' (p. 309), there is required to account for it a set of necessary and contingently sufficient conditions such as the separation of politics from the household, the appearance of 'formally free' men, pragmatism in political thought, the emergence of large-scale political units and the 'sociological competence' of particular social classes, both clerical and lay.

[1] This is to some degree true of Lévi-Strauss, whose assumptions about the workings of the human mind, although not based on any psychological research carried out by himself, are nonetheless more fully articulated than is usual among anthropologists: see Eugène Fleischmann, 'L'Esprit humain selon Claude Lévi-Strauss', *Arch. Eur. Sociol.* VII (1966), 27–57.

has been the basis of a series of brilliant enquiries, ranging from those of his pupils Mauss and Hertz to the studies of Evans-Pritchard and of Lévi-Strauss. Indeed the best advice to those who wish to read Weber on religion would perhaps be "Read Durkheim instead!" [1]

It is undeniable that Durkheim's positive influence has been the greater of the two.[2] Weber still receives most attention on the specific topic of the Protestant ethic, about which competent specialists have repeatedly declared him mistaken;[3] it must be admitted that he never discussed the available ethnographic material in any detail, let alone making a systematic study of any one primitive culture and its religious or magical practices and beliefs;[4] and it can even be argued that in so far as twentieth-century religious sociology has ever been 'Weberian', it is now less so than it was.[5] But for the purposes of this paper, it is immaterial how far Weber is right on matters of substance. The substantive failure of Durkheim's theory of religion is tied, at least in part, to a deficiency of method; the failure of Weber's, even if it is likewise a failure, is not.

It is, of course, possible to argue that the theories of Durkheim and Weber are very much more alike than at first appears. Apart from the plausibility of a general interpretation along these lines[6] and occasional parallels whose significance is at best doubtful,[7] we have the testimony of Raymond Aron that Mauss believed many of Weber's ideas to have been

[1] Alasdair MacIntyre, 'Weber at his Weakest', *Encounter* xxv (1965), 87.

[2] Apart from his influence on the anthropological tradition, see e.g. the invocation of *The Elementary Forms* by Guy E. Swanson, *The Birth of the Gods* (Ann Arbor, 1960), p. vii: 'Like many other sociologists and social psychologists, I have found this book one of the most stimulating in all the literature about society. Its point of view is part of the foundation on which I have built.'

[3] I need not offer a list of these criticisms here; what is perhaps more to the point is that a recent study like J. A. Prades, *La Sociologie de la Religion chez Max Weber* (Louvain, Nauwelaerts, 1966) should concentrate almost exclusively on *The Protestant Ethic*.

[4] Weber did have a better knowledge of the ancient world, and particularly of Rome, than did Durkheim. But the material on it is not, of course, based on trained anthropologists' fieldwork; and Weber is not always reliable—as for example in assuming without argument the existence of an Orphic church (on which see the remarks of Dodds, *op. cit.* pp. 146–9).
Cf. Joachim Matthes, 'Vorbemerkungen', *Int. Jahrb. f. Religionssoziologie*, I (1965), 8: '...ist die vertiefte geschichtliche Perspektive, die von *Max Weber* fur die Religionssoziologie zurückgewonnen ist, der neuren Kirchensoziologie wiederum weithin abhanden gekommen.'

[6] See particularly Talcott Parsons, *The Structure of Social Action* (New York, McGraw-Hill, 1937).

[7] Compare, for example, Durkheim, p. 57, 'Même le Christianisme, au moins sous sa forme Catholique, admet outre la personnalité divine, d'ailleurs triple en même temps qu'une, la Vierge, les anges, les saints, les âmes des morts etc.' with Weber, p. 314, 'der katholische Messen-und Heiligenkult faktisch dem Polytheismus sehr nahe steht'; or some of their occasional remarks on magic and taboo.

borrowed without acknowledgement from *L'Année Sociologique*.[1] But their differences are surely more profound than their similarities, even if this accusation is just. Durkheim, after all, set out quite explicitly to say what religion *is* and to put forward a general theory of its origin. Weber, equally explicitly, did not: in fact, he opens his discussion in *Wirtschaft und Gesellschaft* with the remark that 'Eine Definition dessen, was Religion "ist", kann unmöglich an der Spitze, sondern könnte allenfalls am Schlusse, einer Erörterung wie der nachfolgenden stehen. Allein wir haben es überhaupt nicht mit dem "Wesen" der Religion, sondern mit den Bedingungen und Wirkungen einer bestimmten Art von Gemeinschaftshandeln zu tun . . .' (p. 245).

But what *was* Weber's theory of religion? Often, he was concerned with the effects of religion more than its causes, and was therefore, like many of the ethnographers, not trying to explain it at all.[2] His beliefs about the causal relations between material substructure and ideological superstructure have been very variously represented by different commentators.[3] What is more, his sociology of politics was sufficiently closely intermingled with his sociology of religion for some of his readers to confuse them altogether: Worsley, for example, adds an appendix to *The Trumpet Shall Sound* criticising Weber's 'celebrated theory of charisma', but none of his citations are drawn from Weber's actual sociology of religion, and his attack is chiefly directed against Weber's use of 'rationality' which, as I said at the beginning of this paper, there is no need for his admirers to defend.[4] It is admittedly difficult to establish just what Weber did think about either the causes or the consequences of

[1] Edward A. Tiryakian, 'A Problem for the Sociology of Knowledge', *Arch. Eur. Sociol.* VII (1966), 332 n. 7.

[2] But he was not, of course, so much concerned with the 'functional' consequences of ethical or metaphysical beliefs in maintaining the social order as with the effects of such beliefs in either promoting or inhibiting economic activity of various kinds— for example, leaving aside the Protestant ethic, the beliefs and rituals of both the Jews and the Jains which turned them towards financial and away from industrial capitalism (*GAzR*, II, 212–13).

[3] Contrast, for example, the interpretation of Carlo Antoni, *From History to Sociology* (tr. White; London, 1962), pp. 166–7, who accuses Weber of analysing the evolution of religious and ethical systems entirely in terms of class interests, with that of Reinhard Bendix, *Max Weber: an Intellectual Portrait* (London, Heinemann, 1960), who talks only about a 'very general compatibility between status groups and systems of belief' (p. 115) and about ideas as 'more than intentional or unwitting adjustments to the exigencies of the social situation'.

[4] Worsley, *op. cit.* pp. 266–72. It is noticeable that Talmon, by contrast, does cite Weber's *GAzR* on 'multiple deprivation' as the root of millenarism ('Millenarian Movements', p. 181), and Cohn likewise includes Weber (but not Durkheim) in the bibliography appended to *The Pursuit of the Millennium*.

'religious' beliefs. But the task is made more difficult, not less, by some of his critics.

Weber's clearest statement of his underlying assumptions is in the 'Einleitung' in the *Gesammelte Aufsätze*.[1] But he is more concerned to argue that there can be some reciprocal causal relation between economic and religious beliefs and practices than to set out precisely how he thinks that it operates. The argument of the *Protestant Ethic*, as it has generally been taken, is straightforward enough as a quasi-experimental historical comparison along the lines of the inverse deductive method. The contrast class is defined in terms of those societies, or rather civilisations, in which economic conditions were similar to those of Western Europe but where capitalism in its Western European form did not develop. Given, then, the distinctive nature of Protestantism and its apparent affinities with an ethic of accumulation, it appears to have been a contingently sufficient or possibly a necessary condition (the thesis can be taken both ways) of the otherwise improbable development of European capitalism. But apart from the evidence which tells against this hypothesis, and the objection that economic conditions in the contrasted civilisations (including Catholic Europe) were *not* sufficiently similar for it to be tested so easily, Weber never attempts to formalise his implicit theory of the relation between substructure and superstructure; it tends either to be stated baldly as a fact ('es konnte nicht ausbleiben, dass . . .')[2] or expounded in terms of metaphors, such as ideas being 'stamped' (*geprägt*) by the substructure or in turn functioning as 'signalmen' (*Weichensteller*) who decide along which ideological tracks material interests will be shunted. At the risk of oversimplification, however, and in recognition of the obscurity of much of Weber's presentation, the principal assumptions of his method can be tentatively spelled out as follows:

(1) The identification of beliefs must rest on the claim to have understood the meaning (*Sinn*) of those beliefs to the actors themselves; but this does not mean that the investigator need share them.

(2) Beliefs are not uniquely determined by material conditions and the economic-cum-political interests to which they give rise: in other words, once given a distinctive system of beliefs, the evolution of doctrine is not necessarily or exclusively a function of exogenous social variables.

---

[1] *GAzR*, I, 237 ff.

[2] *Ibid.* II, 400–1: 'Im Einheitsstaat hörten die Chancen der Konkurrenz der Fürsten um die Literaten auf. Jetzt konkurrierten umgekehrt diese und ihre Schüler um die vorhandenen Aemter und es konnte nicht ausbleiben, dass dies die Entwicklung einer einheitlichen, dieser Situation angepassen, orthodox Doktrin zur Folge hätte. Sie wurde: der Konfuzianismus.'

MAGDALEN COLLEGE LIBRARY

(3) There is no one explanation of a system of beliefs: the explanation required must depend on the place at which the investigator chooses to break into the sequence of historical events as well as on the particular relation of cause to effect which he seeks to establish.

(4) To argue that class interests are often decisive in determining whether or in what form a religious ethic will be adopted is not to deny the equally decisive importance of the individual 'charismatic' prophet, magician, priest, etc., in originating or developing that religious ethic.

(5) A system of beliefs can function as an independent variable in the sense that (a) without it, the evolution of the culture in question would be different, or (if that is the contrast at issue) might not take place at all, and (b) following from (2) above, the evolution of the culture and of the system of beliefs cannot both be explained as a common function of some other designated set of substructural variables.

(6) Whatever may have been their origin, and whatever interests they may serve, there seems in fact to have been a unilinear evolution of systems of belief in the direction of a progressive *Entzauberung*; and the sociologist of religion can therefore show not only how the religions of the world have taken the form that they have but also how they either have been or will be both emptied of their 'spiritual' content and deprived of their 'scientific' function.

(7) Despite (1) above, the sociologist (or anthropologist or historian) is not encroaching on the territory of the psychologist ('Die verstehende Soziologie ist nach allem Gesagten nicht Teil einer Psychologie').[1] His task is to explain given social institutions, behaviour and ideas by relating them to their antecedent historical causes, whether social or material, and not to try to explain or even to describe the workings of the human mind.

It will be apparent that these assumptions which I read Weber as having held fit fairly closely to the model of explanation for which I argued

---

[1] *Gesammelte Aufsätze zur Wissenschaftslehre*, 2nd ed. (Tübingen, Mohr, 1951), p. 432. The essay from which this phrase is drawn ('Ueber einige Kategorien der verstehenden Soziologie') is much taken up with the problem of 'rationality'; but it is worth noting that in the course of it Weber makes the point (echoed later in *Wirtschaft und Gesellschaft*) that magic can be wholly 'zweckrational' to the participants. It is also worth noting that Weber does occasionally proffer a psychological speculation, as in his suggestion that the Gnostic mysteries were 'ein sublimer masturbatorischer Ersatz für die Origen der Bauern' (p. 307); and his whole emphasis on the problem of theodicy rests on implicit psychological assumptions about attitudes to suffering. For his acceptance of 'the translatability of deep anxieties, feelings of insecurity and impotence into religiously defined guilt feelings', cf. H. H. Gerth and Don Martindale, 'Preface' to the their translation of *Ancient Judaism* (New York, Free Press, 1952), p. xxi n. 37, and the passages there cited.

in the previous section. The relation of psychological assumptions to sociological explanations; the specification of the contrast class; the idiographic nature of sociological explanation as such; the search for contingently sufficient conditions to account for a particular sequence once certain necessary background conditions have been assumed; all these are both implied in Weber's injunctions about method and exemplified in some of the explanations which he himself puts forward. His assumptions, indeed, can be illustrated by the same example of the cargo-cults which, as we have seen, cannot be explained except by reference alike to material interests, individual prophets, and an autonomous system of traditional beliefs. Moreover, they provide an excellent example of the complexity as well as the inevitability of *Entzauberung*. If Lawrence is right, the cargo beliefs will not be displaced at all easily: they are too well supported both by antecedent beliefs and by continuing experiences which they and only they make comprehensible to the believers (including the Melanesians' experience of Christianity itself). Yet at the same time, we know very well that the anthropologist will not be converted to the Melanesians' beliefs; they, or their grandchildren, will be converted to his. This has nothing to do with question-begging definitions of 'rationality'. It is as readily predictable, whatever one's judgement of value, as that technological evolution will take the Melanesians towards us and not us towards them. So the explanation of the cargo-cults, just like Weber's explanations of Judaism, Buddhism and the rest, accounts not only for their origin, spread and persistence but also their place in the story of world-historical evolution which Weber sought to grasp as a whole.

Three summary examples from *Wirtschaft und Gesellschaft* may serve to illustrate the ways in which Weber's own arguments are characteristically formulated. I cite them, as before, without regard to their plausibility, because they seem to me to bring out precisely the *kind* of hypotheses which need to be formulated and assessed if sociological explanations of religious beliefs, as I have suggested these terms should be used, are to be arrived at. For the same reason, I have deliberately expanded, and perhaps therefore misread, ideas which in Weber's own unrevised formulation are often fragmentary and cryptic:

1. A doctrine of sin did not develop in the ancient world because there was neither an independent class of priests, which is a necessary condition of the rationalisation of religious life (p. 260), nor prophecy, which frequently functions as the contingently sufficient condition of a centralised ethic of salvation (p. 268), although it is true that the priests of the

Delphic Apollo, and perhaps some others, had the chance of establishing themselves during the Persian wars (p. 277), and that Pythagoras must be counted as a prophet (p. 272, cf. p. 298).

2. Once a religion of an ethical and congregational kind has been established, its practical doctrines and their influence will depend to a large degree on the 'cure of souls' (*Seelsorge*). This in turn depends initially on the prophetic revelation and the distribution of grace; but thereafter, there is a general tendency to the 'ossification' (*Verknöcherung*) of prophecy, and the priesthood, in order to control the *Lebenspraxis* of the laity in accordance with the divine will, increasingly compromises with the traditional folk beliefs and practices, as in Egypt, India and (in the case of Islam) Africa. At the opposite end of the scale, the inverse relation of preaching to sacramentalism is shown by Protestantism, which is unique in (among other things) its successful supplanting of the priest by the preacher (pp. 283–5).

3. The ideological rejection of state control by *Manchestertum* can in part be traced to the particular response of Protestantism to the tension with politics which is felt by every ethical religion. It is of course possible for the inner-worldly ascetic to hold that political power is justified if used for the restraint of the sinful; but many Puritan sects have, like some Jews under the Maccabees, held that ethical virtue is wholly incompatible with the political *Gewaltapparat*, and this, when combined with the economic ethic of Puritanism and its altogether easier compromise with *Erwerbsinteressen*, helped to sustain the doctrines of laisser-faire (p. 357 and above). More generally, the development of religious pacifism is argued by Weber (against Nietzsche) to be caused not by a *Sklavenaufstand* but by a complex interplay of social and ideological circumstances including such things as the interests of the priesthood and their following among women and the degree of bureaucratisation of politics.

It could fairly be said that these examples illustrate some of the defects as well as the virtues of Weber's approach. The argument is very difficult to unravel; the implicit definitions and distinctions ('rationality', 'prophecy' and the rest) are never adequately set out; the parallels are very allusive or even severely qualified elsewhere. But at the same time they do show what it is to offer specific sociological explanations within the vast range of ethical-cum-metaphysical beliefs to which different societies or sub-cultures or social strata have adhered in their different fashions. It is not simply that they show how complex, even on questions peripheral to the central problem of the evolution of ethical rationality, are the concatenations of material and ideological conditions within which 'religious' doctrines are to be assigned their place. More specifically, they bring out both the features of such explanations which I have been trying to emphasise: the specification of a contrast class within a common framework of antecedent necessary conditions, and the presumption of unstated laws which justify the claim that one, or several, designated conditions were contingently sufficient within a unique historical sequence to bring about the explanandum.[1] If there are, or are ever to be, adequate sociological explanations of the beliefs of different societies, sub-cultures and social strata, then this is the exercise which needs to be carried out in order to vindicate them. Weber's sociology of religion may be mistaken; but it is not misconceived.

The fundamental defect of Durkheim's sociology of religion, by contrast, is that it *is* misconceived, whatever its incidental merits or subsequent influence. Substantively, the analysis of Australian totemism in *The Elementary Forms* has been subjected to continuing criticism ever since its first appearance,[2] just as has happened with Weber's *Protestant Ethic*. But again, the ethnographic evidence and Durkheim's use of it is not to the point of this paper so much as the way in which his enquiry is framed. As his commentators have not failed to notice, Durkheim's aim is as much to justify religion as to explain it. Already in the introduction to *The Elementary Forms*, he says that 'C'est, en effet, un postulat essentiel de la sociologie qu'une institution humaine ne saurait reposer sur l'erreur et le mensonge ... Il n'y a donc pas, au fond, de religions qui soient fausses'.[3] This curious view, for which Durkheim has been ridiculed often enough, would be much more plausible if he meant only to imply that other people's beliefs are not inexplicable just because they seem, to the representative of a more sophisticated culture, to be

[1] This is perhaps most explicitly stated in the concluding words of the essay on 'Hinduismus und Buddhismus' (*GAzR*, II, 378): 'Das Auftreter dieser [sc. ethische, ihren Alltag rational formende, Sendungsprophetie] aber in Occident, vor allem in Vorderasien, mit den weittragenden Folgen, die sich daran knüpfen, war durch höchst eigenartige geschichtliche Konstellationen bedingt, ohne welche, trotz allen Unterschieds der Naturbedingungen, die Entwicklung dort lecht in Bahnen hätte einmünden können, welche denen Asiens, vor allem Indiens, ähnlich verlangen wären.'

[2] See particularly Robert H. Lowie, *Primitive Religion* (London, Routledge, 1925), ch. VII, and his citation of A. A. Goldenweiser, 'Religion and Society', *J. Philosophy, Psychology and Scientific Methods*, XIV (1917), 121 ff. Lowie does allow some merit to Durkheim's treatment of symbolism, but he is unreservedly critical otherwise.

[3] P. 3; cf. e.g. p. 497: 'Pour que nous soyons fondé à voir dans l'efficacité attribuée aux rites autre chose que le produit d'un délire chronique dont s'abuserait l'humanité, il faut pouvoir établir que le culte a réellement pour effet de reproduire périodiquement un être moral dont nous dépendons comme il dépend de nous. Or cet être existe: c'est la société,' or more generally still, p. 99: 'Qu'est-ce qu'une science dont la principale découverte consisterait à faire évanouir l'objet même dont elle traite?'

'irrational'. But Durkheim means more than this; instead of dismissing any implicit appeal to 'rationality' as irrelevant to the specification of necessary and sufficient conditions, he argues as though making beliefs appear better justified is a part of, or even equivalent to, explaining them. This yields some damaging consequences. Not only does it fail to bolster his theory in the way that he expects—why, after all, is the worship of society any more readily explicable than the worship of gods? It also leads him to substitute *a priori* justification for empirical explanation on points of detail.[1] Furthermore, it leads him, as we have already seen, to pursue two incompatible aims in his demarcation of religion, magic and science: he wishes to justify religion (and with it magic) by marking it off from science under the heading of the 'sacred' at the same time as justifying magic (and with it religion) by showing how closely modern science resembles it.[2] The result, however ingenious or suggestive the particular arguments, is that the usefulness not only of Durkheim's overall hypothesis but also of his definition of religion is, so far from being demonstrated, seriously undermined.

The overall hypothesis rests in any case on the dubious claim that central Australian totemism furnishes a sufficient test for it; and although the attempt to devise a crucial experiment in the social just as well as in the physical sciences may not be fundamentally misconceived, it is altogether too ambitious in the present instance.[3] The presumption that

---

[1] Cf. e.g. pp. 307–8 on the soul: 'Voilà ce qu'il y a d'objectif dans l'idée de l'âme: c'est que les représentations dont la trâme constitue notre vie intérieure sont de deux éspèces différentes et irréductibles l'une à l'autre. Les unes se rapportent au monde extérieur et réel; les autres, à un monde idéal auquel nous attribuons une supériorité morale sur le premier. Nous sommes donc réellement faits de deux êtres qui sont orientés en des sens divergents et presque contraires, et dont l'un exerce sur l'autre une véritable préeminence ... Il reste vrai que notre nature est double; il y a vairment en nous une parcelle des grands idéaux qui sont l'âme de la collectivité'; or p. 513 on 'mimetic' ritual: 'Une erreur aussi manifeste semble difficilement intelligible tant qu'on ne voit dans le rite qu'un but matériel où il paraît tendre. Mais nous savons qu'outre l'effet qu'il est censé avoir sur l'éspèce totémique, il exerce une action profonde sur les âmes des fidèles qui y prennent part ... Comment cette sorte d'euphorie ne donnerait-elle pas le sentiment que le rite a réussi, qu'il a été ce qu'il se proposait d'être, qu'il a atteint le but où il visait?'

[2] Cf. p. 62, n. 2, and p. 63, n. 2, above; and for the virtual identification of science with religion, cf. p. 613: 'la pensée scientifique n'est qu'une forme plus parfaite de la pensée religieuse.'

[3] Cf. p. 352: 'une expérience dont les résultats, comme ceux de toute expérience bien faite, seront susceptibles d'être généralisés', or pp. 593–4: 'quand une loi a été prouvée par une expérience bien faite, cette preuve est valable universellement ... Si donc, dans les très humbles sociétés qui viennent d'être étudiées, nous avons réellement réussi à apercevoir quelques-uns des éléments dont sont faites les notions religieuses les plus fondamentales, il n'y a pas raison pour ne pas étendre aux autres religions les résultats les plus généraux de notre recherche.'

Australian totemism is the archetypal, or rather the original, religion of mankind is never argued; it is merely stated. In any event, apart from the assumption of generalisability, what does Durkheim mean by his claim that 'nous avons l'assurance que cette religion est la plus primitive qui soit actuellement observable, et même, selon toute vraisemblance, qui ait jamais existé' (p. 238)? What sort of assurance is it that we have? What is the implication of the term 'primitive' in this connection? What is the value of an appeal to 'vraisemblance'?[1] For Durkheim's analysis of totemism to sustain the extravagant conclusions which he draws from it, he would have to show either how the religions of the world can all be traced historically back to totemism or how the social and psychological influences by which totemism can be explained serve also to explain both the beliefs and the practices of the other religions. In the event, he does neither;[2] and even if he were entirely right about Australian totemism (which, according to expert testimony, he was not), he would not be entitled to pronounce his analysis of it a sufficient basis for a general theory of 'religion', whether as a psychological or a social phenomenon.

Finally, what about the role which Durkheim attributes to society itself not only in religion but in human thought in general? It is this, after all, which is the principal reason for his influence, and whatever criticisms are to be made of it it is only fair to concede its originality and importance. At the less general level, it has surely to be allowed that there is at least *some* connection of the kind that Durkheim argues between sentiments about God and sentiments about society, or, if you prefer, between religion and patriotism: the flag *is* equivalent to some degree to the totem, 'representative' rituals *are* much as Durkheim describes them and without assenting to Durkheim's theory as a whole it is possible to agree that the forces at work in 'religious' rituals may be present also in rituals of an ostensibly more secular or political kind. More generally, it is equally hard to disagree that there is *some* connection between religion (or, better, 'ideology') and forms of social organisation. Durkheim's famous claim in *L'Education Morale* that if he is told the code of domestic morality he will tell you the form of social organisation should not, perhaps, be put too strictly to

---

[1] For 'vraisemblance', cf. p. 402 n. 2: 'Il resterait à rechercher d'où vient que, à partir d'un certain moment de l'évolution, ce dédoublement de l'âme s'est fait sous la forme du totem individuel plutôt que sous celle de l'ancêtre protecteur. La question a peut-être un intérêt plus ethnographique que sociologique. Voici pourtant comment il est possible de se représenter la maniére dont s'est vraisemblablement opérée cette substitution . . .'

[2] Cf. p. 550 n. 2: 'L'objet de ce livre est d'étudier les croyances et les pratiques élémentaires; nous devons donc nous arrêter au moment où elles donnent naissance à des formes plus complexes.'

the test. But that there are parallels (or 'isomorphisms') between ideology and social organisation which are more than coincidental is something that few sociologists, anthropologists or historians would want to deny.

The objection to be made, however, is once again that Durkheim's claims are much, much too sweeping. That there is, or can be, a causal connection between social organisation as the independent and ideology as the dependent variable is an assumption of Weber's just as much as of Durkheim's. But Weber, for all his reticence about spelling out just what the connection is, is at pains to emphasise how very differently it can operate and how much meticulous research may be necessary to establish it in the particular case. Durkheim, by contrast, is even more sweeping in his dicta than Marx, and his version of 'social being determines consciousness' is at least as recklessly applied. The argument of *The Elementary Forms* is perhaps more carefully worked out than the earlier essay on 'Primitive Classification' which he had written in collaboration with Mauss. But his derivation of the rules of thought themselves from the fact of society still rests on the same logical howler. We are told in *The Elementary Forms* that conceptual and logical thought are social in origin not merely in the sense that individual thinkers are taught and influenced by each other but in the sense that the perception of society precedes and causes the development of logic. But the perception of society as unitary, hierarchical, differentiated and so forth must *presuppose* the concepts of unity, hierarchy and differentiation. To say, in the sense that Durkheim evidently means, that 'L'unité de ces premiers systèmes logiques ne fait que reproduire l'unité de la société' (p. 206), or that 'La hierarchie est exclusivement une chose sociale' (p. 211) or even that 'On peut même se demander si la notion de contradiction ne dépend, elle aussi, de conditions sociales' (p. 17) not merely fails to explain the rules of logic but contradicts them.

It goes without saying that to be at such pains to criticise a book first published in 1912 is in itself to pay tribute to its author. But for all its merits, *The Elementary Forms* remains a warning both of how not to try to explain beliefs and also of how not to classify them. It is true that Durkheim's analysis shares one merit, at any rate, with Weber's: both were rightly determined not to view religion from the standpoint of a parochial European 'rationalism' of the kind of Frazer, and both saw that many of the features of theistic religion would continue to be preserved in the ideologies even of a secular and 'disenchanted' age. Perhaps, too, it could be claimed for both that they realised that the explanation of ideology must be sought by reference to social substructure and that they both interpreted this in a broader, but no less illuminating, way than Marxism. But once this has been said, the differences between them, both in doctrine and still more in method, heavily outweigh the resemblances; and irrespective of their relative merits and demerits of doctrine, on questions of method it is Weber who deserves to be imitated and Durkheim who should be followed only with the most careful reservation.

The argument which I have put forward in the first two sections of this paper does not, as I hope is clear, depend on the acceptance of my interpretation of either Durkheim or Weber. There has been, and no doubt will continue to be, wide divergence of opinion about them, and this applies to their sociology of religion no less than to their general methodology. Nevertheless, the different approaches to the subject which I have attributed to them, whether or not they would have been accepted by themselves, do serve to illustrate the difference between an implicit adherence to the model which I put forward in the previous section and an attempt to provide a general theory of 'religion' of a kind which has not, and in my view never will be, successfully formulated. That we shall one day know very much more about the conditions which determine the origins, acceptance and persistence of different systems of belief about the world and man's conduct in it can, I trust, be taken for granted; indeed, we already know considerably more than did Weber or Durkheim. How far this future knowledge will progress, and to what extent it will come from psychologists on one side or sociologists-anthropologists-historians on the other, only a specialist in the field could usefully attempt to foretell. If, however, the argument of this paper is correct, the future body of validated explanatory theory about systems of belief will have at any rate these three predictable characteristics: it will not be, or embody, a theory of either 'religion' or 'magic' as such; its predictive value will rest on its success in the application within precisely classified social conditions of some more sophisticated psychological theory than is yet available to us; and it will be an evolutionary theory as, the world being what it is, all theories of social behaviour must be. On this final point, indeed, Tylor, Frazer, Durkheim, Weber and even, in their manner, the 'structural-functionalists' have all alike been correct.

*

4. *Class, Status and Power?* *

The notion that societies are stratified in the three separate 'dimensions' of 'class', 'status' and 'power' is thoroughly familiar in the academic literature. But it cannot be said to have established itself as orthodoxy. From time to time it is openly questioned; more often it is tacitly ignored in favour of some other chosen variant; only occasionally is it explicitly adopted as the framework for empirical research. This lack of agreement one way or the other is surprising not only because so much has been written on social stratification but because the question is in any case not one whose answer must necessarily await the results of empirical research still to be carried out. Whatever subsequent research may reveal about either present or past societies, it should be possible to settle already whether or not 'class', 'status' and 'power' can furnish an adequate framework for the classification and analysis of systems of stratification. In this paper I shall not try to review the recent theoretical or empirical literature, but merely to set out and criticise the kinds of argument which require to be established in order to settle whether the three-dimensional framework is or is not, after all, appropriate to its task.

I

Discussion of the problem generally begins by reference to the ideas of Max Weber. But influential though these have been, it can be argued that they have sometimes hindered the progress of the discussion as much as they have helped it. Weber, like Marx, died leaving his work on stratification incomplete, and (again like Marx) it is unlikely that any one interpretation of it will ever satisfy all his readers. A strong, but not conclusive, case can be made for the view that Weber did not regard class, status and power as separate dimensions of social structure; he may rather have thought that, as one of his commentators has put it, 'whatever its form, stratification was a manifestation of the unequal distribution of power'.[1] But at the same time he was at pains to make clear that power is not a direct concomitant of either class or status, and

---

* This paper was first published in *Sociological Studies*, 1 (1968), edited by J. A. Jackson. It is criticised by Geoffrey Ingham, 'Social Stratification: Individual Attributes and Social Relationships', *Sociology*, IV, 1 (1970); but see the rejoinder by myself, *ibid.* IV, 2.
[1] Leonard Reissman, *Class in American Society* (London, 1950), p. 58.

at the end of his life he was increasingly concerned with the origins and effects of political parties and industrial or governmental bureaucracies considered independently from their relation to the market, with whose influence he had been preoccupied in his earlier studies. It is evident that he regarded power as different in kind from either market-situation on the one hand or prestige-ranking on the other. But this much would be accepted by everybody. Beyond this, any attempt to arrive at a definitive summary of Weber's views merely leads to controversies which in the nature of the case are incapable of settlement. The merits of a three-dimensional framework should, and can, be settled irrespective of how far Weber either foreshadowed or would have been disposed to agree with the verdict given.

On similar grounds, it might be argued that the terms 'class', 'status' and 'power' are better dispensed with, since 'class', in particular, is associated with a long history of sterile verbal disputes which should if possible be bypassed altogether. But this ought not to be necessary. The restriction of 'class' and 'status' to the traditional distinction between wealth and prestige is sufficiently familiar that it can be adopted without risk of misunderstanding. These things are matters of convenience, and although 'class' and 'status' should be qualified or abandoned as becomes necessary, there is no warrant for departing from them unless they prove even more unsatisfactory than they have done in the past. It is only necessary to make it clear from the outset that 'class' and 'status' are not being used in the quite different sense whereby 'Class is differentiated from status in that the latter suggests a range and continuum, while class connotes a degree of unity and some form of homogeneity among its members'.[1] In any case, this paper is not concerned to try to settle what terms are most appropriate, but what it means to claim that social stratification is three-dimensional and by what means such a claim might be invalidated.

If social stratification is three-dimensional, it must follow that the position of every person within a society is in principle capable of being designated as a vector in three-dimensional space. Accordingly, society itself will have to be seen as a sort of box, in which the lowest position is the bottom left-hand corner and the highest position the top right-hand one. To make the metaphor of top and bottom more vivid, we could say that society is a box balanced upright on one corner so that that corner is the bottom in all three dimensions and the further end of the diagonal

---

[1] Walter Goldschmidt, 'Social Class in America—a Critical Review', *American Anthropologist*, LII (1950), 491.

the top. Or if the highest position in one or more of the dimensions is indeterminate, then it would be better to describe society not as a box but as an up-ended pyramid with an apex but no base. We could further say that 'social mobility' is a path from any one point to any other point within the space enclosed by the three co-ordinates; and if it were to be found that there is an exact coincidence between the hierarchies of class, status and power then every member of society would be located somewhere along the diagonal (and the society in question would in effect be one-dimensional). It will not follow from this that it is easy or even possible to assign a place to every member of every society even in terms of ordinal rankings. But if we are to say that stratification is three-dimensional, then this is what we must mean by it.

It should be clear, however, that to say this implies nothing about where the dividing lines should be drawn within any given social space between one 'stratum' and another. Once every person, or simply every role, has been assigned a place, it will still be an open question how they should be categorised in terms of 'classes', 'castes', 'estates' or any other concrete collective term used to designate those sharing an approximate common location. An enormous volume of argument has been devoted to this problem. But there is no one answer to it, and the appropriate classification will vary according to the questions which the investigator has in mind and the distinguishing features of the particular society or societies under study. Indeed, it can be argued that in some societies it is wrong to speak of 'strata' at all, if the term is so used as to presuppose a strictly demarcated differentiation of roles. The appropriate criterion may be purely statistical, expressed in terms of percentiles, or standard deviations, or whatever measure is most suitable to the particular distribution found in each dimension; or the distribution in the three dimensions may be such that all, or nearly all, the members of the society seem to fall into one of a small number of clearly separated clusters; or there may be designated points where mobility is drastically restricted; or it may be more useful to distinguish between strata on the basis of some qualitative criterion, such as mode of entry, or ideological rationale, or legal or historical origin. The principle chosen must not, of course, do violence to the actual location of the individual members of the designated category. But for many purposes, it may well be important to classify society in terms of very different dividing-lines. Even if cardinal rankings could be assigned in the three dimensions, different observers would be free to draw different distinctions in terms of 'proletariat' and 'bourgeoisie', 'élite' and 'mass', 'nobility' and 'commoners', *honestiores* and *humiliores*, 'citizens', 'metics' and 'slaves', 'Brahmans', 'Kshatriya', 'Vaishya' and 'Shudra', and so forth. But nothing follows from this one way or the other about the validity of the claim that where we are concerned with stratification and not simply differentiation, there are only three dimensions in which it can operate.

In the same way, it should be clear that a three-dimensional framework is compatible with any view either of 'subjective' class or of the 'dynamics', as opposed to the 'statics', of stratification. It in no way rules out what is implied in such views as that 'class' is a phenomenon which only arises when 'some men, as a result of common experiences (inherited or shared), feel and articulate the identity of their interests as between themselves';[1] or that '*class* is always a category for purposes of the analysis of the dynamics of social conflict at its structural roots, and as such it has to be separated strictly from *stratum* as a category for purposes of describing hierarchical systems at a given point of time'.[2] The term 'class' can quite well be used in some such sense as these if it is found useful, and if it is, it can be perfectly well accommodated within the three-dimensional framework. Further, 'class consciousness', defined as 'implying consciousness of the special interests of the class and actions directed towards preserving those interests' may be marked off from simple 'class awareness'.[3] Nor is there any reason to deny that the 'dynamic' or 'subjective' aspect of stratification is indispensable to the explanation of how and why any system of stratification came to be as it is and either changes or fails to change. The temptation to use 'class' in a general and subjective as well as a limited and objective sense is unfortunate, since it makes it still more likely that disputes about terminology will be mistaken for disputes about fact. But a theory of how people see their situation and interests, and how this affects in turn the structure and workings of the system within which those interests are perceived or neglected, is in no sense a rival to the claim that societies are stratified in three and only three dimensions. On the contrary, it is an essential complement to it.

II

What, then, are the theoretical objections which can be made to the three-dimensional framework? First of all, it will have to be clear that

[1] E. P. Thompson, *The Making of the English Working Class* (London, 1963), p. 9.
[2] Ralf Dahrendorf, *Class and Class Conflict in an Industrial Society* (London, 1958), p. 76.
[3] P. C. Lloyd, 'Introduction', in P. C. Lloyd, ed., *The New Elites of Tropical Africa* (London, 1966), p. 57.

we are indeed dealing with stratification and not merely with differentiation; or in other words, the metaphor of high and low must be appropriate. This question too has sometimes led to confusion. But it should be
self-evident that when speaking of either wealth, prestige or power we are
speaking of something which by definition admits of the notion of
ranking. Of course, there are other human attributes which admit of
ranking, such as physical height, but from a sociological standpoint, these
are individual, not institutional, differentiations. What needs to be clear
at the outset is both that economic class, status and power admit of
ranking and that these rankings, however they are measured or described,
are institutionalised or, in Rousseau's distinction, 'conventional' as
opposed to 'natural'.

That inequalities of wealth are institutionalised is obvious, since they
are in themselves the outcome of a system of regulated co-operation and
competition between interrelated individuals or economic groups. Similarly, inequalities of power must to some degree be institutionalised in
any society where conduct is at all regulated by sanctions, whether or
not overtly coercive; indeed, without some such sanctions it would be
debatable whether we should speak of the existence of a society at all.
Only with inequalities of status is it possible to conceive of a society
where, although they might exist, they were not institutionalised—
where, that is, although some people might be looked up to by some
other people, the distribution of admiration or deference was either so
nearly random, or else so fluid and unpredictable, that it could not be
said to constitute a status-system at all. But even here, it has to be
allowed that no society has yet been found which does not have a status-
system of some rudimentary kind. Explorers and anthropologists have in
the past claimed to have found such societies: Captain Cook, to take
only one example, thought he had found one in Tierra del Fuego. But
more careful investigation has shown that it is a mistake to suppose that
even in the most egalitarian societies there are no attributes, whether
age, or strength, or skill in hunting or battle which are not more highly
regarded than others to a more general extent than would fit a hypothesis of randomness. Accordingly, it seems that it can be said of status
with as much validity as of power or class that it is one of the ways
in which all societies are at once vertically and 'conventionally' differentiated.

If this is so, then a theoretical objection to the three-dimensional
framework can only take one or other of two forms. It will have to be
shown either that societies can be regarded as stratified in other ways

which are not reducible to one or more of class, status and power, or else that one or more of the three is not really, although it may appear to be, a separate dimension.

III

It is evident that we do not mean the same thing by 'class' (in the economic sense), 'status' and 'power'. But it does not follow from this alone that the three are in fact conceptually distinct in the way that is required if we are to talk of separate dimensions, for if one of them is no more than a kind of one of the others, then to talk of dimensions is illegitimate. In order, however, to establish this criticism it becomes necessary to show that any statement about economic class entails some statement about either status or power (or that any statement about status entails some statement about class or power, or that any statement about power entails some statement about class or status). Furthermore, it would not be enough to show that there always is some connection in any known instance; if we are talking about a conceptual and not an empirical relation, any counter-example whatever will be enough to show that the three are distinct after all. For example, it might be an accurate prediction that in any society where the institution of slavery is in operation slaves will be found to enjoy lower status than slaveholders. But this is a contingent relationship only; it is not a logical one. As it happens, there are examples in the anthropological literature of relationships where servitude is claimed not to be accompanied by loss of prestige: Boas, for example, said of the Central Eskimo that where men unable to provide for themselves are adopted by the able-bodied as dependent servants, they 'are not less esteemed than the self-dependent providers',[1] and in Korea during one period in its history slaves, who could be manumitted by purchase, were forbidden by law from associating with members of the hereditary pariah caste. But even if this were never so, it would not follow that the statement that a person is a slave *logically* entails anything about his location in the dimensions of either class or status. Similarly, to say that a man is a pauper does not *logically* entail anything about his power or his status; and to say that he is a pariah does not *logically* entail anything about his power or his economic class. Whatever relation there may be between the three, it does not follow simply from the meaning which we attach to these terms.

It would be truer to say that there are three separate families of related

[1] F. Boas, 'Central Eskimo', in *Smithsonian Reports VI*, p. 581, quoted by Gunnar Landtman, *The Origin of the Inequality of the Social Classes* (London, 1938), p. 11.

terms, such that there are conceptual links within each family but not between one family and another. Thus to the notion of economic class are linked such terms as: wealth, income, price, capital, market. To the notion of status are linked such terms as: esteem, gentility, exclusiveness, deference, condescension. To the notion of power are linked such terms as: command, obedience, autonomy, tyranny, rebellion. But there is not in the same way a logical link between the members of the three sets. There are, it is true, many terms which span the barriers in a way that these do not; perhaps the most obvious are the general words like 'subordination', 'hierarchy', 'dominance', and so forth. But it is only if such other terms cannot be broken down among the three families that they constitute a challenge to the three-dimensional framework; and they then imply not so much that class, status and power are logically linked to each other as that they are not between them all-embracing.

To bring the point out still more clearly, the three may be distinguished in terms of the kind of aspiration which they represent. To want wealth is not necessarily to want prestige or power; to want prestige is not necessarily to want power or wealth; to want power is not necessarily to want wealth or prestige. It can even be said that 'The difference between a rich man, a celebrity and a ruler is something like this: A rich man collects cattle and hoards of grain, or the money which stands for them . . . A ruler collects men. Grain and cattle, or money, mean nothing to him except insofar as he needs them to get hold of men . . . A celebrity collects a chorus of voices. All he wants is to hear them repeat his name.'[1] This imagery is perhaps a little fanciful, but the point which it serves to make is clear. Whether in terms of position or aspiration, there is a self-evident conceptual distinction between the three.

The confusions which arise, accordingly, are due more to the long-standing imprecision of the terminology of stratification than to a genuine conceptual overlap between power, wealth and prestige. This is due not simply to the conflicting uses of 'class' and 'status', which I need not review further here. In addition, not only 'power' but also 'rank' have been responsible for a good deal of unnecessary difficulty. 'Rank' causes difficulty for two reasons. First, it is sometimes used in such a way that to 'rank' one person above another in any respect is by definition to accord him prestige. This is plausible enough when approval or deference is involved—to 'accord someone high rank' is then by definition incompatible with according him low status. But to see that this will not hold in general, it is necessary only to go back to such examples as height and weight

[1] Elias Canetti, *Crowds and Power* (tr. Stewart; London, 1962), p. 397.

where 'ranking' is quite independent of any overtones of prestige. Secondly, 'rank' is sometimes used for particular hierarchies (such, for example, as military hierarchies) where there is a direct link between power and prestige. This, again, is perfectly plausible in the appropriate contexts. But it can be seriously misleading if it is allowed to imply that it is logically impossible, which it certainly is not, for a man to be the superior in status of those whom he is compelled to obey.

'Power', however, raises yet a further difficulty. Not only does it have to be made clear that its relation to status is a contingent and not a necessary one, but the same must also apply to economic class if we are to talk about three separate dimensions. 'Purchasing power', after all, is presumably power of a sort, and the notion of wealth carries with it the notion of power in at any rate the sense that wealth is by definition the capacity to acquire socially valued things. But the important distinction becomes clear as soon as we move from power over things, in this sense, to power over people. It is sometimes said that economic class is necessarily linked to power because, for example, all employers have, simply by virtue of being employers, some measure of power over their employees. But the link is not, in fact, a necessary one. To say 'Jones has £5' means (assuming that the money is not counterfeit, the economy has not broken down, there is not a total shortage of goods on the market, and so forth) that Jones has the 'power' to acquire £5 worth of goods; or if it does not, then the possession of £5 ceases to constitute wealth by definition. But to say 'Jones pays Smith £5 a week for laying bricks' means that Smith chooses, as it happens and for whatever reasons, to take £5 for the work rather than not to. Even if he is compelled to, because in the society in question employers are allowed powers of physical coercion, the power of Jones over him is still not the necessary consequence of Jones's capacity to pay him £5. In other words, what can be called 'reward power' is contingent; it does not logically follow from the possession of wealth[1]. Of course, the notion of power does still raise notorious difficulties of definition, to which I shall return in a later section of the paper. But I hope enough has been said to make clear that conceptually, at least, economic class, status and power are genuinely distinct, however easy it may be in particular contexts to ignore or disguise the distinction.

[1] For a more rigorous analysis of the difference, cf. Robert Nozick, 'Coercion', in S. Morgenbesser *et al.*, eds, *Philosophy, Science and Method* (New York, 1969), pp. 447–53.

IV

But are we entitled to say that there are *only* these three dimensions in which societies can be said to be stratified? Or are there other ways in which their members are institutionally ranked above and below each other which cannot be conceptually reduced to one or other of the three? A question of this form is always difficult to answer conclusively, since it is impossible to go through an exhaustive list of all conceivable candidates. But there are at any rate a few possible contenders about which something should be said before it can be assumed that the three-dimensional framework is valid on purely conceptual grounds.

First of all, it might be argued that in some cultures the most important term in the vocabulary of stratification is one which ties wealth, status and power together so tightly as to be impossible to disentangle. Indeed, it may even be that the language used does not contain the concepts in which such a disentanglement could be expressed. What, for example, are we to say about the Polynesian *mana*, of which Mauss says in his essay on *The Gift* that it 'symbolizes not only the magical power of the person but also his honour, and one of the best translations of the word is "authority" or "wealth" '?[1] But the answer to this is that the distinctions which are not made in a language are not therefore invalid even for the society or culture whose language it is. Where a distinction is made, then we are indeed bound to take it seriously whether or not it is one which our own language is able to accommodate. But the reverse does not hold. The investigator of Polynesian society is entitled to place its members within a three-dimensional framework whether or not they can grasp what he is up to. It may be, of course, that there is a good reason for their lack of the distinction since it may be that the correlation between the three dimensions in Polynesian society is so close that the positions to be described are all located along the diagonal. But again, this is not evidence one way or the other for the validity of a threefold distinction. If valid, it can meaningfully be applied to Polynesian society just as much as to any other, whatever may be the ideas about stratification entertained by the Polynesians themselves.

A different kind of candidate for a fourth dimension of stratification is what has been called 'informational status'—that is, the 'amount of skill or knowledge possessed'.[2] But it is not difficult to demonstrate that where knowledge and skill do constitute an advantage which 'conventionally' ranks their possessor above his fellows, this is precisely because it

---

[1] Marcel Mauss, *The Gift* (tr. Cunnison; London, 1954), p. 36.
[2] Kaare Svalastoga, *Social Differentiation* (New York, 1965), p. 16.

constitutes an advantage in the hierarchies of either class, status or power. Education does not by definition stratify society, it only differentiates it. Polymaths do not constitute a high-ranking stratum in the way that the rich, or the social aristocracy, or the holders of governmental office do. Where education does stratify rather than differentiate, this is because of its contingent association with economic *Lebenschancen*, or social prestige, or influence and authority, or possibly all three. Without such an association, the distinction between the educated and the uneducated is not stratification any more than is the distinction between the tall and the short or the fat and the thin. It is perfectly true that education, knowledge and skill do as a rule secure advantages for their possessors in a way that physical height does not. But this is merely to say that education is a significant determinant of social location. It is not thereby a separate dimension. On the contrary, the educated man might in some conceivable societies be lower in all three dimensions than the uneducated. The millionaire, the celebrity and the ruler enjoy a high social position by definition; it is one or other of these three kinds of things that having a 'high' social position means. The same cannot be said to be true by definition even of the most talented or knowledgeable members of a social system.

A third candidate might be the so-called 'leader-follower' relationship which is clearly unequal but which cannot be unequivocally assigned to the dimension of power. It is a kind of power to the extent that the leader is able to influence his followers in such a way that they carry out his will. But it is also a kind of prestige, since the relationship is not a coercive one and the superiority of the leader to the led consists precisely in his ability to elicit from them a willing and even eager obedience. As it is described, for example, by Freud (summarising Le Bon), the 'prestige' of the leader is a 'mysterious and irresistible power', a 'sort of domination' which 'entirely paralyses our critical faculty, and fills us with wonderment and respect'.[1] Stated in these terms, the relationship may seem one which belongs to the study of individual psychopathology more than of social inequality. But in its institutionalised aspect, it is one which might be argued to be impossible to break down within the simple dichotomy of status and power.

Certainly, leadership is complex and often difficult to explain. But it does not follow from this that the sense in which leaders must be ranked higher than followers is a sense over and above status and power

[1] Sigmund Freud, *Group Psychology and the Analysis of the Ego* (ed. Strachey; London, 1959), p. 13.

(however these may be intertwined in leader-follower relationships).To say that a man is a leader is to say (by definition) that he enjoys both status and power. It is not to say that he enjoys something else which ranks above his fellows. A leader is different from a ruler because of the element of willing obedience—a ruler's power may be entirely coercive whereas a leader's is not. But this does not mean that if we were to be able to rank leaders themselves in order—that is, to treat leadership as though it *were* a separate dimension—their ranking could not at once be translated into a ranking in the hierarchies (however measured) of status and power. This, in turn, is not to say that the identification of leaders and the explanation of their influence and its consequences may not be of importance in analysing the dynamics of stratification. But as I have already emphasised, the importance of such categories within the three-dimensional framework is not evidence against its validity. Before saying that the phenomenon of leadership invalidates it, it would be necessary to show not that some kinds of power are directly tied to status (or, for that matter, vice versa) but that some kinds of leadership rank leaders above non-leaders in yet a further way. But this is not a conclusion to which the study of leadership in its social context has so far been held by anyone to lead.

An altogether different line of attack might be by way of the notion of 'rights'. The rights of citizenship can, perhaps, be directly contrasted with the system of 'social class', and the resulting distinction between 'civil', 'political' and 'social' rights on the one hand and inequalities of 'social class' on the other might be a more valid one than the simple addition of 'power' as a third dimension to class and status. This is the argument of T. H. Marshall's *Citizenship and Social Class*, in which the rise of the 'Welfare State' is described in terms of 'the impact of a rapidly developing concept of the rights of citizenship on the structure of social inequality'.[1] On this view, equality of citizenship is not only distinct from economic equality or equality of social esteem, but is itself very much more complicated than simple equality of 'power'. As Marshall points out, the trend towards equality of citizenship covers a progressive transition from liberty of the person, equality before the law, and the rights of property and contract, to the franchise, the right to membership in elective assemblies, and the eligibility to membership in any body invested with authority, and thence to the right 'to share to the full in the social heritage and to live the life of a civilised being according to the standards prevailing in the society'.[2] The historical importance of the

[1] T. H. Marshall, 'Citizenship and Social Class', in *Citizenship and Social Class and Other Essays* (Cambridge, 1950), p. 85.
[2] *Ibid.* p. 11.

difference between these three stages is unquestionable; so might it not be argued on the strength of it that the three-dimensional view of stratification falls down?

The answer, however, is the same as in the previous case. To invalidate the three-dimensional framework, it would be necessary to show that one or more of the rights of citizenship enumerated by Marshall ranks a man relatively to his fellows in some way which cannot be classified as an inequality of economic class, status, or power. This might have some force if the definition of economic class were to be restricted purely and simply to wealth instead of to what are generally called 'life-chances', or if the definition of 'power' were to cover only powers of direct physical coercion over other men and not the capacity of a more general kind to determine the actions of oneself as well as other people. But there is no warrant for imposing such restrictions; and without them, it is easy to show that where the possession of rights of citizenship does constitute a ranking in the system of social stratification it is a ranking in one or other of the three dimensions. Thus, liberty of the person and the right to vote are both aspects of inequality of power; the right to own property and the right to draw national assistance are both aspects of equality of economic *Lebenschancen*; and the right to 'live the life of a civilised being', if so vague a term can be more precisely specified, presumably covers equalities in all three dimensions, including the right not to be debarred from social relations with other members of the same society on such grounds of status as colour or race. Once again, it would have to be demonstrated that 'citizenship' denotes an equality with the other members of the same society which cannot be assigned to any one of the three dimensions; and although the several kinds of citizenship may for some purposes be more important than the three fundamental kinds of social equality, there does not seem to be any one aspect of citizenship which constitutes an equality or inequality in some fourth dimension of stratification.

Finally, we should perhaps briefly consider whether any of the evidence furnished by the study of animal societies serves to invalidate the three-dimensional framework on conceptual grounds. Much more is now known about the social life of animals than even a few decades ago, and it is perhaps significant that stratification in animal societies is generally discussed in terms not of 'class', 'status' and 'power' but of 'dominance', 'hierarchy', 'peck-order', 'supersedence' and so forth. Should we therefore conclude that animal societies are stratified in terms of relations of superiority and inferiority which fall outside the three-dimensional classification?

It may be rash for the non-specialist to give too confident an answer to this without detailed knowledge of the present state of ethological research. But the best-known evidence does not seem to suggest that the stratification of animal societies in any way invalidates the three-dimensional framework. The vocabulary in which animal hierarchies are described is guided by a proper caution against the dangers of anthropomorphism, and where the terms taken from human behaviour seem out of place this is more because of the greater simplicity of the 'peck-order' or 'dominance hierarchy' studied than because there is some further dimension in which it would make sense to speak of animal societies as stratified. Animal hierarchies may be of many different kinds, and may be described in many different ways. But they have not (as far as I know) supported the existence of an additional dimension of stratification beyond those in which human societies are stratified. Animal hierarchies often rest on force, or the threat of force, and in this sense are relationships of power, even where the threats have been highly ritualised and thus serve the function of inhibiting fights to the death. But given ritualisation, there can be an additional element of what it is perhaps legitimate to call 'status' in the relationship, as is seen in the gestures of positive and respectful submission shown, for example, by wolves and some monkeys towards their superiors, or in the non-coercive leader-follower relationships observed among ducks, sheep and deer. Similarly, property rights and hence 'economic' advantages may be established and maintained not only by fighting but also by custom as, for example, among rooks. Or again, status may be established not merely by force or threat but by display, as in 'leks' in which low-ranking birds are ignored altogether and from which they seem to accept their exclusion with acquiescence and even humility. In general, the biological function of animal hierarchies in apportioning territory, inhibiting intra-group aggression and restricting indiscriminate breeding lead to composite rank-orders for which a general term signifying an unspecified dominance is likely to be the most appropriate. But it does not follow from this that animal hierarchies are ever of a kind to suggest that the threefold distinction between 'class', 'status' and 'power' is conceptually invalid. On the contrary, the more sophisticated societies can even be argued to illustrate it, provided that it is not applied in terms which presuppose the existence of specifically human institutions.

V

It would seem, then, that there is no convincing argument for rejecting the three-dimensional framework on conceptual grounds. But it could still be claimed that it is not empirically valid, for it might be either that one of the three is strictly reducible to another or that one is a consistent function (even if a lagged function) of another. Both these, however, are strong claims, and to substantiate them would require a more convincing demonstration than has yet been offered.

If the first is to be substantiated, it will have to be shown not merely that there is an isomorphism between the relations holding for the two classes of phenomena but that there is a strict interchangeability between the respective terms. Now this possibility cannot be ruled out entirely, since it is always possible that further research will show that a reduction can be made, however unlikely this may have seemed at one time. In the way that, for example, it has been suggested that rules of marriage are reducible to rules of information exchange (although there is not, of course, an identity of meaning between the two), so it might be suggested that the laws governing inequalities of status, say, are reducible to the laws governing inequalities of class, that the constants in both are identical, and that 'status' and 'class' are interchangeable throughout. But nobody has yet claimed this; and indeed it would be easy to assemble much evidence against it.

Perhaps some examples can be cited which show how a reduction of this kind might operate: thus, the 'potlatch' can perhaps be interpreted as an instance of an ostensible status phenomenon which is reducible to a phenomenon of economic class in the sense that status is here a purchasable commodity acquired by the surrender of an amount of material goods equivalent in value. The same could be said to be true of all instances of 'conspicuous consumption'. Indeed, if in all known communities status in the eyes of a man's fellows could only be acquired in this way, and in strict accordance with the rules of the market, then the case for treating status as a separate dimension of stratification might disappear. But it is enough to show that there are, at any rate, some status phenomena where this does not hold, and where the explanation of the status order cannot be plausibly fitted to what is thought the best explanation of the order of economic class, for the reductionist claim to be very implausible at best.

In the same way, it is perfectly possible that a model for the distribution of power might be found to fit closely in a large number of instances with the distribution of wealth. But it would not follow from this fact by itself that the reductionist case had been established. Once again, a single example where an inequality of power could not be explained by direct reference to the laws of economic class, or where the empirical terms in the two relationships were not interchangeable, would be enough to show the reductionist case to be untenable. In any case, the more obvious inference from a close fit to a common model would be not that power 'is' wealth in the sense that, to take a classic example from the physical sciences, electromagnetic waves 'are' light waves, but simply that for a number of well-known reasons there is in practice a close correlation between the two.

The different claim that one or other of the three kinds of inequality has a general causal priority is more familiar. It has never, as far as I know, been seriously advanced on behalf of status (although status has, of course, often been treated as an independent variable in the analysis of social structure, notably by Weber and Tocqueville). But priority has often been claimed both for class, in the sense of relation to the mode of production or, as Marx himself sometimes puts it, 'the property question', and for power. For the present argument, it does not matter which of these is more convincing than the other, since if either can be vindicated this will furnish sufficient grounds for rejecting the three-dimensional approach. But conversely, the claim of economic class will fall down if even a single instance of autonomous inequality of power or status can be put up against it, and the claim of power will similarly fall down if confronted with an autonomous inequality of status or class.

In a sense, the rival claims of class over power and power over class serve to cancel each other out. If there is the least plausibility in both of them, then the claim by either to universal priority becomes to that degree impossible to sustain. Indeed, it may well be that there is nowhere in the contemporary literature on stratification a claim to priority for either of them which is as extreme as it needs to be to undermine the validity of the three-dimensional scheme. Nobody is now likely to deny the importance of relations to the mode of production; but at the same time nobody is now likely to claim that every possible inequality of status or power is a function of them. Similarly, many inequalities of wealth or access to it can be argued to result from some initial superiority in the means of coercion; but this is very different from claiming that the distribution of wealth in any and all societies can be traced back exclusively to violence and conquest or (as some versions of the power theory have maintained) to the legal controls which the dominant group first laid down and which then governed the subsequent allocation of property. There is no unified doctrine of the primacy of power in the way that there is, or has been, of the primacy of class, and it is often difficult to tell how far statements such as 'The type of stratified society that develops in a situation of contact depends largely on the relative power of the contending groups'[1] or 'because sanctions are necessary to enforce conformity of human conduct, there has to be inequality of rank among men'[2] are compatible with a three-dimensional framework. It is probably true that among contemporary writers, at least, even those most anxious to emphasise the causal importance of relations of power, capacities for physical force, and the strength of legal and therefore ultimately coercive sanctions would not want to argue that absolutely all institutional inequalities are functions of them. But in any case, if we want to refute the claim that either power or economic class is the sole determinant of all other inequalities, it will already be enough to show that inequalities of status can arise, however rarely, on their own.

The examples most commonly cited to show that prestige can be independent of either wealth or power are those of priests, shamans, teachers and intellectuals in general. In the case of priests or shamans, the complete independence of their status may be debatable since their status may well derive from the imputation to them of supernatural powers. But the point can be readily demonstrated by reference to secular activities, despite such blanket assertions as are sometimes made to the effect that 'prestige is essentially determined by power'[3] or that status 'derives from the attempt of those with power to legitimise their position'.[4] Public entertainers furnish the most obvious example. How is the prestige accorded them to be shown to be either synonymous with or derived from one of the other dimensions? When Wright Mills says that 'the "power" of the celebrity is the power of distraction'[5] his own use of inverted commas shows that he is merely playing with words. In some cultures, artists and musicians are highly esteemed and well rewarded; in others, they are recruited only from an inferior caste. But the cases where their status is curiously low cannot be traced to variations in power or wealth any better than the cases where their status is curiously high.

More generally still, the autonomy of status can be demonstrated from the study of play itself, and particularly agonistic play. This point is well made by Huizinga when he describes the 'honour and esteem' which accrues to the 'winner' and thence by extension to the group to which he belongs. There are, of course, many instances where a competitive game,

---

[1] Tamotsu Shibutani and Kian M. Kwan, *Ethnic Stratification* (New York, 1965), p. 250.
[2] Ralf Dahrendorf, 'On the Origin of Social Inequality', in Peter Laslett and W. G. Runciman (eds.), *Philosophy, Politics and Society*, 2nd ser. (Oxford, 1962), p. 104.
[3] Stanislaw Andrzejewski, *Military Organisation and Society* (London, 1954), p. 21.
[4] Kenneth Prandy, *Professional Employees* (London, 1965), p. 174.
[5] C. Wright Mills, *The Power Elite* (New York, 1959), p. 360.

even if carefully regulated, is a competition for power or wealth and not merely for status. But equally, there are many instances where status and only status is what it is the purpose of the game to determine. As Huizinga says, 'the competitive "instinct" is not in the first place a desire for power or a will to dominate. The primary thing is the desire to excel others, to be the first and to be honoured for that. The question whether, in the result, the power of the individual or the group will be increased takes only a second place. The main thing is to have won.'[1] Indeed, the point hardly needs to be laboured. Rousseau, for all his emphasis on the institution of private property as the root of 'conventional' inequality, is also very much aware of what he calls 'cette ardeur de faire parler de soi, cette fureur de se distinguer'. This ardour is at least somewhere present in all societies, and in some it is absolutely overriding: it has been said of the Mestizos of Aritama, in Colombia, that to be 'respected' is 'the ultimate goal of life, and all human activities are essentially oriented toward achieving this end'.[2] It is only necessary to reassert its existence when it is being denied that *any* institutionalised difference of status can arise except as a function of inequality of either class or power.

To be sure, it is always possible that (as with a reductionist argument) further research will vindicate a claim which does not at the moment look plausible. If, for example, the historical evidence were adequate—which it is not—to show how the Indian system of caste came into being, it might turn out that causal priority should, after all, be assigned either to property and the division of labour or to political and military dominance or to status derived from religious conceptions of purity and pollution. But it would still be necessary to prove that the primary dimension in this instance was also the primary dimension over the whole range of systems of stratification. If there is any general conclusion to be drawn from the mass of heterogeneous and often conflicting evidence with which the student of stratification is confronted, it is surely that inequalities of all three kinds can under at least some circumstances arise autonomously, and that the causal relations between the three are sometimes in one direction and sometimes in another. Thus the relation between wealth and power may be directly reversed depending on the stage of economic or political development reached by the society in question. For example, it has been said both that 'in pre-market societies wealth tends to follow power; not until the market society will power tend to follow wealth'[3]

[1] Johan Huizinga, *Homo Ludens* (Boston, 1955), p. 50.
[2] Gerardo and Alicia Reichel-Dolmatoff, *The People of Aritama* (London, 1961), p. 441.
[3] Robert Heilbroner, *The Making of Economic Society* (Englewood Cliffs, 1962), p. 27, quoted by Gerhard E. Lenski, *Power and Privilege* (New York, 1966), p. 229.

and, conversely, that 'in the emergent countries, the Party, rather than being the expression of the economic interests of a class, is itself the opening to economic opportunity. Wealth derives *from* political power; it does not create it'.[1] It is only under limited conditions that a simple one-way model giving primacy to class or power is likely to fit the facts. To say this is not to decry the importance of theories which assert that under given conditions of, say, industrialisation, or expansion of population, or military conquest, or cultural diffusion the resulting system of stratification will be determined by the relations holding between the respective groups in one dimension rather than another. But it is, I think, safe to say that no claim for the consistent and universal primacy of one dimension over the others has yet been successfully put forward. If, therefore, the three-dimensional framework is invalid as such, it is not on empirical any more than on conceptual grounds.

VI

To have established, however, that the three dimensions are both conceptually and empirically distinct does not mean that it is therefore possible to assign a precise location to each member even of a small organisation, let alone a large and complex society. It might seem plausible to regard class, at least, as lending itself to straightforward measurement and analysis (and in fact I shall say less about it than either status or power). But although it is easy to say that by economic 'class' is meant every aspect of a person's relation to the commodity and labour markets expressed in terms of money or the probability of obtaining money or its equivalents, it is by no means easy to define and list these aspects in such a way as to yield a cardinal ordering.

In principle, it should be possible to ascertain the distribution of income, or wealth, and then to fit it to the Pareto or lognormal or whatever is the most appropriate curve. But there are still serious difficulties. There is not merely the technical difficulty that there may be societies in which the units of money are not such as to furnish an adequate measure of utility and therefore of wealth. More important, there are aspects of class-situation which do not lend themselves to satisfactory quantification even in societies with a sophisticated market economy.

The first difficulty can, perhaps, be dismissed as of increasingly little importance. There do exist societies where there is not a stable and reciprocal unit of currency, or where 'wealth' consists in the possession or

[1] Peter Worsley, *The Third World* (London, 1964), pp. 192–3.

accumulation of objects which have no exchange value, like the famous 'stone money' of the Yap Islanders, so that it becomes impossible to draw comparisons even in terms of a basic unit of goods or the work-time required for its acquisition. The same could be said, indeed, of Europe in the early middle ages, when the coinage was limited in supply and locally variable in value, or of any society where the development of currency has not reached the point at which a 'market-situation' can properly be said to exist. But even where a fully developed money economy is in operation, it is impossible to express all the various aspects of class-situation precisely in terms of it. In practice, significant economic inequalities can be calculated well enough to furnish many useful comparisons both within societies and between them. But a full assessment of class-situation will have to include not merely earnings and possessions but net real reward related to labour time, all gifts, receipts, benefits in kind or remissions of expenditure, allowance for any expenses regarded as mandatory, such as the maintenance of dependants, and allowance for all potential or expected benefits which are a function of present position in relation to the market. Further, in any economy in which public funds are held in some sense on behalf of the population at large, these should be somehow credited to the presumed beneficiaries; but this is as problematic in sophisticated societies, where costly social services (including national defence) are centrally financed, as in simpler societies where there is no clear line between the public funds and the ruler's private purse. Finally, the definition of 'class-situation' may need to be broadened to include what has been called 'work-situation',[1] or in Weber's words the 'allgemeinen typischen Lebensbedingungen' consequential on market-situation, such as the need to submit to the discipline of the workplace.[2] Perhaps it can be assumed that any aspects of 'work-situation' which do not fall under either status or power can be expressed in monetary terms. But even so, it is as well to remember how far we are, even in the dimension of economic class, from the cardinal rankings which the monetary yardstick and the market mechanism would appear to make possible.

VII

The difficulties raised by the notion of status, however, are (as is well known) more formidable still. Not only does status rest by definition on

---

[1] David Lockwood, *The Blackcoated Worker* (London, 1958), p. 15.
[2] Max Weber, 'Die Wirtschaftsethik der Weltreligionen', in *Gesammelte Aufsätze zur Religionssoziologie*, I (Tübingen, 1922), 274.

subjective attitudes which may not be susceptible to precise description and measurement; but even if these attitudes can be unambiguously expressed, there will remain the problem of deriving an ordering from them. It may be that for some purposes a cardinal ranking will not be called for. To establish, for example, the existence in the status hierarchy of post-medieval Europe of a middle stratum of 'bourgeoisie' with its own life style, ideology and pattern of social contacts between the aristocracy on one side and the proletariat on the other, it is not necessary to measure by just how much it is either below the one or above the other. Further, it is perhaps only in ordinal terms that some distinctions of status can be said to have meaning at all. But inequalities of status can take many forms, and if we are to assign to each member of a society a place in the dimension of status, let alone to compare one society with another, then it will be necessary somehow to decide the relative weight to be assigned to one distinction as against another and to measure the social distance by which individuals or strata are accordingly separated.

The investigator of a status-system needs in principle to know only the criteria by which its members rank each other and the scores which they assign. He can then plot the distribution of the population studied, and if he is satisfied that the scorings are capable of being related to a common scale he can compare one population with another. Moreover, he can make comparisons in terms not only of the height and scatter of the several distributions, but also the number and consistency of criteria used, the degree of unanimity underlying the composite scores, and the changeability both of the criteria themselves and the rankings assigned by reference to them. It is sometimes said in criticism of the analysis of status in terms of reciprocal rankings that it presupposes a face-to-face community in which the antecedents and attributes of every member are known to every other member. But although this is a self-imposed limitation in studies in which status is deliberately defined in terms of actual relations between designated individuals, it is hard to see why it should be necessary in principle to speak of inequalities of status only in face-to-face terms. If we wish to speak of the distribution of status in a large community or even a nation, then what we mean is presumably the different prestige rankings which people would accord to each other on the basis of their possession or lack of the attributes which merit prestige in the scorer's eyes.

The difficulties arise when it comes to constructing a status distribution in practice. In the first place, the criteria by which status is accorded are often incommensurate. It is all very well to say that the status of X is measured by the ranking which Y and Z assign to him and that if they are asked to rank him relative to A, B and C then the weighting of the various criteria finds expression in the final score which they give. But Y and Z may quite properly refuse to give a single score of this kind; and even if they are prepared to, the investigator may have doubts as to whether, let us say, their disparagement of X on grounds of racial purity ought not to be given more weight relative to their professed admiration for his attainments in other spheres than they themselves are disposed to give it. Furthermore, the criterion of ranking is likely to vary qualitatively not only over time but also within even a single culture at a single time. The prestige of the distinguished celebrity is not like the rich man's wealth: as one French author has put it, 'L'éminence se définit par la réputation, donc par un phénomène social qui varie selon le milieu et les échelles de valeur.'[1] How, therefore, can it ever be legitimate to construct a uniform, let alone a cross-culturally valid, prestige scale?

Secondly, it may in any case be impossible to translate behaviour symbolic of inequality of status into the sort of prestige scale required. The existence of distinguishable status-strata is generally held, following Weber and others, to involve differential life styles and upbringing, commensalism and endogamy, and social exclusiveness in general. But how is a distribution of status to be constructed from these, even where there is no question that the several groups are vertically, and not merely horizontally, differentiated? It may be possible, for example, to construct a 'ritual pollution scale' for the ranking of Hindu castes,[2] or to establish the existence of a 'hierarchy of preferences among shades of skin color' among Negroes by means of an appropriate psychological experiment and non-parametric statistical test.[3] But what are we to say if the castes are not after all amenable to Guttman scaling, or the results of the psychological experiments conflict? And in any case, it will only be within a caste-like system where status-equilibration is rigidly maintained that a single scale of exclusiveness will be capable of furnishing all the answers required. In the same way, sociometric choice may in some situations furnish an operational index of prestige. But it is only where 'popularity', in this sense, is a sufficient criterion of status that no further questions

---

[1] Claude Lévy-Leboyer, 'Les déterminants de la supériorité', in Alain Girard, *La Réussite sociale en France*, Institut national d'études démographiques, Cahier no. 38, (Paris, 1961), p. 32.

[2] Pauline M. Mahar, 'A Ritual Pollution Scale for Ranking Hindu Castes', *Sociometry*, XXIII (1960), 292–306.

[3] Sidney Seigel, *Nonparametric Statistics for the Behavioral Sciences* (New York, 1956), pp. 49–50.

will arise. In general, it is only where exclusiveness can be assumed to correlate directly with esteem that anything like a distribution of status analogous to the distribution of wealth can be plotted at all.

Thirdly, there may be a difference in kind not merely between the attributes selected as relevant to status or the forms of behaviour to which the recognition of these attributes gives rise but also in the nature of the recognition itself. There may be significant differences between societies where status is awarded in terms of, say, 'esteem' (defined by reference to performance in a specified role) as opposed to 'prestige' (defined by reference only to the role itself),[1] or 'praise' (defined as zero-sum) as opposed to 'respect' (defined as non-zero-sum),[2] or differentials of prestige deriving from 'sacred' values, in a Durkheimian sense, as opposed to 'secular' values (the distinction which, rather differently expressed, underlies G. M. Young's description of 'the philosophic man, like Mill and Fawcett, who will admit no inequality of status unless some utilitarian cause can be shown'.)[3] These are not differences in the choice of attribute to which high or low status is assigned, although they may in practice correlate with one type of attribute rather than another. They are differences, broadly speaking, in the nature of the ideology which underlies the choice of attributes. Sometimes these differences are very difficult to locate and define, even with a thorough knowledge of the history and culture of the society under study. But even if we assume that the investigator is sufficiently knowledgeable to detect not only the attributes held relevant to status and the forms of behaviour in which it finds expression but also the nature, in this sense, of those forms, how is he to express this in measurable terms? How, for example, could he compare the distribution of status in a modern industrial community with that in ancient Sparta, or among the Kalahari Bushmen, or in feudal Europe, even if we assume that he has available to him all the evidence that he could ask for? It is not that different attributes are taken to be relevant or that different modes of speech and behaviour are culturally prescribed so much as that the kind of status itself is different. We still wish to speak of inequality of status in each of its divergent forms; but there is no common yardstick which will make it possible to speak of the social distance between superiors and inferiors in one case as greater or smaller than in another. Even when all the evidence is in, there will be no way to

---

[1] K. Davis, 'A Conceptual Analysis of Stratification', *American Sociological Review* VII (1942), 309–21.
[2] See chapter 9, below.
[3] G. M. Young, *Victorian England* (London, 1960), p. 155.

describe the different distributions of status except in terms more or less valueless for the purpose of precise comparison.

Fourthly, there is the difference between those systems in which the members of the inferior strata do, and those in which they do not, accept the ranking which they are assigned by the strata above them. This is not a difference which will be reflected in the investigator's map of prestige rankings or sociometric choices. Where the criteria of ranking are not in dispute the problem of intensity of feeling is solved by the translation of esteem or prestige into a score whose range will reflect the extent of variation among those whose rankings constitute the status-system in question. But what are we to say when the dominant ideology is passionately rejected by those whose inferior position it is held to justify? Indeed, it may be that in no society can those at the lowest level of status be said to be satisfied with their position, for even if they do not reject the ideology which assigns this rank to them they will envisage the possibility of securing at least a slightly higher rank within the accepted system. To pursue these differences of attitude further would lead into problems in the psychology of relative deprivation which are outside the scope of this paper. But they raise yet a further difficulty in the classification and comparison of hierarchies of status. It may be said that a man's resentment of the feelings of others towards him is irrelevant to the location to which those feelings consign him; although, in the words of Hobbes, 'every man looketh that his companion should value him at the same rate he sets upon himselfe', he cannot in any way require his companion to do so. But it is at the same time difficult to argue that where the members of an inferior stratum reject either the criterion by which they are ranked or the rank which they are assigned there is not an important difference of kind from a status hierarchy in which they are willing to accept their place.

This leads on to a fifth difficulty. When the ideology of the dominant stratum is rigidly exclusive and strongly held, the legitimacy of upward mobility may be denied altogether. It is this denial which is sometimes held to mark the difference in kind between 'class' systems and 'caste' systems: Myrdal, for example, in *An American Dilemma*, defines caste as consisting in 'such drastic restrictions of free competition in the various spheres of life that the individual in a lower caste cannot, by any means, change his status except by a secret and illegitimate "passing" '.[1] The phenomenon of passing is in a sense only a symptom of the previous difficulty: it arises only because the members of an inferior stratum

[1] Gunnar Myrdal, *An American Dilemma*, 2nd ed. (New York, 1962), pp. 674–5.

refuse to accept the place assigned to them. But it raises a further problem for the investigator who is trying to locate every person, or at any rate every group, along a continuum of status. To treat those who pass as members of the stratum to which they are aspiring is to reflect correctly (for as long as they are not discovered) the prestige assigned to them by their fellows. But it is surely a distortion of the reality to categorise them as though they were, so to speak, 'genuine' members of the superior stratum. The problem is particularly acute when there are no overt signs by which those of inferior social origin can be recognised. The Burakumin of Japan, for example, are indistinguishable as members of a pariah caste except to the extent that their origin may be betrayed in such nuances of manner and attitude as are the product of their own awareness of their origin. Their difficulty in passing lies in concealing their place of birth or residence which others will be able to identify as a ghetto. Hence a distinction has to be made between 'lateral mobility', where the anonymity of a new milieu conceals but does not abolish the home ties of a Burakumin, and 'true vertical mobility' which will require a transfer of family registry as well as a permanent change of residence.[1] In other cultures, 'passing' may require a change of name. Indeed, if a person can conceal his family, then 'passing' can become relatively easy even within a caste system: thus, it has been said of outsiders in a Sinhalese village that 'if their kinship connections are unknown, and if they choose not to state their caste, then by changing their caste-linked names and occupations they can pretend to be anything they fancy. And they can get away with it'.[2] If, of course, the characteristic is unmistakable, like colour, individual mobility is only possible by overriding the fact of origin as opposed to denying it (whence the saying in Brazil that 'money whitens'). But the phenomenon of passing is one which is peculiar to the dimension of status, and makes it curiously difficult to say whether a person does or does not occupy a certain position. People cannot in this way pretend to have wealth or power; but if they can behave in such a way as to be treated by their fellows as other than they are, then they have to this extent to be accorded *de facto* equality of status.

Sixthly, there is the difference between those systems where there is, and those where there is not, an explicit legal sanction which underlies and sustains differences of status. However true it is that social recognition

[1] George De Vos and Hiroshi Wagatsuma, *Japan's Invisible Race* (Berkeley and Los Angeles, 1966), p. 248.
[2] Nur Yalman, 'The Flexibility of Caste Principles in a Kandyan Community', in E. R. Leach, ed., *Aspects of Caste in South India, Ceylon and North-West Pakistan*, Cambridge Papers in Social Anthropology, no. 2 (Cambridge, 1960), p. 99.

and esteem are not matters which are subject to legislative regulation, where mobility between strata which are distinguished from each other in social prestige is restricted not merely by custom but by law, there is an evident qualitative difference from those systems where custom alone furnishes the sanction. It is this difference which underlies the remark of Marc Bloch that 'If in France we speak today of the upper middle classes as a capitalist aristocracy, it is only in irony'.[1] Where every person is treated by law as inheriting the privileges of his father, and where those privileges serve to define a family's rank in terms of status as well as wealth or power, the very notions of exclusiveness, mobility, *déclassement* and so forth take on a different meaning. Of course, it is possible for the members of the society to deny the implications of the law in the sense that they may refuse to accord social esteem to the holders of inherited privilege. But it is a significant fact that they have, as it were, actively to refuse it. Thus when, for example, in imperial Rome it was ruled that a free woman cohabiting with a slave could be claimed, together with any child of the union, by the slave's owner, this will have served institutionally to reinforce the exclusiveness of which endogamy is a characteristic symptom and thereby to increase the social distance separating slaves and free. It will be difficult, and perhaps impossible, to tell just what importance changes of this kind may have in determining the distribution of status within the society at large, given that the attitudes and feelings of individual people never do correlate precisely with those tacitly enshrined in the law. But it can hardly be denied that the role of the law as it bears upon the hierarchy of status constitutes yet another difference of kind which undermines the validity of any ostensibly quantified comparison between one system and the next.

This list of the difficulties is not exhaustive, and will in any case have probably struck the reader as obvious. But it serves to show how the most intractable difficulties in the analysis of stratification arise within the three separate dimensions rather than in the relations between them. The analysis of inequalities of status is problematic not so much because they cannot be described in isolation from inequalities of power or economic class, but because they so seldom lend themselves to the kind of description which would make measurement and comparison possible.

[3] Marc Bloch, *Feudal Society*, tr. Manyon, 2nd ed. (London, 1962), p. 283.

VIII

If this is true of inequalities of status, it is hardly less true of inequalities in the dimension of power. The distribution of power is strictly speaking the province of political science, just as the distribution of wealth is the province of economics; but whether from the inherent difficulty of the subject-matter or because of the relative backwardness of political science, we are scarcely better placed than Aristotle or Hobbes to measure and compare inequalities of power between man and man or stratum and stratum. This has led some writers to voice the suspicion that the term 'power' is somehow inherently inaccurate or misleading, and would be better dropped altogether. But, as with status, it is difficult to deny that the many forms of special relationship habitually labelled in terms of it do all manifest an inequality of a common kind, however difficult to specify precisely. It would, of course, be absurd to suggest that the distribution of power in a society or even a relatively small organisation could be plotted on a Lorenz curve as though it were an inequality of wealth. Even an ordinal scale analogous to a social distance scale can be plausibly constructed only under extraordinarily restricted conditions which have little application outside the psychological laboratory. But the various definitions of power which are current in the recent literature, however far they may be from being entirely adequate, all presuppose the meaningfulness of a distribution of power such that some people can be ranked above others by reference to it. The difficulty, as in the dimension of status, lies in the precise allocation of these rankings.

So difficult is it, in fact, to place the members of even a single community in an order of power that many of the writers on 'community power structure' have been justly criticised for falling into the error of simply assuming *a priori* that there is a correlation between the hierarchy of power and the hierarchy of economic class. But to rank the members of a community in order of power it will be necessary to show empirically and in detail both that some are better able than others to bring about actions and decisions on the part of others which conform to their wishes and also that those actions and decisions can be of a kind which those carrying them out are more strongly disposed to resist. The various definitions of power which are offered all agree, whatever their differences, that it has something to do with the capacity to bring about intended states of affairs; and most of them agree that what we mean in speaking of power in terms of more and less is that the more powerful man is both able to determine more actions of more people against stiffer resistance on their part and also to resist more successfully any such attempts made by others on himself. But it is not at all easy to say just what evidence is needed to answer these questions or how it might make possible even an ordinal ranking. Even worse, to the extent that we do know what evidence is called for we are likely to find that it is impossible to obtain.

The researcher cannot restrict himself to the actual performance of those whom he is studying, since the notion of 'having power' involves by definition a capacity to do, or bring about, something if one wishes (which one very well may not). It is not difficult in principle to discover a person's wealth, if he is prepared to co-operate in the inquiry, and even his status can in principle be ascertained by asking the right questions of the other members of his society or group. But it is impossible to discover a person's power without experimental evidence. Where there are satisfactory precedents, or where the scope and limits of the power attaching to a specific role are clearly laid down within a fixed institutional framework, then a person's power can to some degree, at least, be measured. We can say that he can decide more actions of more people than can others of his fellow-citizens; or that for a given number of such actions and people he can call on such agencies as will overcome stronger resistance should those affected be moved to put it up; or that he is able where others are not to avoid arrest or detention, the forced levy or extortion of goods, compulsory or directed labour, military service, and things of this kind. But although it is differences in these respects which justify the assertion that in a given social system one group or stratum has more power than another, they leave us still a long way from the precise description and assignment of weights which would be necessary for the purpose of comparison; and to establish these it would be necessary to have available an enormous number of examples in which the whole range of analogous conditions were precisely and systematically varied and which even then would only furnish a quasi-experimental justification for a ranking in order of power.

There is thus at best a limited value in attempting a quantified analysis of the distribution of power whether defined in the generally accepted sense which I have tried to summarise or reformulated in such more sophisticated terms as the probability of an outcome which would not otherwise come about[1] or the latent capability to inflict sanctions[2] or the ability to adopt those courses of action which will show the maximum

---

[1] Robert A. Dahl, 'The Concept of Power', *Behavioral Science*, II (1957), 201–15.
[2] Karl W. Deutsch, *The Nerves of Government* (New York, 1963), pp. 120 ff.

pay-off.[1] The last of these approaches, which derives from the mathematical theory of games, has the advantage of yielding very precise differences in winning capacity between one player and another in the situations to which it can be applied. But the problems of bluff, coalition, log-rolling and so forth which have been shown to be amenable to formal treatment along these lines merely constitute a further difficulty in an attempt at a broader appraisal of the power of one person or group relative to another. It is not impossible that a market model which draws on primarily economic notions of cost, benefit and equilibrium may turn out to be applicable over a broader field than has been shown hitherto. But in general it seems likely that success will be bought only at the price of reducing its bearing on those conventional relationships of power which people tend to have more often in mind when speaking of the power of one person or group 'over' another. Indeed, this is one reason why there are so many other terms which are employed to characterise particular kinds of relations of power—influence, threat-advantage, control, authority and so on. All fall somewhere under the broad intuitive definition, but none furnishes an adequate criterion of measurement.

Two further general difficulties are related to these: first, the varying importance of numbers, and, second, the problem sometimes posed by intensity of feeling. Inequalities of either class or status can in general be much more adequately described by reference to roles than can inequalities of power. Power tends to be a function either of personality and circumstances or of numbers and organisation, and to learn a person's role may tell the researcher surprisingly little about where he stands relative to others in the hierarchy of power. Not only does the power attaching to a role vary with number in the sense that in an open pluralist society the member or official of a large organised group has in general more power than the member or official of a small one; but even within the Indian caste system, the relative power of Peasants and Brahmins may be a function of their numerical proportions within their community. This might seem at first sight to make the problem of measurement and comparison easier. But even where the significance of number is not influenced by variations in the structural context, there is no way of weighting aggregation, in the sense of the ratio of actual members of a group to possible members, with either concentration, in the sense of the ratio of members to sub-groups or leaders who can be said effectively to speak for them, or numerical importance in the simple sense of the ratio of members of the group to the society at large. And once the structural

[1] William H. Riker, *The Theory of Political Coalitions* (New Haven, 1962), pp. 21–3.

context is taken into account, number itself in the sense of number of members may become less important than the number of non-members, or in other words the public at large, whose interests the members are in a position to affect: to borrow an example from Gerth and Mills, the elevator boys of Manhattan, whatever their relative wealth or status, are a more powerful group than its violinists.[1] Thus although numbers are indeed important and although they automatically make possible comparisons of a certain kind, they serve in effect only to complicate still further the problem of elaborating how far one person, or role, or group, or stratum can be said to be higher or lower in power than another.

The problem of intensity is in one sense accommodated by defining a person's power not only by reference to the number of people or actions he can modify but by reference to the strength of the resistance which he may encounter. But this may, if feelings run strong enough, give rise to a paradox, for as Tawney observed, to destroy power 'nothing more is required than to be indifferent to its threats'.[2] If X is in a position to require Y to do whatever he wishes on pain of death, and Y is unable to offer resistance to him, then it would be natural to say that X has absolute power over Y. But suppose that Y feels so strongly about being made to do what X wishes that he not merely tries unsuccessfully to escape from X, or evade his instructions, but submits to being killed by X rather than compromise his pride, or his religious principles, or whatever it may be. X may well decide to modify his instructions in this circumstance for he may recognise that if his aim is that Y should do as he wishes he is not achieving it any better by killing him. But do we then have to say that so far from X having more power than Y, Y has more power than X? This sort of paradox is, of course, familiar in formal theories of non-cooperative games. But as I suggested above, to interpret power strictly in these terms is to restrict its meaning too far. Power is not simply the chance of winning, but a relation between persons. If it is interpreted entirely in terms of probabilities of winning, it will merely create still further paradoxes of its own. For instance, it can be formally shown that under certain conditions a war of all against all will give the weakest player the best chance of survival. But it would be at least as absurd to say that he is therefore the most powerful person as to say in the hypothetical example just given that Y had, after all, more power than X.

Yet a further difficulty is that even where the power vested in a

---

[1] H. H. Gerth and C. Wright Mills, *Character and Social Structure* (London, 1954), p. 329.

[2] R. H. Tawney, *Equality*, 4th ed. (New York, 1961), p. 176.

particular role can be readily assessed, the power of individuals in the society in question may be held to be measured relative not merely to that role but to their chance of occupying it. Whatever the prerogatives of office, the individual citizen will presumably be said to be less unequally placed if he has a chance, however slight, of occupying the position himself than if he has none whatever. The most egalitarian system, on this basis, will be one in which all offices are filled by lot. The least egalitarian will be one in which political decision rests with one man only, and only the one successor designated by him is eligible to take his place. In between is a whole complex of gradations of what is sometimes called 'politicization' according to which the adult citizen is more or less involved in the processes of decision-making and more or less likely to become so either by standing for office himself or by coming to be in a position where he may influence others who do. The likelihood of office can then be used as itself an index of the relative power of any chosen category of citizens. If an overwhelming majority of successful candidates for office are drawn only from certain restricted groups, whether in terms of wealth, race, occupation or anything else, then this will furnish an obvious criterion for saying that the members of that group should be collectively ranked above others in the hierarchy of power. In a way, this is an analogous measure to the probability of future wealth which requires to be built in to any measure of economic inequality. But where in the economic case the value of this future wealth can be directly related to the monetary yardstick in whose terms a person's position in the commodity and labour markets is expressed, in the political case the chance of office cannot be simply added to the other information acquired about the relative power of a person or group. Once again, although a quantitative measure is possible it does not significantly help to yield the cardinal ordering which an effective three-dimensional model of stratification would require.

Even if a political structure can be clearly described in terms of the power assigned to the various offices within it and the chances of the representative member of any designated group coming to hold one of these offices, it will still be possible to make only a limited and partial comparison between the distribution of power in one society and another. Even such a relatively simple, relatively homogeneous and relatively well documented set of cases as the traditional kingdoms of Africa cannot be compared with each other except in very broad and largely qualitative terms. When it comes to societies as large, complex and sophisticated as those of the advanced industrial nations, then the advantage of greater possibilities of quantification within limited areas is more than offset by the intricacy and incommensurability of the other areas which the researcher must take into account if he is to attempt to plot inequalities of power on even the most rudimentary kind of scale. This is not to say that progress will not be made in the comparative morphology of political systems. But it is hard to see how the generalisations to which subsequent research may lead will ever make possible the rigorous measurement, explanation and comparison of institutionalised inequalities of power.

As in the discussion of status, this review of the difficulties will probably have struck the reader as not only sketchy but obvious. But its moral is the same. The notion of power raises difficulties which make the construction of a satisfactory theory of social stratification exaggeratedly difficult not because we cannot isolate inequalities of power from inequalities of class or status but because having done so it is virtually impossible to make the kinds of comparison and measurement which would be necessary to justify it.

IX

Accordingly, we are now in a position to ask why it is that the three-dimensional framework, although both conceptually and empirically valid, is neither universally accepted nor widely used. The first answer follows directly from the discussion in the preceding sections: the difficulties which arise within the separate dimensions are by themselves enough to undermine any hope of adequately representing the structure of a society in terms of the box on its corner which I described at the beginning. But there is a further reason. In the present limited state of our knowledge, the three-dimensional framework is all too often unnecessary.

It is often unnecessary simply because of the closeness of fit between the three dimensions alike in industrial and pre-industrial societies. Wealth, power and prestige tend to go together, and this tendency itself is reinforced by a continuous feedback. One obvious example is the position of women. As anthropologists since Lowie have reminded us, their inferior position can be significantly discrepant even as between very similar cultures. But it is still true that women are less privileged than men in almost all known societies; they are less highly regarded, less able to participate in political decision-making, and less wealthy; only in a few cases do they even enjoy the unfettered right to direct inheritance from their fathers; and the separate inferiorities of class, status and power each serve to make the other more difficult to remedy. In some societies, indeed, the three dimensions are so closely interwoven at all levels and in all respects that the system is virtually one-dimensional, particularly where role differentiation is slight. To take only one example, it has been said of Peru in the Inca period that 'the degree of fit between the three sub-cultures (of "wealth", "authority" and "prestige") was so close that they scarcely had any independent meaning'.[1] Often, moreover, the mechanisms for maintaining the fit are quite explicit. A recent study of Ruanda describes how the 'pretence to natural superiority' on the part of the Tutsi is upheld when one of them is unable to maintain himself in the style of life appropriate to his caste by making him the client of a richer Tutsi and thus in turn the patron of a few inferior Hutu.[2] Even where it might be less readily expected, the fit is still apt to be preserved. In ancient Athens, despite its notoriously democratic constitution, voters tended to elect as generals men of wealth and aristocratic birth rather than seasoned professional soldiers: democracy or not, 'the Athenian people', in the words of A. H. M. Jones, 'were rather snobbish in their choice of leaders'.[3] Indeed, the example of Athens serves to show how the fit may be preserved as much by the attitudes of the less privileged as by the policies and ambitions of the élite.

In industrial societies, the index of fit is furnished above all by the hierarchy of occupations. There are, of course, some familiar exceptions. An aristocracy of birth may retain much of its status even when its wealth and power has declined; some bureaucratic or organisational roles may carry undue power relative to their status or pay; some highly regarded occupations may still be badly paid. But on the whole, a man's occupation is a fairly reliable index of his relative position in all three dimensions. Perhaps, because of the peculiar difficulties raised by power, it would be safer to say that if and where occupations can be ranked in terms of power, their rank will generally correspond to their rank in the hierarchies of wealth and prestige. But occupations can on the whole be very adequately graded in terms of a 'composite of social and economic attributes that tend to cluster together':[4] in the United States there has been shown to be a correlation as high as ·91 between the prestige of occupations and a

[1] Eugene A. Hammel, *Wealth, Authority and Prestige in the Ica Valley, Peru*, University of New Mexico Publications in Anthropology, no. 10 (Albuquerque, 1962), p. 96.
[2] Jacques J. Maquet, *The Premise of Inequality in Ruanda* (London, 1961), pp. 141–2.
[3] A. H. M. Jones, *Athenian Democracy* (Oxford, 1957), p. 49.
[4] Joseph A. Kahl and James A. Davis, 'A Comparison of Indices of Socio-economic Status', *American Sociological Review* xx (1955), 321.

combined measure of education and income.[1] It is not surprising, therefore, that many researchers have deliberately chosen to work with an index of 'socio-economic status' rather than with separate measures of status and class.

The analysis of social stratification in terms of occupation is equally justifiable whether it is the causes or the consequences of the nature and distribution of occupations which are to be assessed. To explain the distribution of occupations is largely to explain the social inequalities found in industrial societies, and to explain its consequences is to explain how it is that these are modified or preserved. Occupations are the mechanism by which the influences of natural endowment, upbringing and education are translated into differences of wealth, power and prestige, and the most significant moves which the individual can make in all three dimensions will be by means of a change from one occupation to another. Thus occupations are at once the most obvious symptom and the most effective predictor of differential location within the structure of social inequalities, whether considered in terms of income and economic *Lebenschancen*, or life-style, commensalism and endogamy, or autonomy and authority. Whether occupation or some more elaborate measure of 'socio-economic status' is used, there is often no need to sift out the separate elements of class, status and power in any of the usual areas of social research in education, politics, demography, criminology and the rest. The fit is too close, and a composite indicator is too useful, for it to be called for.

But quite apart from the convenience of occupation as indicator, the three-dimensional framework is often irrelevant simply because many of the most interesting problems in the study of social stratification are so far from being resolved that an accurate distinction of types of inequality is still premature. To see this, it is only necessary to draw up a more or less haphazard list of topics in the field and then count how few of these involve more than very indirectly the distinction between the three dimensions. A number of topics of which this is true have already been touched on in the earlier sections, and the reader will no doubt be able to think of many of his own. But such questions as the following may serve as examples: Why did the Greeks base citizenship on birth but the Romans on residence? Why was the rate of manumission very much higher in Rome than in Athens? How far can the relations of dependence in feudal Europe be accounted for in military terms? Why is the

[1] O. D. Duncan, 'A Socioeconomic Index for all Occupations', in A. J. Reiss *et al.*, *Occupation and Social Status* (New York, 1961), p. 124.

organisation of pastoral societies more hierarchical than that of hunting and gathering societies? How important are patron-client relations in pre-industrial societies? How did Denmark, which had had a feudal system, become as egalitarian as Sweden, which had not? What is the importance of religion in sustaining the acceptance of inequality by the under-privileged? How far is this importance related to the stage of technological development? What in general is required to engender a perception of joint interest among those who share a common social location? Does the permeability of adjacent strata during industrialisation depend on whether urbanisation is 'orthogenetic' or 'heterogenetic'?[1] Does industrialisation diminish or exacerbate racial discrimination? Under what circumstances will the privileges of a bureaucratic élite within a centralised state be maximised? What are the principal psychological determinants of occupational mobility? In none of these questions is the distinction between class, status and power more than marginal. Furthermore, this will hold even if large-scale cross-cultural comparisons are to be attempted. The relevant column entries in Murdock's world ethnographic sample[2] are based not on class, status and power but on the presence of slavery, of a hereditary aristocracy, of 'important' distinctions of wealth, and of a complex subdivision into three or more 'classes' or 'castes'. As it happens, these headings are far from adequate for the sorts of comparisons from which valid and useful large-scale generalisations about stratification could ever be extracted. But such a search might in practice be just as useful if conducted along these lines as if conducted along the lines of an elaborate and careful distinction between inequalities of class, status and power.

X

It almost seems, then, as though we are left with the paradox that a fundamental distinction which is conceptually and empirically valid is either inapplicable or simply irrelevant. But this conclusion would be mistaken. If it is easy to construct a list of topics to which the distinction is ostensibly irrelevant, it is no less easy to construct a list of topics to which it is indispensable. What is more, many of these are topics which are difficult or contentious largely because the distinction has been given less attention than it deserves.

[1] Robert Redfield and Milton Singer, 'The Cultural Role of Cities', *Economic Development and Social Change*, III (1954), 53–73.
[2] G. P. Murdock, 'World Ethnographic Sample', *American Anthropologist*, LIX (1957), 664–87.

This applies not least to the ordering of occupations, which I have just cited as the most familiar example of closeness of fit between class, status and power. It is perfectly true that the familiar exceptions are, indeed, exceptions. But their significance is often out of proportion to their frequency, and they call in any case for explanation no less than do the more usual cases from which the rule has been constructed. It is not simply that as between different occupations the correlation of class-situation with status-situation may not always be exact, or that, as it is sometimes put, the separate 'statuses' bound up with a single occupation are not 'congruent'. Sometimes, an explicit condition of status is the diminution or loss of superiority in economic class; and conversely, sometimes an explicit condition of advantages of class or power is an inferiority of status. An example of the latter is the position of court eunuchs in imperial Rome and China; an example of the former is the position of the *sanyasi* within the Indian system of caste. These cases should not be confused with those where status or power are purchased at a relatively small cost to those who are already rich. Thus, decurions in the later Roman Empire (after 390) were more than willing to bear the very heavy expenses which senatorial rank then entailed because it also brought them both elaborate privileges of precedence and address and also effective immunity from the orders of the provincial governors. But this is closer to the sale of privilege as practised by, say, François I or Lloyd George, which serves more to illustrate how status and power can follow wealth than how a serious forfeiture of economic class can be a condition of it. The more interesting cases are those where there is not simply a lag which is in due course either personally or institutionally remedied, but a permanent discrepancy, such as the wealth accruing to members of despised but essential professions, the rejection of economic gain by the ruling élite in favour of martial glory, or the refusal of commensurate reward to highly esteemed occupations. These can all be documented for a wide range of societies both pre-industrial and industrial, and they call for explanation precisely because they involve an intrinsic and significant non-correlation between two or more of the three fundamental dimensions of stratification.

Where, in particular, there is a discrepancy between the status of a person or group and either their power or their economic class, it is essential to maintain the distinction. Perhaps the most important example is the study of race relations. No explanation will be adequate which attempts to account for this form of stratification simply by assuming *a priori* that inequalities of status are a function of economic exploitation or political dominance without reference to the psychology of purity and pollution. Indeed, this can likewise be said of the position of women. How far it may be possible to generalise on these matters is an open question. The psychology of pollution is by no means fully understood; nor are the social conditions by which the practice of segregation is more or less likely to be broken down. But without precise analysis of the interrelation between the separate dimensions of stratification it will be impossible to understand either the nature of the inequalities to which such relationships give expression or the prior inequalities from which they derive.

More generally, the importance of the three-dimensional distinction becomes clear whenever stratification requires to be discussed in terms of greater or less inequality as opposed to a specific analysis of a qualitatively distinct form of unequal social relationship such as that between master and slave or patron and client. This is true most of all in the discussion of 'classes'. Of course, a part of the difficulty here may be ideological. The views of even the most self-consciously academic observers are likely to be coloured by their approval or disapproval of the particular society in which they live, and there is a persistent tendency for the spokesmen of all kinds of regimes to overstate the degree of egalitarianism within them. Thus, as has often been pointed out, in the Soviet Union there has developed a doctrine of 'non-antagonistic classes' according to which the abolition of private property has eliminated the conflict of interest between hostile strata; and in the United States, correspondingly, there has developed a doctrine of 'classlessness' according to which the absence of hereditary privileges on the European model has allegedly made it meaningless to speak of 'class' membership at all. But there is in fact no need for such apologetics to confuse the issue once the distinction between the dimensions of stratification is strictly maintained. It is only necessary, first, to distinguish stratification from differentiation and, second, to establish as an empirical matter how far some people must be ranked above others in class-situation, status-situation and power. It is true that there will remain the practical difficulties which I have already described. But it is at least roughly clear what sort of evidence we need to answer the question how far state ownership of property in the Soviet Union has diminished inequalities of economic class, or how far the United States, although still permitting marked inequalities of economic class, has (among Whites) a more egalitarian status-system than other countries. The two further questions where, and on what grounds, a division should be made between one particular 'class' and another, and how far the members of these 'classes' perceive and act on a common interest, are, as always, a separate matter.

As before, the reader will be able to think of many instances for himself where the distinction between the three dimensions is appropriate and useful. But it may be worth citing a few current topics of controversy where a thoroughgoing recognition of the validity and application of the distinction could help to sift out much, if not all, of the purely verbal confusion which bedevils the argument. Consider, for example, the following questions: How far is the social structure of the Soviet Union going to become like that of the United States? Have British manual workers and their families become middle-class? Does the Negro population of the United States constitute a separate caste? Can social stratification be shown in some way to be functional for social systems as a whole? Are all societies controlled by an élite? These questions are, to be sure, very ill-defined. But they are very ill-defined in the literature where they are fully and extensively discussed. Once it has first of all been established to what extent they do relate to stratification and not simply to differentiation, then they will be effectively answered only by reference to the distinction between class, status and power. Theories of 'convergence' between advanced industrial nations must take account of how far similarities in the distribution of wealth within a highly differentiated occupational system may be compatible with marked dissimilarities in the distribution of power. Theories of *embourgeoisement* must show how far similarities in style of life made possible by equalization of class-situation may be compatible with continuing hierarchical distinctions of commensalism, endogamy and relations of friendship. Attempts to include the position of the American Negro within a more general theory of 'caste' must show how far the relation between the economic, political and status hierarchies found in the Indian system are paralleled in the United States. A 'functional' theory of stratification will have to show whether and to what extent it is an unequal distribution of economic rewards, social esteem, or institutionally vested authority which is claimed to be necessary for the adaptation of societies to changes in their environment. The argument between 'élitists' and 'pluralists' must establish empirically not only how power is distributed and governmental decisions influenced but to what extent this distribution is or is not causally related to the distribution of wealth and status. These remarks may seem so obvious that they ought to be wholly unnecessary. But it is precisely because the distinction between the three dimensions of stratification has often been neglected that the discussion of these topics has often been unnecessarily confused. The fact that, for the reasons we have seen, the distinction cannot be rigorously applied is in no way a sufficient reason to ignore it.

Whether there will ever be a general theory of stratification is of course a further question. But if there will, it follows from the validity of the three-dimensional distinction that any general theory will have to be expressible in terms of it. Unless it is somehow shown that class, status and power are not conceptually and empirically distinct, or else that there is some further dimension in which organisations and societies are stratified, then the content of a general theory of stratification can be nothing other than such general propositions as will furnish an adequate and comprehensive explanation of any institutionalised inequalities observed anywhere and at any time—that is, of any and all 'conventional' relations of class, status and power. This would include, moreover, all those relations which I have cited as qualitatively distinct, for even if the explanation of, say, patron/client relationships were to require the application of terms not found elsewhere within the theory, it would still be true that the superiority of the patron and the inferiority of the client can only consist in some combination or other of the three fundamental kinds of inequality. Even those questions which may not appear to require direct reference to the distinction could be conclusively answered only by reference, as more or less special cases, to the laws from which all variations in the nature and degree of institutionalised inequalities would in principle be predictable. To this extent, therefore, the irrelevance of the distinction to many of the specific problems with which students of stratification are concerned is simply a mark of the present inadequacy of our knowledge of the necessary and sufficient conditions of the phenomena we are attempting to observe.

In any event, there is little purpose in speculating about what a general theory of stratification might look like. The necessary limitations on the extent of rigorous, comprehensive and publicly testable knowledge which the historian or sociologist is ever likely to attain renders the hope utopian from the start; and the extent to which it will ever be fulfilled is an empirical matter which, as the relevant knowledge increases, will take care of itself. For the moment, we are not even in a position properly to answer the elementary question by which the social theorists of the nineteenth century were so strongly divided: does industrialisation increase inequalities, as was believed by Marx and Engels, or decrease them, as was believed by Tocqueville and J. S. Mill? When there is so much still to be learnt, it may seem less important to argue about terminology than to set about collecting the facts. But in the field of stratification, as in others, many of the facts that we have would be much more useful to us if they had been collected with closer attention to avoidable confusions of terminology and logic. If the argument of this paper is correct, it will have shown that the researcher who ignores the distinction between the three separate dimensions of stratification must show good reason for doing so; and even if it is not, I hope that it may at any rate put the onus of argument on those who deny that this is so instead of those who assert it.

PART II

5. 'Embourgeoisement', Self-rated Class and Party Preference*

In a widely-read paper published in *The Sociological Review* in 1963,[1] John H. Goldthorpe and David Lockwood convincingly argued against the then fashionable view that post-war affluence had made British manual workers and their wives 'middle class' in attitudes and styles of life, and put forward a model designed to give the notion of *'embourgeoisement'* a precise and testable meaning. Their scepticism about *embourgeoisement*, however, was based in part on a disbelief in the value of figures for self-rated class as evidence either for the *embourgeoisement* thesis in general or for the use of *embourgeoisement* as an explanation of working-class Conservatism. The present paper sets out to show that figures for self-rated class can, on the contrary, be used to elucidate both these questions once respondents have been asked about the meaning of their self-rating, and that when this has been done the results support much of Goldthorpe and Lockwood's own argument. The data on which this conclusion is based are taken from a national sample survey carried out by Research Services Ltd in the spring of 1962.[2]

I

The *embourgeoisement* thesis was of course not new, even in the early 1950s. Before the Second World War many different observers had spoken of a visible assimilation between the manual and non-manual classes. Orwell remarked in *England Your England* that 'in tastes, habits, manners and outlook the working class and the middle class are drawing together',[3] and Carr-Saunders and Caradog Jones in the 1937 edition of

---

*This paper was first published in *The Sociological Review*, n.s. XII (1964).
[1] John H. Goldthorpe and David Lockwood, 'Affluence and the British Class Structure', *Sociological Review*, n.s. XI (1963), 133–63, cited hereafter as *GL*.
[2] The results of this survey have been published in greater detail in W. G. Runciman, *Relative Deprivation and Social Justice: a Study of Attitudes to Social Inequality in Twentieth Century England* (London, 1966).
[3] George Orwell, *'England Your England and Other Essays* (London, 1954), p. 223.

their statistical survey of the social structure of England and Wales claimed that 'in respect of dress, speech, and use of leisure all members of the community are obviously coming to resemble one another'.[1] Such comments multiplied in and after the war. By the beginning of 1948, the *Economist* was speaking of the middle class 'expanding and extending itself as the wage-earner assumes bourgeois habits and standards'.[2] By the 1950s, the changes in income differentials between clerical and manual workers were becoming well documented. So were many changes in working-class styles of life. In the later 1950s, these various observations took on a further overtone when the advance into so-called affluence was accompanied by successive Conservative victories at the polls. In 1955, David Butler came to the guarded conclusion that 'If prosperity was rapidly driving the working class into middle-class habits of consumption, it was only very slowly driving them into middle-class attitudes to voting'.[3] But by 1959, Butler and Rose were prepared to describe traditional working-class attitudes as having been 'eroded by the steady growth of prosperity'.[4] This theme became particularly insistent after the election of 1959. More or less explicitly, and with or without a direct reference to voting, the *embourgeoisement* thesis became almost a commonplace.[5]

It is, however, a thesis which, as Goldthorpe and Lockwood have made clear, is a good deal more ambiguous than it appears at first sight. In the first place, none of its proponents ever made a sufficiently clear distinction between class and status.[6] Even if we leave aside the difference in security, as opposed to income, which still distinguishes the class-situation of the manual from that of the non-manual worker, an equivalence of class-situation need not make manual workers the status equals of the middle

---

[1] A. M. Carr-Saunders and D. Caradog Jones, *A Survey of the Social Structure of England and Wales*, 2nd ed. (Oxford, 1937), p. 67.

[2] *Economist*, 24 January 1948.

[3] D. E. Butler, *The British General Election of 1955* (London, 1955), p. 264.

[4] D. E. Butler and Richard Rose, *The British General Election of 1959* (London, 1960), p. 2.

[5] For examples, see the references given by Goldthorpe and Lockwood. It may be worth remarking, however, that many of the cruder statements of the *embourgeoisement* thesis have come from writers who are not professional sociologists or social historians. For additional examples to those cited by Goldthorpe and Lockwood, see e.g. Graham Turner, *The Car Makers* (London, 1963), section II; or George Steiner, 'The Decline of the Labour Party', *The Reporter*, 29 September 1960, quoted by R. R. Alford, *Party and Society* (Chicago, 1963), p. 161.

[6] Goldthorpe and Lockwood state their position on the use of these terms in an appendix to their article (*GL*, pp. 157–9), where they argue that much of the present confusion derives from a 'gross misunderstanding' of the well-known distinctions drawn by Max Weber. I am not sure how far they are right, either in general or about Weber; but for my own views, see chapter 4, above.

class. Not only can their style of life still be different in important respects, but they can also remain a long way from full mutual recognition of social equality as exemplified in commensalism, endogamy and relations of friendship. It is true that 'status' has featured in the *embourgeoisement* argument to the extent that the manual worker who acquires the consumer goods formerly restricted to the middle class is sometimes accused for this reason of 'status-seeking'. But in the first place, as Lockwood already argued in 1960,[1] the evidence has not yet been presented which would demonstrate that status-seeking, rather than the simple wish for what is obviously useful, is the motive behind the acquisition by manual workers of consumer goods; and in the second, even if it is true that some manual workers buy a car or a television set because they want to be regarded as 'middle class' this need not make the middle class regard them as such. Indeed, if the finding of Willmott and Young in Woodford is typical, then it is just such things as these which may make the middle class more anxious to preserve the status difference between manual and non-manual workers.[2] The *embourgeoisement* thesis has, in fact, been disputed often enough, particularly by commentators on the 'New Left'. But the sensible questions for the social historian to ask have only been clearly formulated in the two papers published by Lockwood in 1960, and Goldthorpe and Lockwood in 1963.

There is, however, one difficulty which confronts the critics of the *embourgeoisement* thesis no less than its proponents, and that is the difficulty of comparison. Not only is there no survey evidence which could yield comparisons with the 1930s or even 1940s; but there is almost no comparative evidence at all. There is no way of estimating the frequency of friendships between manual and non-manual workers, the extent of acceptance by manual workers and their families of middle-class norms of behaviour, and so on. A good deal of evidence has been presented in reports of community studies showing that among the manual workers of certain localities relative affluence and change of residence have brought about a modification of 'traditional' working-class norms and behaviour. But these studies still do not make unequivocal comparisons possible; and as Goldthorpe and Lockwood point out, some of the features of the 'new' working-class way of life were by no means unknown in the 'traditional' working-class sub-culture.[3] But although unequivocal comparison is

---

[1] David Lockwood, 'The "New Working Class"', *Archives Européennes de Sociologie*, I (1960), 248–59.

[2] Peter Willmott and Michael Young, *Family and Class in a London Suburb* (London, 1960), p. 122.

[3] *GL*, p. 141.

impossible, this does not mean that no arguments about the *embourgeoise-ment* thesis, whether for or against, can be substantiated. I am not suggest-ing—nor, as I understand them, do Goldthorpe and Lockwood—that it cannot be shown that substantial changes have taken place within the British working class. The point is rather that whatever these changes have been (and they can be measured only in very few respects), they have not been so great as to vindicate ambitious generalisations about a 'fusion' of the classes, or an 'irreversible' trend towards middle-class psychology among the working class, or a widespread 'erosion' of tradi-tional working-class norms. Goldthorpe and Lockwood effectively show not only what evidence would be required to substantiate such claims; they also show how little evidence of this kind has yet been produced.

It may be convenient at this point to summarise Goldthorpe and Lockwood's own thesis. For a manual worker to 'turn middle class' involves, in their view, a move in three stages. First, the worker becomes socially isolated from his fellow-members of the working class. He still retains, however, his normative identification with the working class, and at this stage is only what Goldthorpe and Lockwood call 'privatised'. The second stage is reached when the worker adopts a set of norms which are primarily 'middle class' but is not yet integrated into middle-class membership groups. He is now what Goldthorpe and Lockwood call 'aspiring'. He reaches the third and last stage only when he belongs to middle-class groups in which he is accepted as an equal. The process of *embourgeoisement* is then complete, and the manual worker has become what Goldthorpe and Lockwood call 'assimilated'.

This model makes explicit what is, or should be, meant when we speak of manual workers 'becoming middle class', and I shall use the terms 'privatised' and 'aspiring' in this sense throughout the rest of this paper. My disagreement with Goldthorpe and Lockwood comes when they deny that people's 'class' identification as ascertained through a poll-type interview can furnish any evidence of value for (or, presumably, against) the *embourgeoisement* thesis. Their view is that 'the pollster's overriding concern with easily obtainable and easily quantifiable results must be abandoned',[1] and they quote with approval the remark of Milton M. Gordon that 'self-identification as to class made in a poll-type interview may be safely calculated to be the least reliable method of ascertaining class structure, even psychologically defined'.[2] Now it is perfectly true

[1] *GL*, p. 145.
[2] Milton M. Gordon, *Social Class in American Sociology* (Duke University, 1958), p. 197, quoted *GL*, p. 143, n. 24.

that the responses to such questions as 'what social class would you say that you belong to?' vary markedly depending on whether a multiple-choice formula is used and, if so, what alternatives are offered. It is also true that the answers given may have widely different meanings to different people. But it does not follow from this that nothing whatever can be inferred from poll-type responses. It follows only that nothing can be inferred from comparisons between responses to differently worded questions, and that to be able to draw any solid inferences from the pattern of responses to any of the possible forms of question it is necessary to ask a further question about what is meant by the replies. In the two following sections I shall try to show, first, how a procedure which meets these conditions can throw light on Goldthorpe and Lockwood's general argument, and second, how it may at the same time help to elucidate the relation between party preference and self-rated class among manual workers and their wives.

II

The sample on which the evidence to be presented is based is a stratified random sample of the adult population of England and Wales. The interviewing was carried out between April and June of 1962 and 1415 responses were obtained after an initial 2000 names had been drawn from electoral registers. Respondents were assigned to the 'working' or 'middle' class on the basis of manual or non-manual occupation. Wives were classified by husband's occupation, whether or not they themselves had jobs. By this criterion, the distribution of the two classes was 919 working and 496 middle.

The form of question about self-rated class used in the questionnaire was as follows: people were first of all asked 'Which social class would you say you belonged to?'. Those who did not reply by any variant of either 'middle class' or 'working class' were then asked 'If you had to say middle or working class, which would you say?'. All respondents were then asked first, 'What sort of people do you mean when you talk about (respondent's) class?' and second, 'What sort of people do you mean when you talk about (the other class, working or middle as the case might be)?'. This sequence of questions not only avoids the major dangers of multiple-choice technique but also furnishes some evidence on how widely the meanings given to the terms 'middle' and 'working' class may differ. All but 17 per cent of the sample gave an answer to the initial question, 'which social class would you say you belonged to?', which came under the heading of either 'working' or 'middle', and of that 17 per cent all but one per cent assigned themselves to either one or the other when explicitly prompted. The distribution of self-ratings within 'objective' classes was as follows: non-manual class, 74 per cent self-rated middle, 25 per cent self-rated working; manual class, 33 per cent self-rated middle, 66 per cent self-rated working.

This form of question also makes it possible to compare the proportion of working-class respondents describing themselves as 'middle class' in answer to the first, open-ended question with the proportion found in other studies where an open-ended question was also used. There is evidence to suggest that whatever people may mean by it, the proportion of manual workers and their wives who describe themselves (without prompting) as 'middle class' varies with the social composition of the community in which they live. The upper and lower limits can be plausibly taken from the study of Woodford by Willmott and Young and the study of Dagenham by Willmott. Since both are districts in the London area, it may be unwarrantable to generalise from them to the whole of England. But they are districts which were chosen for study because of being in the first case a suburban, and in the second case a proletarian community, and the difference in the responses given by working-class people in the two places is certainly striking. In Woodford, 34 per cent of working-class respondents described themselves as 'middle class' in answer to the question 'Which class do you belong to?'. In Dagenham, the proportion was 13 per cent.[1] In the present survey, the figure for England and Wales was found to be 29 per cent. If, therefore, a middle-class self-rating is a good deal likelier among working-class people when they live in a predominantly middle-class community, the figure for England and Wales as a whole appears to be nearer to that for a predominantly middle-class community than a homogeneous proletarian one.

An assessment of the influences behind this figure, however, requires a more detailed breakdown. If—still leaving aside the question of meanings —the prompted are combined with the unprompted, certain clear correlations are visible within the sample as a whole. A national poll-type survey does not permit a cross-tabulation by the class composition of the immediate neighbourhood in which people live. But a number of more or less predictable correlations can be shown with other social variables. Manual workers and their wives are likelier to describe themselves as middle class in urban districts than in rural, in the Midlands than the South and the South than the North, and if their fathers were in

[1] See Peter Willmott, *The Evolution of a Community* (London, 1963), p. 102.

non-manual occupations than if they were in manual occupations (the difference here is as much as 23 per cent). If the total sample is divided into three groups by income (or, in the case of married women, husband's income), then the proportion of working-class people describing themselves as middle class rises from 27 per cent in the bottom group to 36 per cent in the middle to 41 per cent in the top. Sex, however, makes no difference whatever, despite the popular allegation that women are more status-conscious than men. It makes a noticeable difference to self-assigned class among non-manual workers and their wives, but none among manual, even if father's occupation is held constant. Age shows certain differences, but the pattern of variation is sufficiently haphazard for it to appear unlikely that any inter-generational influence is at work. The big and obvious differences are made by where people live, what their fathers did, and how much they (or their husbands) earn.

It is difficult, surely, to dismiss these comparisons as altogether valueless. It is unfortunate that no comparison is possible with 1938 or 1945. But even comparisons within the same sample at a given date are suggestive of the influences which may make manual workers and their wives think of themselves as in some sense 'not working class'. Moreover, once these people have been asked what they mean by 'working' and 'middle' class, it may be possible to relate these answers to the stages of the threefold transition outlined by Goldthorpe and Lockwood. Even without a quantified comparison with the past, it should be possible to show how far a state of *embourgeoisement* can be plausibly attributed to the English working class of 1962.

It was found that nearly all the replies to the two questions 'Who do you mean when you talk about the (middle or working) class?' could be coded into one or more of seven categories. For the question 'Who do you mean when you talk about the middle class?' these seven categories were as follows: first, non-manual workers (either specific examples being given, or a more general description like 'white-collar'); second, a literal definition, such as 'those between top and bottom'; third, a mention of actual manual jobs; fourth, an explicit reference to money; fifth, a reference to middle-class style of life; sixth, a personal criterion of approval (such as 'self-respecting'); and seventh, a personal criterion of disapproval, which was only given by people who described themselves as 'working class'. Of the total sample, 14 per cent gave an answer which could not be coded into one of these, either because some other criterion was given or because they said they didn't know. For the question 'who do you mean when you talk about the working class?' the seven categories were as follows: first, manual workers; second, 'ordinary' people; third, a mention of actual non-manual jobs; fourth, a reference to poverty or low income; fifth, 'everybody'; sixth, a personal criterion of approval; seventh, a personal criterion of disapproval. Of the total sample, 12 per cent gave an answer which could not be coded into one or the other of these seven categories.

For the *embourgeoisement* argument, the most interesting category of people is, of course, the 33 per cent of manual workers and their wives describing themselves as 'middle class'. First of all, what do they mean by this self-rating? And second, who do they think of as the 'working class'? The table below shows the distribution of answers among this group as compared with those manual workers and their wives who described themselves as 'working class'.

Table 1. *Definitions of 'middle' and 'working' class; manual respondents by self-rated class*

	Self-rated middle	Self-rated working		Self-rated middle	Self-rated working
Definition of 'middle' class as:	%	%	Definition of 'working' class as:	%	%
Non-manual workers	16	43	Manual workers	34	42
Literally 'middle'	14	6	'Ordinary' people	13	29
Actual manual occupation cited	6	0	Actual non-manual occupation cited	0	2
Rich	8	27	Poor	9	9
Personal criterion of approval	27	2	Personal criterion of approval	5	12
Personal criterion of disapproval	0	6	Personal criterion of disapproval	15	1
Middle-class style of life	12	10	Everybody	7	1
Other	16	5	Other	7	5
Don't know	6	10	Don't know	16	4
Total	105	109	Total	106	105
Number of cases	303	610	Number of cases	303	610

The first point that emerges from a comparison of these tables is that, as one would expect,[1] the self-rating chosen by working-class respondents makes a good deal of difference to the meanings which they assign to 'working' and 'middle' class respectively. Even more interesting for the *embourgeoisement* argument, however, is the pattern of responses among those who describe themselves as 'middle class'. Of those who described themselves as 'working class', over four out of ten meant non-manual workers when they spoke of the middle class; but of those who described themselves as 'middle class' only just over three out of twenty did so. This may be set against the further finding that among those respondents describing themselves as 'middle class' who were in fact non-manual workers or their wives, the proportion was 65 per cent. The largest single category among manual workers and their wives describing themselves as 'middle class' is some personal criterion of approval—a response, that is, which has no explicit reference to any social or economic boundary between the working and the middle class. There seems, therefore, to be little ground for imputing to working-class people who describe themselves as 'middle class' an overt feeling of membership of the non-manual occupational category. The majority may be conscious of being in some sense different from the 'traditional' working class; only the 6 per cent who mentioned actual manual jobs as their definition of 'middle class' do not suggest even 'privatisation' by their reply. But the only ones to whom it is plausible to impute an identification with the non-manual stratum as such are the 16 per cent who directly referred to it. The rest (except for the 6 per cent mentioning actual manual jobs) may to some extent be 'privatised'; but there is no warrant for supposing them to be 'assimilated' or even 'aspiring'.

A similar conclusion is suggested by the answers of the self-rated 'middle' class to the question about the meaning of 'the working class'. If there is any group whose answers suggest a conscious wish to distinguish themselves in norms and standards from the 'working class', it is presumably those who gave a criterion of disapproval. But this proportion (15 per cent) is virtually the same as the proportion identifying with non-manual workers in their definition of the 'middle' class (16 per cent). The proportion giving a personal criterion of approval (and therefore, by implication at least, not wishing to distinguish themselves overmuch from

[1] Cf. the findings in Hertford and Greenwich in 1950 reported by F. M. Martin, 'Some Subjective Aspects of Social Stratification', in D. V. Glass, ed., *Social Mobility in Britain* (London, 1954), pp. 59–60. A comparison with the present figures, however, is not possible since not only the form of question but also the coding categories are different in the two studies.

the 'working class') is virtually the same as the proportion mentioning manual jobs as 'middle class'. The replies of the rest suggest, once again, that although a middle-class self-rating by manual workers and their wives may be symptomatic of some degree of 'privatisation', it is unlikely that more than a small proportion of them are 'aspiring', let alone 'assimilated'.

It is, of course, perfectly possible for people to be uncertain and even ambiguous in their answers about self-rated 'class'. This has been amply demonstrated in studies which have set out to examine in detail the models of the social structure which underlie people's views about 'class',[1] and further evidence is furnished by the present survey. A single example, chosen for the apparent contradictions which the respondent expresses, will serve as an illustration. The wife of a hospital head porter who described herself as 'middle class' said that she meant by this people 'kind of thoughtful, not stuck up and of reasonable income'. But she described the working class as 'people who do genuine jobs and not money on the fiddle', and gave as her reason for supporting the Labour party 'because they are for the working-class interest'. When asked who she meant by 'people like yourself' in the context of voting, she replied 'middle class—working people'. It is obvious from this somewhat anomalous sequence of replies that it would be wrong to infer from this person's description of herself as 'middle class' that she identifies herself with the non-manual class in any ideal-typical 'bourgeois' way. But it is also obvious that it would be wrong to suppose that her self-rating is therefore meaningless. Except in cases where people have no idea what they mean by 'middle class' or mean by it what everyone else understands by 'working class', a middle-class self-rating can be plausibly interpreted as an indication of some minimal sense of not belonging with the main body of 'ordinary' manual workers and their families. It is true that a middle-class self-rating cannot be as over-simply interpreted as it has by those whom Goldthorpe and Lockwood criticise.[2] But this does not destroy its interest as an independent variable in the analysis of sample surveys. It means only that we must qualify any conclusions drawn from such analysis in the light of what these self-ratings can be shown to mean. In particular, we must beware of assuming without further evidence that when manual workers and their wives describe themselves as 'middle class' anything more than 'privatisation' is likely to be involved; and this applies, as I shall try to show, in

[1] See particularly Elizabeth Bott, *Family and Social Network* (London, 1957), ch. VI; and A. Willener, *Images de la Société et Classes Sociales* (Berne, 1957).
[2] Particularly Mark Abrams: for references see *GL*, pp. 144–5 and n. 33.

looking at party preferences just as much as in examining the *embourgeoisement* thesis in general.

III

In considering the relation of party preference to self-rated class, the underlying problem is, as many commentators have emphasised, that of explaining working-class Conservatism as such. As Birch observed in discussing a finding made at the beginning of the 1950s swing to the Right, 'The fact that needs explaining is that 33 per cent of the industrial workers voted Conservative in 1951'.[1] Of course, not even the most vehement advocates of the *embourgeoisement* thesis would claim that it provided more than a part of the explanation of working-class Conservatism. But it does have a demonstrable bearing on it; and even if self-rated class should not be used as it is by Mark Abrams in those of his writings which Goldthorpe and Lockwood most strongly criticise, it may still help to some degree in the elucidation of why the British working class votes as it does. When Birch, in the same sentence from which I have quoted, goes on to say that 'it is no help to show that if those who rate themselves middle-class are excluded from the analysis the proportion is reduced to 31 per cent' he becomes no less misleading on one side than Abrams on the other. The smallness of this difference is a function of the ratio of self-rated middle-class to self-rated working-class manual workers in Birch's sample. The percentage difference in Conservative vote between the two groups is 13 per cent, even in a sample drawn in Glossop in 1953. In my national sample, drawn nine years after Birch's local one, the difference is 20 per cent. The figures for both classes are shown in Table 2, the question having been asked in the form: 'If there was a General Election tomorrow, which party would you support?'

Whatever they may mean, these differences are surely larger than can be dismissed as not requiring further analysis; and the obvious procedure is to test the effect of different definitions of 'middle class' on the party preferences expressed. It will then be possible to see how far we must modify the claim that a middle-class self-rating correlates with working-class Conservatism; at the same time, it will become clear whether the *embourgeoisement* argument can be sustained to the extent that some, at least, of the manual workers and their wives who describe themselves as 'middle class' are strongly predisposed to Conservatism. The figures are given in Table 3.

It turns out that when the meanings given to 'middle class' have been

[1] A. H. Birch, *Small-Town Politics* (London, 1959), p. 110.

Table 2. *Party preference; non-manual and manual respondents by self-rated class*

	Non-manual		Manual	
	Self-rated middle	Self-rated working	Self-rated middle	Self-rated working
	%	%	%	%
Conservative	52	23	36	16
Liberal	25	23	19	16
Labour	11	37	31	55
Other	1	0	0	1
Don't know *or* refuse	11	17	14	12
Total	100	100	100	100
Number of cases	365	124	303	610

Table 3. *Party preferences of manual respondents describing themselves as 'middle class'; by definitions of 'middle class'*

	Non-manual workers	Liter-ally 'middle'	Actual manual occu-pation cited	Rich	Per-sonal criter-ion of approval	Middle-class style of life	Other	Don't know
	%	%	%	%	%	%	%	%
Conservative	47	28	22	37	43	47	33	11
Liberal	14	17	11	17	21	25	16	26
Labour	23	38	56	33	25	22	33	42
Don't know *or* refuse	16	17	11	13	11	6	18	21
Total	100	100	100	100	100	100	100	100
Number of cases	49	42	18	24	82	36	49	19

152

allowed for there are three categories of respondents who, far from approximating to the middle-class pattern of party support, are noticeably likelier to be Labour than Conservative supporters. The most predictable is the category of those who mentioned actual manual occupations as their definition of 'middle class'. These, as I have already remarked, must clearly be excepted from any generalisation about *embourgeoisement*, and it is no surprise that they should be as likely to be Labour supporters as those working-class respondents who described themselves as 'working class'. The second category likelier to be Labour than Conservative supporters is the category of those who said they did not know what they meant in assigning themselves to the middle class. It is, perhaps, significant that this group is likeliest of all to support the Liberals. But it too must be excepted from generalisations about either *embourgeoisement* or the correlation of middle-class self-rating with Conservative support. The third and most puzzling category is the category of those giving a definition of 'the middle class' as 'in the middle'. Further analysis discloses that out of this group it is those aged 50 and over who are nearly three times as likely to be Labour as to be Conservative supporters, while those under 50 are slightly more likely to be Conservative than Labour. Thus it may be that the old tend to give a purely literal answer; but any proffered explanation can only be a guess. In any event, whatever the explanation, this category also must be excepted from the generalisation about self-rating and Conservatism. Finally, those whose definition of 'middle class' could not be coded into one of the seven categories are exactly as likely to be Labour as Conservative supporters; they thus show slightly more predisposition to Labour support than the total of working-class people who described themselves as 'middle class'. This group of 'others' should, perhaps, be excepted from any generalisation whatever. But even if we take only those three groups which are a good deal likelier to be Labour than Conservative supporters, they still comprise a quarter of all the working-class respondents describing themselves as 'middle class'. To this extent, therefore, that variant of the *embourgeoisement* thesis which sees working-class Conservatism as causally connected with a middle-class self-rating on the part of manual workers is demonstrably untenable in its unqualified form.

We are still left, however, with the substantial majority of working-class respondents describing themselves as 'middle class' for whom the correlation holds. Those who defined the middle class in terms of affluence are only slightly more likely to be Conservative than Labour supporters. But the remaining three groups, who comprise over half the total, are roughly twice as likely to be Conservative as Labour supporters. If we remember also that the frequency of middle-class self-rating rises with income, then to this extent the *embourgeoisement* thesis appears to be vindicated. But we must, if we can, relate it to the three-stage model of *embourgeoisement*. If it is true that those who define the middle class in terms of non-manual occupation are those who are closest to full *embourgeoisement*, then closeness to *embourgeoisement* does correlate with a high propensity to Conservative support. But there is an equally high propensity among those who define their membership of the middle class in terms of style of life and may or may not be 'aspiring' in Goldthorpe and Lockwood's sense; and the propensity is only a little less high among those whose definition of 'middle class' is based on purely personal criteria and to whom there is no warrant for attributing more than 'privatisation', if that. The conclusion, therefore, is that for most of those working-class people who rate themselves 'middle class', their self-rating (or the social attitudes of which it is a symptom) does predispose them to Conservative support; but this self-rating need not be an index of any more than some degree of 'privatisation', nor, as I shall argue in a moment, need this group be as fixed in their party loyalty as those working-class Conservatives who describe themselves as 'working class'.

Proper examination of the *embourgeoisement* thesis requires, however, that the relationship with income should be more fully considered. The *embourgeoisement* thesis would presumably lead us to expect that the frequency of Conservative support should be highest among those manual workers (or their wives) who have reached the top third of the overall income distribution; and perhaps it would also lead us to expect that the correlation with self-rating should hold within all three levels of income. In fact, the second is true, but not the first. Taken by itself, income (or husband's income) makes virtually no difference in the present sample to the likelihood of working-class Conservatism. The manual workers and their wives in the top third of incomes were likeliest to be Liberal supporters—a finding which may suggest that they are 'privatised' to the extent of being unable to identify their interests with the Labour party, but at the same time not so far 'aspiring' or 'assimilated' as to become 'bourgeois' Conservatives. But the most interesting finding is that when both income and self-rated class are held constant, Liberal support is most frequent among those working-class respondents in the top third of incomes who rate themselves 'middle class', whereas Conservative support is most frequent among those in the bottom third of incomes who likewise rate themselves 'middle class'. This pattern results in part from the Liberal revival which coincided with the time at which the interviews were done. But even so, it is not what the *embourgeoisement* thesis would naturally lead one to predict.

The frequency of Conservative support among the working-class respondents in the bottom third of incomes who described themselves as 'middle class' was found to be 41 per cent as against 18 per cent of those describing themselves as 'working class'. In the middle third of incomes the figure was 36 per cent as against 14 per cent and in the top third 27 per cent as against 18 per cent. This persistent influence of self-rated class among all three income levels perhaps bears out one implication of the *embourgeoisement* argument. But the inverse correlation, among those who describe themselves as 'middle class', between income and Conservative support is hardly compatible with the supposed relation between working-class Conservatism of an 'aspiring' kind and working-class affluence. The assumption that working-class Conservatives must be 'aspiring' if they describe themselves as middle class, and 'deferent' if they describe themselves as working class, will in any case not stand up to examination.[1] Why may not some of the working-class Conservatives describing themselves as middle class be 'deferent'? And why may not some of the working-class Conservatives who describe themselves as working class not be 'secular' or 'prosperity' voters?[2] It is outside the scope of this paper to consider the validity of 'deference' as an explanation of working-class Conservatism. But if either 'aspiration' or 'deference' provides the explanation why 41 per cent of working-class people in the bottom third of incomes if they think of themselves as 'middle class' support the Conservatives, then some further evidence is needed. Without such evidence it is equally plausible to describe them as either. The present figures suggest only that if a middle-class self-rating implies, as it often seems to, some detachment from felt membership of the traditional proletariat, then although such a self-rating rises with income, the Conservative support associated with it does not.

[1] For an oversimple dichotomy between 'deferent' and 'aspiring' working-class Conservatives, see apart from Abrams, S. M. Lipset, 'Must Tories Always Triumph?', *Socialist Commentary*, November 1960. This article is criticised also by Goldthorpe and Lockwood (*GL*, p. 145 n. 35).

[2] The 'prosperity' voter is, as the name suggests, the voter who identifies his economic interest with the Conservative Party; he may describe himself as 'middle-class' (see *GL*, p. 145), but there is no reason why he should necessarily do so. The 'secular' voter is the voter distinguished from the 'deferent' voter by the type of leader he would prefer—a self-made success rather than a member of the traditional élite; the distinction is refined and discussed in R. T. McKenzie and A. Silver, *Angels in Marble : Working Class Conservatives in Urban England* (London, 1968).

The final point on which the present survey furnishes some evidence is the stability of this kind of working-class Conservative support. Goldthorpe and Lockwood suggest that the 'privatised' worker is likely to vote out of calculation and opportunism, and therefore to have only conditional or even tenuous Conservative loyalties.[1] The present survey cannot definitively demonstrate this; but as far as it goes, it appears to bear it out. Respondents were asked if their party allegiance had been always the same, or whether they had previously supported another party. They were not asked the date of their change of allegiance (although changes before 1945 were excluded); but although their previous pattern of party support cannot be reconstructed as it was at any one point of time, some inferences can still be made about the sort of working-class voters who had changed in any given direction.

It was found that three-quarters of working-class respondents had been consistent in their support of one or another party. An analysis by self-rated class bears out the *embourgeoisement* thesis in one respect: more changes from Labour to Conservative have occurred among those who describe themselves as 'middle class'—3·1 per cent as against 1·8 per cent. But the net loss to the Conservatives is larger, and the net loss to Labour smaller, among this group than among those who describe themselves as 'working class'. The net Conservative loss (including those who have become 'Don't Know's') is 10·9 per cent, as against 4·5 per cent for those describing themselves as 'working class'. The net Labour loss is 4·5 per cent as against 6·8 per cent. These figures must, of course, be seen against the Liberal revival of 1962. But it is just this wave of Liberalism which helps to confirm Goldthorpe and Lockwood's suggestion that 'privatised' workers are likely to be conditional Conservatives. If a middle-class self-rating is, except in a small minority of cases, an index of some minimal 'privatisation', then 'privatised' workers and their wives are more likely to have abandoned an allegiance to the Conservatives as well as more likely to have acquired it. Once again, the implications of the *embourgeoisement* thesis are to a limited degree borne out, but only if it is defined and modified along the lines put forward by Goldthorpe and Lockwood; and once again, Goldthorpe and Lockwood's argument is supported by evidence of the kind which they reject.

[1] *GL*, p. 156.

6. Charismatic Legitimacy and One-Party Rule in Nkrumah's Ghana*

In the first section of this paper, I briefly discuss Max Weber's notion of charismatic legitimacy and its routinisation. In the second and longer section, I try to suggest how Weber's discussion may be applicable to the course of Ghanaian politics between 1949 and 1962.

I

Weber's notion of charisma and its routinisation, though unclear at two important points which I shall return to in a moment, is apt nevertheless to be misrepresented by his critics on three major issues.[1] It is important to remember first, that his explicit concern in his discussions of charismatic authority is with the problem of legitimacy and not the separate problem of leadership which he treats elsewhere.[2] Secondly, Weber is at pains to stress that charismatic authority is seldom if ever found in its ideal-typical

*This paper was written in the early months of 1962, following two visits to Ghana in the winter of 1961–2, and was published in the *Archives Européennes de Sociologie*, IV (1963) pp. 148–65, who have authorised reprinting. I am indebted to the Smuts Memorial Fund for a grant which covered my travel, and to the staffs of the Ghana Government Archivist and Government Statistician for their help. Since the paper first appeared, I have discovered from an earlier notebook that I owe the interpretation of 'charismatic' *Herrschaft* as a fusion of the source and agent of authority to a seminar conducted by Professors R. Bendix and S. M. Lipset at the University of California in 1960. I am sorry not to have included this acknowledgement in the original publication.

[1] Unfortunately a good deal of Weber's writing on charisma was still not available in English at the time when this paper was first written. References to *Wirtschaft und Gesellschaft* are to the 4th ed. (Tübingen, 1956), cited hereafter as *WuG*. Other abbreviated references are to *From Max Weber: Essays in Sociology*, ed. H. H. Gerth and C. Wright Mills (New York, 1946), cited as *Essays*; and to *The Theory of Social and Economic Organization*, ed. T. Parsons (New York, 1947), cited as *Theory*.

[2] Leadership in a parliamentary democracy is several times discussed apart from charisma in Weber's political essays. The basic problem here, as he himself formulates it, is this: 'in welcher Richtung entwickelt sich die *Führerschaft* in den Parteien unter dem Druck der Demokratisierung und der zünehmenden Bedeutung der Berufspolitiker, Partei- und Interessenten-Beamten, und welche Rückwirkung hat das auf das parlamentarische Leben?'; and again 'gestatten die Parteien in einer voll entwickelten Massendemokratie überhaupt Führernaturen den Aufstieg?' (*WuG*, pp. 868, 874, reprinted also in *Gesammelte Politische Schriften*, 2nd ed. (1958), pp. 378–9, 389). The different problem of the role of charismatic leadership in a democracy is discussed in *WuG*, pp. 674 ff., *Theory*, pp. 387–9.

MAGDALEN COLLEGE LIBRARY

form, but that all authority-systems are likely to be based on some combination of his three ideal-typical elements.[1] Thirdly, the charismatic element does not exist only in pre-industrial societies, nor is it appropriate only to rainmakers and medicine men.[2] In Weber's own words, 'Charismatic authority rests upon the uncommon and extraordinary devotion to the sacredness or the heroic force or the exemplariness of an individual and the order revealed or created by him'.[3] In other words, where authority is charismatic, the legitimacy accorded to the agents of that authority derives directly from the source of it: it is impossible to criticise the actions of the regime without attacking its legitimacy, for the actions of the charismatic leader and of the order created by him are precisely what that legitimacy rests on. Under a traditional system, the servants of, say, a hereditary monarch may be pronounced wrong without questioning the monarch's title to rule. Similarly under a rational-legal system, an elected official may be removed from office without thereby endangering the constitution. But under a charismatic system this separation of source and agency is impossible. For this reason, charismatic legitimacy must always be unstable (in Weber's word, *labil*).

The problem of leadership is a separate one from this. Although it is fashionable to refer to strong or popular leaders such as Nkrumah[4] as 'charismatic', it does not follow either that a charismatic leader must be a strong one or vice versa; what makes a leader charismatic or not is the basis on which his legitimacy rests. Under a bureaucratic or rational-legal system, the situations where charismatic leadership still finds expression are those where a leader can by his personal and exemplary qualities create a further legitimacy for actions going beyond his stipulated office: in a

[1] *Theory*, pp. 329, 382–3; *WuG*, p. 678.

[2] *WuG*, pp. 676–8, where Weber gives a series of examples of the role of charisma in modern representative democracy, and then explicitly remarks (p. 678) 'Wie diese Beispiele zeigen, gibt es charismatische Herrschaft keineswegs lediglich auf primitiven Entwicklungstufen'; cf. p. 683 and *Essays*, pp. 295–6.

[3] Weber gives several slightly different definitions: the one quoted its taken from *WuG*, p. 124, as translated in M. Rheinstein, ed., *Max Weber on Law in Economy and Society* (Harvard, 1954), p. xl. A slightly different translation is given by Parsons (*Theory*, p. 328). See also *Essays*, pp. 295–6, *Theory*, pp. 358–9, *WuG*, p. 555.

[4] The concept of charisma is applied to Nkrumah and to the political development of Ghana by David Apter, *The Gold Coast in Transition* (Princeton, 1955). He sees charismatic legitimacy as necessary to the transition from traditional to secular norms, with which I agree. However, I do not find his attempt to link this to the structural-functional notions of the American theorists successful, and it is never clear from his use of charisma quite what he understands the term to mean (see, e.g., p. 213 n.18, where the difference between a leader and a charismatic leader is confused, and p. 303 where 'charisma itself' seems to be treated as a reified object).

democracy, this may often be what Weber calls *Charisma der Rede*, deriving from the leader's oratorical powers.[1] There may well be less scope for charismatic leadership in a bureaucratic constitutional democracy than in less 'developed' political systems. But it may still be important to our understanding of how authority is acknowledged as legitimate: and it is a criticism only tenable by disregarding Weber's text to assert that the notion of charismatic legitimacy is not relevant or useful except in pre-industrial societies.[2]

Weber stresses that the inherent instability of charismatic legitimacy is shared by neither of his other ideal types: though they are in many ways polar opposites, traditional and bureaucratic systems both have the essential quality of *Alltagsgebilde*,[3] that is, the stability of routine. Of course, in a 'mixed' authority structure where charisma plays only a part, the wholly unorganised, irrational and anti-economic character of 'pure' charisma finds little or no expression.[4] But even here, charismatic instability persists to the extent that the agents of governmental authority derive their own authority from the charismatic leader or institution. Until the incumbent can be wholly divorced from the office, the system whereby he holds that office is liable to be threatened by his mistakes. Thus, it is this separation of the incumbent from the office (or of the agent of authority from its source) which is crucial to the successful process of routinisation.

It is here, however, that Weber is far from clear; and indeed, on his conception of 'routinisation' his critics have not done him great injustice. It is easy enough to see his central point: to take an example he gives, the Catholic Church has evidently succeeded in routinising its charisma so that the *Gnadengabe* which it inherits and transmits is not impugned by the imperfections of its ministers. Routinisation, in fact, becomes virtually synonymous with institutionalisation, for an institution presupposes by definition a routine and if charisma is successfully transferred from a person or set of persons to a dynasty, or a church, or a party, as such, then routinisation may be assumed to have succeeded. The trouble comes, however, when we try precisely to relate the routinisation of charisma to

---

[1] *WuG*, p. 676.

[2] This assertion is made, e.g. by Arthur Schlesinger, Jr., in his article 'On Heroic Leadership', *Encounter* (December 1960), pp. 3–11. Schlesinger also misrepresents Weber on both the other issues to which I have referred.   [3] *Essays*, p. 245.

[4] Edward Shils, however, has argued that the emphasis in underdeveloped countries on purely political charisma does inhibit economic initiative and the attitudes necessary for the creation of a rational, advanced economic structure. See his 'The Concentration and Dispersion of Charisma: Their Bearing on Economic Policy in Underdeveloped Countries', *World Politics*, XI (1958), 1–19.

the rest of Weber's ideal typology. Two difficulties in particular arise which require some mention.

First of all, the borderline between charismatic and traditional authority is harder to delimit than Weber's almost pedantic definitions would suggest. Once obedience to charismatic authority has become a habit, what does it mean to say that it is charismatic? If it means (as in the case of a church) that it retains some sort of 'magical' attributes, this is equally true of many rulers who are by Weber's definition traditional. If, on the other hand, it means that it remains in some sense personal, then so, once again, can traditional authority; and to say that stability is the distinguishing criterion is to turn Weber's basic insight on this topic into a circular definition. Of course, as has already been remarked, Weber emphasised that his ideal types are likely to exist in combination; but he gives no account of a procedure which would enable us to analyse a combination into its components.

The second difficulty is the notion of institutionalisation itself. Weber uses the term *Amtscharisma* for the case where charisma is vested in the office and not the man. But this raises an objection similar to the preceding one. What, we may ask, is the difference between a charismatic institution and an institution? Given that an institution is necessarily routinised (whether traditionally or rational-legally or more probably both), what does it mean to talk about its continued possession of charisma? It may be that for the successful founding of any institution a period of charismatic legitimacy is necessary, but to speak of a permanently charismatic legitimacy is on the basis of Weber's own analysis to come close to a contradiction in terms. If any and all institutions of authority, even when traditionalised and legalised, are to be allowed without contradiction to be described as charismatic, then the term loses the significance which made it of interest.

It may be that Weber's analysis can be somehow rescued from these difficulties, but I do not propose to make the attempt. I wish merely to concede them while claiming that they do not undermine the use or validity of the greater part of Weber's discussion. His diagnosis, for instance, of the plebiscite as remaining a charismatic recognition rather than a legal selection until such time as it becomes the basis and not the consequence of legitimacy,[1] is no less shrewd because of the ambiguities of

[1] *WuG*, p. 673, 'Das Plebiszit ist keine "Wahl", sondern erstmalige oder (beim Plebiszit von 1870) erneute Anerkennung eines Prätendenten als persönlich qualifizierten, charismatischen Herrschers'. However, 'when the organization of the corporative group undergoes a process of progressive rationalization, it is readily possible that, instead of recognition being treated as a consequence of legitimacy, it is treated as the basis of legitimacy. Legitimacy, that is, becomes "democratic"' (*Theory*, p. 386).

'routinisation'. In particular, his analysis of the instability of any authority which rests on a person or a newly founded institution and his emphasis on the need for the source of authority to be somehow immunised from failure are both, as I shall argue, relevant to a situation such as Ghana's irrespective of any confusions in the ideal typology. In addition, of course, much of what Weber has to say about bureaucracy and about law is also applicable to Ghana. However, I shall merely recapitulate some of the more relevant of Weber's remarks on charismatic legitimacy before going on to consider whether Ghana may not in fact furnish a specific case.

Charismatic leadership, says Weber, is typically manifested by expansive political movements in their early stages.[1] Where a transfer of power is to take place to a regime opposed by the incumbent bureaucracy the development round the leader of a group of charismatic followers becomes essential.[2] The instability of charismatic authority requires that the leader constantly prove himself by fresh successes.[3] In addition, the succession problem is crucial unless the system has been successfully routinised.[4] In any charismatic *Herrschaftsverband*, parties must necessarily be schismatic sects.[5] The elective principle may help to transform charismatic into rational-legal legitimacy[6] so that recognition by plebiscite does become selection.[7] Where, however, a democratic system is such as still to allow scope to the leader, he tends to arouse an emotional devotion to himself and to succeed by making more spectacular promises than his rivals.[8] Finally, in a passage which is worth quoting in full, 'If a ruler is dependent on recognition by plebiscite he will usually attempt to support his régime by an organization of officials which functions promptly and efficiently. He will attempt to consolidate the loyalty of those he governs either by winning glory and honour in war or by promoting their material welfare or, in certain circumstances, by attempting to combine both. Success in these will be regarded as proof of the charisma. His first aim will be the destruction of traditional, feudal, patrimonial and other types of authoritarian powers and privileges. His second main aim will have to be to create economic interests which are bound up with his régime as the source of their legitimacy.'[9]

With these remarks in mind, I shall in the next section turn to Ghana itself. My intention is not to construct an explicit model from Weber's discussion in order to try to fit the Ghanaian case to it, nor shall I try to relate everything in my account to Weber's remarks. I do, however, mean

---

[1] *Theory*, p. 370. [2] *Theory*, p. 385. [3] *Essays*, p. 248.
[4] *Theory*, p. 371. [5] *Theory*, p. 410. [6] *Theory*, pp. 386–8; *WuG*, p. 674.
[7] See p. 160, n. 1. [8] *Theory*, p. 389. [9] *Theory*, p. 390.

to suggest that what Weber says is at several important points directly relevant to the understanding of Ghana's politics between 1949 and the time of the writing of this paper.

II

In assessing the relevance of Weber's analysis of charismatic authority to the Ghanaian case, it is necessary to remember at the outset that the extraordinary rapidity of social and political change throughout Africa makes comparison with apparently analogous cases often misleading. The problem of legitimacy which arose in Ghana from the moment that the hand-over of power by the colonial government was seen to be imminent involved the attempt to establish or transfer a form of rational-legal legitimacy in a much shorter time than in any of the examples that Weber had in mind. It is true that the policy of the colonial government was based on the assumption that such a programme would be successful, even to the point of its being able to bequeath to an independent Ghana a working two-party system on the Westminster model. It can, however, be strongly argued that this assumption misconceived the extent to which, after the departure of the colonial authority and the breakdown of the pre-colonial traditional authorities (which had never been unified at a national level in any case), effective legitimacy could only rest on a charismatic authority whose stability would depend on the success of its subsequent routinisation.

It is true that after Nkrumah's breakaway from the United Gold Coast Convention (UGCC) in 1949, and the subsequent formation of the Convention People's Party (CPP), the leading Ghanaian politicians can more or less be classified in Left and Right terms so as to suggest the opposition of parties as in a developed rational-legal system. But this apparent distinction was at no time reflected in the electorate or the nation at large. Differences of opinion on national issues were marginal—the twin aims of political independence and economic advance were universally shared. No class differences existed among the population sufficient to lead to the formation of national class-based parties competing for economic benefits according to rational-legally legitimised rules. The effective opposition parties were all regional movements centred on the traditional authorities: the United Party was merely the fusion of all the opposition groups which was effected in 1957, and the Ghana Congress Party, which was more or less the remainder of the old UGCC, secured only one seat (Dr Busia's) in 1954 before being assimilated to the Ashanti-based National Liberation Movement. The retention of traditional power and legitimacy by the chiefs was never a programme with which to recruit a national mass party, but only a basis for regional separatism. Adequate differences of ideology or of interest on a national level simply did not exist.[1]

In this situation, the first party to capture power and thereby to appear to be responsible for the achievement of independence was likely to retain the charismatic authority accruing to proved success. In an electorate without literacy or property qualifications this retention could be all the better effected by organisation and propaganda. Moreover, the control of patronage by the victorious organisation was likely to mean both that amenable power-seekers could be induced (as many were) to join the charismatic following and also that dissatisfied power-seekers would be more likely to consider resorting to unconstitutional (and thus anti-rational-legal) objectives. Nkrumah's personality and its successful projection were of course important to his electoral success. But even without a leader of Nkrumah's qualities, the first party victorious was likely to remain the embodiment of the charisma derived from achieving the national aim. An electorate brought up under tribal-cum-colonial authority may, as some observers believe, be in any case unfamiliar with or indifferent to the functions of a parliamentary opposition. But whatever weight should be assigned to this, the control of patronage and propaganda, together with the claim to have forced the concessions granted by the colonial power, meant that the first party to mobilise the necessary electoral support on some sort of national basis would be unlikely to be ousted by any rival national movement. Only a drastic failure to achieve its promulgated objectives could bring this about by depriving it of the manifest and recognised success necessary to counteract the instability inherent in all charismatic authority.

It is, of course, important to remember that the anti-colonial 'revolution' for which the CPP claimed credit was only a revolution in a limited sense of the term. Power was peacefully handed over by the colonial administration, and although the speed of the hand-over was certainly the achievement of Nkrumah and his party, they inherited as much as they created of the apparatus and personnel necessary to the exercise of government. Moreover, some of the deliberate 'charismatisation' or

---

[1] The authors of the pre-election survey conducted in Accra in 1954 were of the opinion that kinship ties were the only effective inducement to voters to support the opposition: see W. B. Birmingham and G. Jahoda, 'A Pre-Election Survey in a Semi-literate Society', *Public Opinion Quarterly*, XIX (1955), 152. The extent to which elections in Northern Ghana were guided by purely local factions and interests is clearly shown by Dennis Austin, 'Elections in an African Rural Area', *Africa*, XXI (1961), 1–18.

'messianisation' of Nkrumah followed rather than preceded his accession. Nevertheless, the legitimacy deriving from success which is characteristic of charismatic authority may be traced through his career, both before and after his attainment of total leadership. The notion of charismatic legitimacy becomes particularly relevant when we consider the real source of the threat to the authority of Nkrumah and the CPP. This was never the colonial power so much as the traditional authorities and their tribal or regional support. It was against these as much as against the colonial power that there was a 'revolution' in Ghana after the end of the Second World War, and it was in place of these that a charismatic authority was needed as the focus of legitimacy on a national level.

In considering the nature of the opposition in Ghana, it is as well to go back briefly over the events of 1949 and the immediately following years. Throughout the whole period, the effective opposition to the CPP was, as already emphasised, based on regionalism.[1] The CPP, of course, never hesitated to use regionalism in its own favour (as, for instance, in benefiting from the traditional hostility of the Brong chiefs to the Ashanti); but this did not render invalid the claim of the CPP to stand for national identity against the 'tribal chauvinism' consistently attacked in their speeches by Nkrumah and other party spokesmen. As early as the break-up of the UGCC, Nkrumah's opponents were attempting to discredit him in the eyes of the Ga people of Accra by harping on his Nzima origin.[2] The three principal regions of Ghana (the coastal 'Colony', Ashanti and the formerly so-called Northern Territories) have always been very different and on occasion hostile to each other. Indeed, the political frontiers of Ghana, deriving as they do from an arbitrary decision of the colonial powers, follow neither tribal nor economic lines. Any national mass party was therefore bound to have difficulty in fostering an allegiance based on national statehood. Such an allegiance, by competing with and indeed setting out to replace the allegiance owed to the traditional authorities,[3] had to depend on the achievement of national aims shared by

[1] The Moslem Association Party, which won one seat in the 1954 and 1956 elections, should perhaps be described as a confessional rather than a regional party, although its support came mainly from the Moslem communities of certain particular localities.
[2] Kwame Nkrumah, *Autobiography* (Edinburgh, 1957), p. 105. The regional basis of the opposition continued to be emphasised: see e.g. the Ghana Government's *Report of the Commission appointed to enquire into the Matters disclosed at the Trial of Captain Benjamin Awhaitey*, and the statement thereon (1959), pp. 23–4.
[3] There are, of course, great differences among the types of political system covered by the term 'traditional authorities' (e.g. between the Ashanti as described by Rattray and the Tallensi as described by Fortes). Moreover, the success or failure of the CPP in a given district often depended on the personal popularity and following of particular individuals (e.g. Krobo Edusei in Ashanti, or W. A. Amoro in the Northern

or made meaningful to a sufficient proportion of the total society; that is, on the manifest success from which charismatic legitimacy could derive as the necessary supplement to the rational–legal legitimacy taken over with, perhaps, a certain precariousness from the colonial power.

When the first general election was held under the Coussey Constitution in 1951,[1] only 38 out of a total of 84 seats in the Legislative Assembly were popularly elective. But of these the CPP won 33, and thus became enabled to press successfully for more far-reaching constitutional reform than had been envisaged by the Coussey Committee in 1949.[2] It was in this period that the personal charisma of Nkrumah was most important, and this not so much in his role as Leader of Government Business (from 1952, Prime Minister) as in his role as leader of his party—a party which in its enthusiasm and its devotion to its leader approximated closely to the sort of movement or following described by Weber as necessary to charismatic authority. Ironically, the demand among Nkrumah's followers for the immediate achievement of the party's promised goal was perhaps the greatest strain on his personal authority and, therefore, his retention of charisma. The successful transition from 'Positive Action' (organised non–violent resistance to the colonial power) to 'Tactical Action' (co-operation with the colonial power where serving the ultimate aim of independence) must be largely attributed to the charisma of Nkrumah himself. It was in this spirit that the constitutional reforms were effected[3] whereby a general election was held in 1954 for a directly elected assembly of 104 seats.[4] The CPP won 72 seats (later increased to 79). From this point, the practical achievement of independence was the CPP's primary goal, and regionalism the principal threat to its partly rational-legal but also partly charismatic legitimacy.

It must be remarked that the victory of the CPP in the elections of 1954 and 1956 does not indicate quite so much unanimity as the resulting

constituency of Bongo). However, the conflict of allegiances between the CPP and the traditional authorities, however different these may be, is sufficiently clear-cut for the use of the term to seem justifiable: all rest primarily on 'traditional' legitimacy in Weber's sense.

[1] For an account of the 1951 election, see J. H. Price, *The Gold Coast Election* (West African Affairs No. 11, n.d.).

[2] Col. No. 248, *Gold Coast : Report to His Excellency the Governor by the Committee on Constitutional Reform*, 1949. Neither Nkrumah nor any radical nationalist was invited to serve on the committee.

[3] See *The Government's Proposals for Constitutional Reform*, 1953, and Col. No. 302, *Despatches on the Gold Coast Government's Proposals for Constitutional Reform*, 1954.

[4] For an account of the 1954 election, see G. Bennett, 'The Gold Coast General Election of 1954', *Parliamentary Affairs*, VII (1954), 430–9.

distribution of seats would suggest. In both elections, the CPP received a minority of votes in the North. Its overall majority was increased in 1956, but out of a total vote of roughly 700,000 the majority was still under 100,000. Moreover, only about a half of the registered electors voted, and these were themselves only a proportion (for which no reliable statistics are available) of the potential voters.[1] This hardly constitutes an overwhelming mandate. The important fact, however, is that these figures cannot be interpreted as representing the sort of genuine national opposition occurring under a long-standing rational-legal parliamentary system. No unequivocally reliable measure of this is available, but even a simple ecological analysis of the two elections suggests that the greater part of the votes cast against the CPP should not be interpreted as the expression of a positive choice for an alternative national policy.[2] It was not a case of a choice of policies or national interest-groups in a rational-legal system, but rather a recognition or rejection of the leader and his following in a still largely charismatic one.

It is this plebiscitary quality in both the 1954 and 1956 elections, as well as the subsequent referendum, which provides one of the principal grounds for seeing Ghana's politics in the decade after independence in Weber's terms. Votes cast against the CPP involved a rejection (for whatever personal or other reasons) of Nkrumah as the charismatic leader rather than support for an alternative rational-legal government deriving its legitimacy from the constitution. Although a conclusive interpretation is impossible on the basis of the brief summary being given here, the limited sources available do seem to make it plausible to see Ghana as a case of what Weber had in mind. Such a view may be further confirmed by the way in which Nkrumah and the CPP acted after the successful vindication of their claim to national leadership. The establishment of a group of followers who could be used to counteract the incumbent bureaucracy—a policy described by Weber as essential to the charismatic leader—was as far as feasible attempted by Nkrumah both before and after independence.[3] The propaganda of the CPP continued to portray it as having achieved precisely the economic gains and quasi-military

---

[1] In 1954, with 3 seats uncontested, 50 per cent of the registered electors voted. In 1956, with 5 seats uncontested, the proportion was 48 per cent.

[2] The only figures which might be used to draw conclusions about a national opposition are those of the 1960 presidential referendum: Danquah, 124,643; Nkrumah, 1,016,076. But even when regionalism may be presumed to be a less important factor, the referendum remains a choice of leader rather than policy. If (which some observers have questioned) the referendum was accurate, it must be regarded as a measure of Nkrumah's popularity rather than of opinion on issues.

Autobiography, p. 147: 'It has always been my conviction that after any political

success[1] which Weber argues that a charismatic authority will try to emphasise or exaggerate in order to consolidate its hold over the loyalty of the people at large. The creation of economic interests bound up with the regime as the source of their legitimacy—Weber's 'second main aim' of the charismatic leader—may be illustrated by the creation of numerous offices which did not exist prior to independence. For instance, the revised CPP constitution of 1959 provided for the creation of full-time Regional Propaganda Secretaries, and in 1961 the reorganisation of administrative districts to correspond with electoral districts led to the appointment of 28 new District Commissioners. Such measures as these may, indeed, be seen as realising both Weber's 'main aims' of the charismatic leader: first, the destruction of traditional powers and privileges, and second, the creation of loyalty through patronage. Finally, Weber's contention that under a charismatic regime parties will necessarily be 'schismatic sects' is amply illustrated by the behaviour both of the other parties or movements and of the CPP towards them.

The strongest and most disruptive of the several 'schismatic' movements was the National Liberation Movement, which was formed after the CPP's victory in the General Election of 1954. It should, as its name implies and as Weber's argument suggests, be regarded more as a mass movement than as a parliamentary party, although it did win 12 seats in 1956 and also contested some outside of Ashanti. Founded by the Asantehene's linguist and with the Asantehene's backing, it was based on traditional Ashanti separatism sparked into organised opposition by government pegging of the cocoa price paid to the Ashanti farmers and by the breakaway from the CPP of a group of militant dissidents. It constituted the biggest threat both to the legitimacy of Nkrumah and the CPP and to the national unity of Ghana as such: neither the Northern People's Party nor the Togoland Congress were as powerful, nor did they represent so economically indispensable a region. The political violence which took place in Ashanti shows how serious the threat became. In addition, the NLM's boycott of the Bourne Committee on constitutional reform, the subsequent Achimota conference[2] and finally the Legislative

revolution, non-violent or violent, the new government should immediately on coming into power clear out from the civil service all its old leaders. My own experience taught me that by failing to do so, a revolutionary government risks its own destruction.'

[1] The continued commemoration of the 1948 riots in terms of the achievement by organised force of a self-conscious political objective may be cited as illustrative of this.

[2] See the *Report of the Constitutional Adviser*, 1955, *Report of the Achimota Conference*, 1956, and the *Government Report on the Achimota Conference*, 1956. In fact, strong but unavailing representations were made by the Joint Provincial Council delegation to persuade the Asanteman Council and the NLM and its allies to join.

Assembly itself were self-evidently 'schismatic' in intention. In the end, as it happens, this policy probably did the opposition more harm than good. It did not prevent the CPP from carrying through its plans for unicameral elected government, and it ultimately reinforced the CPP's arguments in favour of one-party rule. The pressure brought to bear on the British government did not serve either to secure a federal government or significantly to delay independence; it only forced a General Election by which the opposition gained nothing. The events of 1954–7 did not seriously alter the CPP's claim to be the sole national party; what they did was to show both how violent and how regional the opposition was, and how far the country as such still was from a stable rational-legal system.

On Weber's analysis, such a state of affairs must, even with an ineffective or incompetent opposition, constitute a persistent threat to the legitimacy of a central government. No appeal to traditional authority is possible; rational-legal authority cannot be successfully established when its constitutional basis is unacceptable to those whose loyalty it is intended to retain; and the charismatic authority which is thus necessary for legitimacy must be inherently unstable until it is successfully routinised. The central government may be sure of winning a show-down by force, but unless this force is recognised as the only legitimate force by the nation at large, then the danger is immediately created of a succession of attempted *coups d'état* by any group in pursuit of power.[1]

Such dangers are likely to be particularly acute where the claimed successes and continuing promises of the charismatic leader or group are both a cause and a symptom of heightened popular expectations. A competitor for leadership under these conditions is likely to behave as described by Weber—that is to try to arouse an emotional devotion to himself and to make more spectacular promises than his rivals. Both of these will be less necessary in a more stable and institutionalised system. That the expectations of the Ghanaian electorate were heightened by the benefits hoped for from independence can be evidenced by the propaganda of the CPP. Indeed, the CPP could perhaps be seen not as the principal claimant to charismatic legitimacy in a period of imminent transition but also as in some aspects a millenarian-type movement embodying Utopian expectations centred on (in the CPP slogan) 'free-dom' and resulting in part from rapid social change. This is not to say that the CPP can be

---

[1] That one *coup d'état* is likely to lead to another is a danger explicitly recognised in the *Statement by the Government on the Recent Conspiracy* (1961), p. 1, although 'any revolution which is based on real and genuine mass support is justified' (p. 2).

fitted to the usually accepted definitions of a millenarian movement. But it could be argued to have exemplified several millenarian characteristics, of which the most important for the present argument was the expectation of its followers that independence would lead to the quicker fulfilment of more utopian aims than was likely in practice. There is thus the risk of a vicious circle of expectations and promises for as long as legitimacy remains charismatic and the authority of the successful competitor for leadership rests upon their continued achievement of success.

There is only one answer to these difficulties: the institutionalisation of charisma in the single party itself. The party must become at once the symbol and the focus of the national consciousness towards which loyalty can be directed above and even irrespective of loyalty to particular persons. Thus the agents of the party's authority may be acknowledged to fail or defect and ministerial heads may be seen to roll, but this must never be equated with any failure by the party as such. When the source and agency of authority are successfully separated in this way, it can then become true that 'le parti règne mais il ne gouverne pas'. In other words, charisma will become successfully routinised once the separation of the source from the agency of authority immunises it against the failure which would bring about the collapse of a 'pure' charismatic system.

This process may be seen in Ghana in the years following independence. The establishment of the CPP as the source of authority was consolidated by such enactments as the Municipal Councils (Abolition of Traditional Members) Act, which was explicitly declared by Mr Kofi Baako in the Legislative Assembly to be 'consistent with our policy of keeping the chiefs away from politics'.[1] At the same time, the party's propaganda constantly stressed the identification of the nation with the CPP. Since well before independence, the CPP set out to bring under its control such other organisations as the Ghana ex-Servicemen's Union and the Trade Unions,[2] and it subsequently created a whole series of subsidiary organisations such as the Builders' Brigade and the Young Pioneers to extend and consolidate its influence. It was to the party, and to the president as head at once of the party and the nation, that allegiance was to be owed. It is, of course, true that the president was the principal agent

---

[1] *Parl. Debates*, vol. XVI, No. 25 (1959), cols. 348–9.
[2] The two Trades Union Congresses which had jointly existed up to 1962 were amalgamated at Nkrumah's insistence (*Autobiography*, p. 178). The Gold Coast ex-Servicemen's Union (the more radical of the two ex-Servicemen's organisations) played a considerable part in the events before and after the 1948 disturbances, which may be regarded as the starting-point of the accelerating constitutional reforms which led ultimately to independence. See Col. No. 231, *Report of the Commission of Enquiry into Disturbances in the Gold Coast* (1948), pp. 7, 20–3.

of the governmental authority of which he remained to some extent the charismatic source. But the president, like the party, was never to be seen as the agent of failure; blame must always be laid on lesser agents when mistakes are acknowledged to have taken place. Only such a separati n of the source of authority (the party) from its agents (the government) could make it possible for the problem of succession, which Weber sees as crucial, to be resolved from within the party.[1]

In the process, which Weber envisages, of deliberately circumventing or replacing the influence of the traditional authorities, the CPP extended its control by the creation (which I have already touched upon) of a bureaucracy superimposed by the central authority on the pre-existing structure.[2] To some extent, of course, this followed the pattern laid down by the colonial power. But the centralising policy of the CPP was diametrically contrary to the British pattern of 'indirect rule' and the consequent retention of power by the traditional authorities. The CPP's principal legal measure diminishing the chief's potential influence in politics was the Chiefs Recognition (Amendment) Act whereby power over enstoolment and destoolment was given to the Ministry of Local Government.[3] In addition, commissions of inquiry modelled on the Lynskey Tribunal were used against the traditional authorities. The Akim Abuakwa Commission set up in 1957 and the Kumasi Commission set up in 1958 brought to light evidence of the misuse of their powers by Nana Ofori Atta II, Omanhene of the Akim Abuakwa State, and some of his councillors, and by the Kumasi State Council; in both cases, evidence was produced that considerable sums of money had been improperly transferred to the organisation of opposition to the central government. It is worth remarking that both reports stress that the functions of the chieftaincy are traditionally non-political.[4] This means only, however, that politics based on parties are unknown to the structure of traditional or customary institutions; to deny to the chiefs the right to exercise their authority in

[1] I have here deleted two sentences suggesting that Nkrumah would be succeeded from within the CPP, although I did also recognise, in 1962, the possibility of a military coup (see p. 172, n. 1, below). This, however, does not affect my suggested interpretation of the events of the period covered in the paper.

[2] It is worth noting that this also fits closely with Weber's analysis in his discussion of bureaucracy; see, e.g. *Theory*, pp. 224–5 and cf. p. 163 and elsewhere.

[3] The Leader of the Opposition (by then called the 'Minority Group'), Mr Dombo, directly accused the Government in the debate on the bill of intending to abolish chieftancy; see *Parl. Debates*, vol. XVI, no. 35 (1959), col. 1682. This was denied by the Government, however.

[4] *Report of a Commission appointed to enquire into the Affairs of the Kumasi State Council and the Asanteman Council* (1958), para. 121; *Report of a Commission appointed to enquire into the Affairs of the Akim Abuakwa State* (1958), para. 66.

the context of the new political institutions is thus to make clear that the new are to supplant, not coexist with, the old. Though the chiefs might retain an administrative or judicial function, as they continued to do in many Northern areas, where the District Commissioners had to work with or through the chiefs if they were to carry out a proposed measure successfully, nevertheless it was not to them or even through them that national allegiance was to be owed. The chiefs, in fact, were to be the agents, not the source, of a centralised national authority which was claimed to embody the popular will and thereby constitute the charismatic source of acknowledged legitimacy.

The legitimacy of the CPP and of Nkrumah was thus partly rational-legal but still partly charismatic, even if this charisma was becoming increasingly institutionalised. As we have seen, Weber's notion of 'routinisation' is not as clear as one would wish; but it may be suggested that the charisma of the CPP was likely to become both traditionalised as it became longer accepted as the source of authority and at the same time increasingly legalised as the constitutional provisions under which its position was retained became accepted as an adequate criterion of its legitimacy. It might thus have aquired the *Alltagsgebilde* without which charismatic authority must remain inherently unstable. In 1962 it still retained an element of 'pure' charisma, for its legitimacy did still depend in part on the 'exemplariness' of itself and of its founder. But the institutionalisation of Nkrumah's charisma in the CPP and the consequent separation of the source of authority from its agency were reducing the instability of 'pure' charisma to a point where it was becoming unlikely that the party as such could be seen so to have failed that its authority would be seriously questioned. Only the total failure of 'Nkrumaism' as such was going to bring this about. This is not to say that both the persons and policies of a CPP government did not radically change from time to time; but what was crucial to the regime's stability was that they should change within an established pattern of legitimacy and derive their authority from a legally constituted institution which could grow more secure as its charisma became increasingly routinised.

It may still be questioned, however, how complete routinisation was to occur—how, that is, the Ghanaian system could come to approximate closely to the ideal type of rational-legal system at all, even if civilian rule were to be retained in the long term. The revised constitution, the replacement of the traditional authorities as the focus of popular allegiance, the increasing rate of urbanisation and industrialisation and the emergence of economic classes might suggest an increasing irrelevance of charismatic authority (although, as already remarked, Weber's analysis gives scope for charismatic authority not only in pre-industrial systems). Nevertheless, it may be argued that a charismatic element must persist in the institutional-ised charisma of the dominant party under any non-military regime. Where the party, rather than the constitution or tradition under which rival parties compete for office, is the source of legitimacy, it is only an appeal to the party's charismatic authority which can be made if there is a threat to the stability of the regime as such.[1] Such an appeal, moreover, will continue to carry the risk of collapse to which charismatic authority is always liable. If the party's reputation must be staked as such in the attempt to sustain its legitimacy, it cannot afford to be unsuccessful in the way that it could if it were only the agent of an authority deriving its legitimacy from elsewhere. The continuance of a charismatic residue, as it were, in the Ghanaian system therefore depended largely on whether or not a charismatic party system could develop into a rational-legal party system with the constitution as the source of legitimacy and an alternation of rival parties in power.

One parallel for such a development immediately suggests itself, namely the evolution of Turkey's politics since Ataturk.[2] The Democrat party in Turkey emerged in opposition to the policies of Ataturk's party, but not to Ataturk's personal achievements as the charismatic founder of the modern Turkish regime. The two parties were, therefore, posing as rival heirs to the legitimacy of the charismatic founder and claiming to be chosen by the electorate as the agents, but not the source, of that legitimacy. This approximate precedent might appear to suggest that a similar pattern could have been followed in Ghana. In Ghana's case, the organised dissatis-faction of some section of Ghanaian society or of the CPP itself might have led to the emergence within the framework of 'Nkrumaism' of national parties competing for office on the rational-legal model. However, several features of the Turkish case were not present in the Ghanaian, and it seems worthwhile to cite these as evidence for the unlikelihood of the emergence of a multi-party system from the single-party system of Nkrumah, even if we suppose that Nkrumah had died or retired before he was overthrown.

---

[1] The note appended here read in the original: 'Such a threat might come at some later date from the army, although this topic raises separate issues which I shall not pursue here. It could, however, be argued that a potentially dissatisfied generation of young officers may have been created by the abnormally rapid promotion of the party-favoured candidates chosen to replace the departing expatriates.' For such promotions, see the *Ghana Gazette*, 13 October 1961, p. 724.

[2] I have here relied largely on Kemel H. Karpat, *Turkey's Politics: The Transition to a Multi-Party System* (Princeton, 1959).

First, the Second World War produced hardships and shortages in Turkey which the Republican government (like the colonial government in Ghana) was unable to cope with; and whereas post-war difficulties helped the nationalist movement in Ghana to agitate against the colonial authorities, in Turkey it was the ruling single-party system which bore the opprobium. Secondly, the Turkish government was under strong pressure to conform ideologically to the West, particularly in view of the chances of aid from the Truman government; Nkrumah, by contrast, was able to secure aid from both blocs without any compromise in domestic policy. Thirdly, Ataturk himself claimed always to be in favour of Western parliamentary government, a free press and non-totalitarian party organisation; his effort to arrange an opposition led by Fethi Bey, however unsuccessful, may still have helped to make the events of 1947–50 possible.[1] Fourthly, Inonu's Multi-Party Declaration of 12 July 1947 and his willingness when both President and Republican party chairman to see himself as head of state in a genuine two-party system was crucial to the emergence of the Democrat party; it was clear by 1961 that Nkrumah would not be prepared to do the same. Finally, despite all these considerations, the multi-party system in Turkey cannot be said to be working well or to rest on established class-based national parties; this would by itself seem an argument for saying that the transition to a rational-legal multi-party system from a single charismatic party system will in any circumstances be difficult.

It might still be urged, however, that the accelerating industrialisation of Ghana had created the interest-groups on a national level on which alternative parties might be based, and that urbanisation, bureaucratisation and a deliberate revival of liberal-democratic ideology might between them create a situation in which charismatic authority could give way altogether to rational-legal. Certainly, these processes may be amply documented: the number of wage and salary earners increased during the 1950s from at least 186,000 in 1950 to at least 277,413 in 1958—an increase of over 40 per cent;[2] the number of trade unions had risen from

---

[1] Professor Duverger makes the crucial point in his observation that 'The Turkish single party had a bad conscience' (Maurice Duverger, *Political Parties* (London, 1959), p. 277). The same does not seem true of the CPP.

[2] The figure for 1958 is taken from the *Annual Report of the Ministry of Labour 1957–8* (1960), which was the latest available at the time of writing. On the 1951 figures, see D. A. Sutherland, *Memorandum on Mining in the Gold Coast* (Accra, 1951), p. 26. It is, however, worth noting that in the mines the African labour force had shrunk from 41,270 in 1951 to 29,945 in 1960; see *Report of the Mines Labour Enquiry Committee* (1953), p. 43, and *Report of the Mines Department for the Period 1st April 1959–31st March 1960*, p. 13.

73 in 1953 to 153 by 1958;[1] the projected increase needed in high-level occupations by 1965 was already calculated at 59 per cent in 1960;[2] and the successful completion of the Volta Project entailed a long-foreseen increase in the labour force.[3] In addition, an increasing differentiation of styles of life has inevitably accompanied economic development.[4] Nevertheless, the development of a fully bureaucratised and politically articulated system on the rational-legal model might still be steadily impeded by such factors as the continuance of the extended family system and the regional loyalties bound up with it, the tradition of authoritarian (even if not wholly undemocratic) leadership inherited from the tribal systems, and the predisposition (whatever its causes) to a greater emotionalism in politics than is generally observed under more bureaucratised systems, though this is not, of course, a universal or even very tangible rule. It is thus possible that the legitimacy accorded to parties and their leaders must remain to some extent conditional on their charismatic success.

This must, however, remain speculative. Not only does it involve unverifiable guesswork about the future course of Ghanaian politics, but it also leads into problems where, as we have seen, Weber's notion of 'routinised' or 'institutionalised' charisma becomes progressively more ambiguous and less useful. It is in the separation of the single party as the source of authority from the government as its agent and in the institutionalisation in this sense of the party's necessary charisma that I have tried to suggest that Weber's discussion applied directly to Nkrumah's Ghana. The deliberate breaking-down of the traditional authorities and the lack of a sufficiently established rational-legal authority to be by itself a substitute meant that the national legitimacy of the CPP had to be to some extent charismatically sustained, and, if stability was to be achieved, routinised. The way in which this was done during the period of Nkrumah's rise to power accorded almost exactly at several points with Weber's analysis, and it therefore seems plausible to suggest both

---

[1] *Annual Report of the Ministry of Labour 1957–8*, p. 94, table IX (*b*).

[2] *Survey of High-Level Manpower in Ghana* (1960), p. 11. This calculation assumed an annual population growth of 3 per cent and economic growth of 5 per cent (*ibid.* p. 10).

[3] Already in 1952, the Seers-Ross report estimated a labour force increase of 10,000 per annum if the project started in 1952 or 1953. See D. Seers and C. R. Ross, *Report On Financial and Physical Problems of Development in the Gold Coast* (1952), p. 93.

[4] Seers and Ross (*op. cit.* p. 7) comment on the even greater increase in 'luxury' than 'semi-luxury' imports between 1938 and 1950. This led J. Boyon, *Le Ghana* (Paris, 1958), p. 94, to speak of the evolution of an 'haute bourgeoisie'; but the phrase needs to be treated with care.

that Weber's analysis is upheld by the actual Ghanaian case, and that the Ghanaian and, perhaps, other similar cases may be better understood by reference to Weber's view of the causes, symptoms and consequences of a situation of charismatic legitimacy.

7. Status Consistency, Relative Deprivation, and Attitudes to Immigrants*

(WITH C. R. BAGLEY)

I

The idea of equilibrium, or consistency, between different status ranks is a thoroughly familiar one. It can be traced, under other names, at least as far back as Aristotle;[1] but the recent discussions of it by academic sociologists have been largely prompted by the two papers of Benoit-Smullyan (1944) and Lenski (1954). One problem to which it continues to give rise is that a satisfactory definition of 'status' itself is exceedingly difficult,[2] but leaving this aside, the underlying notion may be summarised by saying that not every member of a group, organisation or society is equally ranked by his fellow-members on all of the several criteria by which they assign status to each other. Once given a discrepancy of this kind, two related consequences are alleged typically to follow. First, the individual will attempt to bring his two (or more) discrepant ranks into equilibrium either by raising his rank on the attribute where his status is lowest or by denying the validity of the criterion according to which this low rank has been assigned. Second, until he has succeeded in this (and the second alternative depends in any case more on others

---

*This paper was first published in *Sociology*, III (1969). For some additional references to the extensive recent literature on 'status consistency', see Steven Box and Julienne Ford, 'Some Questionable Assumptions in the Theory of Status Inconsistency', *Sociological Review*, n.s. XVII (1969), 187–201.

[1] In the Politics (1266b–1267a), Aristotle observes that the well-educated agitate ($\sigma\tau\alpha\sigma\iota\acute{\alpha}\zeta o\upsilon\sigma\iota\nu$) if their political status, in the sense of their share in the distribution of offices, is not congruent with their educational status. Precisely this hypothesis is tested and confirmed for present-day Iran by Ringer and Sills (1953) in a paper sometimes cited in discussions of 'status equilibrium'.

[2] Two confusions are commonly found: first, 'status' is sometimes used synonymously with prestige and sometimes as a generic term whereby prestige becomes a *criterion* of 'status'; second, it is sometimes taken to be measured by fellow-members of a group and sometimes by fellow-members of the society who are *not* members of the group. For a further brief discussion, see Runciman (1967).

than on himself), he will remain in a state of psychological stress. It accordingly follows that the many people whose ranks are not all in equilibrium[1] may be expected to evince social attitudes and behaviour significantly different from those whose ranks are 'congruent'.

The difficulties begin, however, as soon as we ask: what attitudes and behaviour? and in what way? It will have to be specified first, in what direction their attitudes will differ, whether towards tolerance or intolerance, liberalism or conservatism, activism or quietism; second, whether the same attitudes will be found to correlate with the same discrepancies, or whether different discrepancies will engender contradictory attitudes; and third, whether those whose statuses are discrepant will differ in the same direction and to the same degree from those who are above and those who are below them in aggregate status. It will not be surprising to find a difference of some sort or other between those who are and those who are not 'in equilibrium'. But there is no warrant for citing such a finding in support of a 'theory of status congruence' unless it is shown from what specific premises it could have been predicted in advance. Two risks are particularly apparent. The first is that it may turn out that the correlation is to be explained not by the discrepancy of status as such, but by a particular feature of the situation which may happen to coincide with a discrepancy of status. The second is that even where discrepancies of status are precisely matched with differences of attitude, the difference may be such as can be statistically accounted for by the cumulative independent influence of the two or more 'status factors' involved.

The recent advocates of a 'theory' of status consistency, or congruence, have, in our view, been notably unsuccessful in meeting these difficulties. The suggestion put forward by Lenski (1954) was that what he called 'low crystallisation' was associated with liberal political responses, and this finding seemed subsequently to by confirmed by Goffman (1957) and Jackson (1962). But Kenkel (1956) was unable to repeat Lenski's result,[2] and Kelly and Chambliss (1967) subsequently lent support to Kenkel's conclusion by a study in which no significant association between status inconsistency and political liberalism was found. In addition, Rush (1967) found an association between status inconsistency and extremism of the Right. The difficulty in reconciling these findings is not lessened by the

[1] Treiman (1966), p. 653, points out that it is a mistake to suppose that only a small number of people are in general in a situation of disequilibrium; the study he quotes showed that two-thirds of heads of American households were status discrepant.

[2] Lenski (1957) then suggested that the discrepancy might result from the possibility of defining 'inconsistency' in different ways.

notorious ambiguities of the classifications of political attitude used and the need to disentangle the separate dimensions of Left-Right and liberal-authoritarian.[1] But whatever the reasons, it cannot be said that a convincing overall generalisation linking status inconsistency with political attitude has yet been put forward.

Furthermore, there is a similar lack of a convincing generalisation if the analysis is extended from static to dynamic by the introduction of changes in ranks relative to each other. Bettelheim and Janowitz (1964) argued that if race and education were held constant, those who moved into status disequilibrium as a result of downward occupational mobility would be more likely to exhibit attitudes of racial prejudice. But Silberstein and Seeman (1959) had found a contradictory result, and this was later borne out by the studies of Hodge and Treiman (1966) and Seeman *et al.* (1966). We shall be presenting some figures which bear on this topic in a later section; but neither they, nor the other findings known to us, lend support to any effective 'theory of status congruence'.

It is fair to say that those who have wished to retain status inconsistency as an independent explanatory variable have recognised that the social context must be taken into account. Thus, Sampson (1963) points out that more importance is generally attached to some of the criteria on which status is assigned than to others. But this is already to concede that status inconsistency as such may mean many different things; and it ought in any case to be sufficiently obvious not to need saying. A more ambitious attempt to preserve status inconsistency as a theoretical term is made by Geschwender (1967),[2] who sets out to link it to the notion of cognitive dissonance. But to move in this way to a still higher level of generality is to preserve it only at the cost of a further loss of explanatory power. To say that status inconsistency generates psychological stress of specified kinds when, or because, people are in general eager for social certitude merely defers once again the question what sort of attitude is produced by what sort of incertitude. To answer it, it is necessary to formulate some very much more specific generalisations which will relate particular attitudes to particular historical and cultural conditions on the basis of equally specific and well-validated psychological assumptions.

[1] See the remarks of Rush (1967), p. 92; and such discussions as that of Shils (1954).
[2] Geschwender at the same time invokes the idea of 'distributive justice' as formulated by Homans (1961) to show how particular discrepancies of status will be viewed. Homans's discussion has been criticised in some detail by Runciman (1967); for our present purposes, it suffices to say that to the extent that this approach helps to explain why some discrepancies of status and not others give rise to feelings of resentment, it replaces, rather than preserves, the hypothesis that the inherent stressfulness of status inconsistency generates predictable differences of attitude.

Geschwender suggests that his model may make it possible to predict how people will behave if inconsistently ranked in particular ways. But inspection of the chart in which these predictions are set out (p. 170) shows how little the notion of 'cognitive dissonance' can help to give these notional predictions the precision they need. Like the assumption that everyone acts to maximise utility, the catch-all assumption that everyone acts to minimise dissonance is, as the basis for a 'theory', either circular or false.

A variety of instances can readily be cited to show that very different reasons may underlie the association of status inconsistency (and therefore, by definition, cognitive dissonance) with differences of attitude. One recent example should be adequate to illustrate the point. Abramson (1966) found that among immigrants into Israel aged 30 and over, those whose status was either high on occupation and low on education or vice versa scored significantly higher on the Cornell Medical Index of mental disorder than those whose education and occupation were consistent. This relationship did not hold, however, either among those under 30 or among the native-born Israelis (most of whom were, in fact, under 30 too). Now the evidence presented by Abramson is not enough to furnish a test of possible explanations of these results. It is clear already that the simple hypothesis that status inconsistency engenders anxiety will have to be severely qualified. But beyond this, all that can be said is that perfectly plausible explanations at once suggest themselves which depend in no way on the notion of status inconsistency as such. That those immigrants of high education and low occupation should have high C.M.I. scores could well be explained by the familiar generalisation that well-educated people in routine or menial jobs are likely to feel both frustrated by their inability to use their talents and resentful that they are not being rewarded in accordance with those talents. That those of high occupation and low education should have higher scores could well be explained by the familiar generalisation that those who are uncertain whether they are fully qualified for their jobs will be likely to feel insecure on that account. It may be that in the case of Abramson's sample these are not the generalisations which do in fact apply. But some reason or other must be given for the greater anxiety found among these two groups, and it is not provided by the blanket assertion that they are anxious because they need to establish a greater measure of status consistency.

In the same way, nothing is added by the invocation of status inconsistency when the fact of low (or high) status by itself is already all that is needed. It should again be enough to cite a single example, which

MAGDALEN COLLEGE LIBRARY

in this case is furnished by the discussion in Malewski (1966) of a finding reported by Menzel (1957). Menzel found that doctors of doubtful professional competence tended to pretend to interviewers that they were using more up-to-date drugs than in fact they were. Doctors of recognised competence, on the other hand, felt no need to conceal this. Menzel professed himself puzzled by this result, which seems in itself surprising. Malewski, however, cites it in a discussion of the effects of 'status incongruence' to show that 'people whose status is very high *and stable* (our italics) pay less attention to behaviour as the visible symbol of higher status' (p. 307). Why is it necessary here to bring in 'stability', by which Malewski means that 'an individual has a great many congruent status factors'? No doubt, over the range of their status ranks the less competent doctors were (other things being equal) more inconsistent in their statuses than the more competent doctors. But it is not the incongruence between their low status as doctors and their high status by other criteria (or in the judgement of other groups) which explains their disingenuous replies about the use of up-to-date drugs. Their simple unwillingness to risk a further diminution of their status by being thought old-fashioned is a sufficient explanation by itself.

It is also possible that the invocation of status inconsistency as an independent variable can be shown to be spurious on purely arithmetical grounds, as has been suggested on the topic of racial prejudice by Treiman (1966). Suppose that we contrast those whose economic and educational statuses are consistent with those whose are not. If we find that those of high income and low education and those of low income and high education both differ in their responses from those whose income and education are consistent, then this may seem to lend *prima facie* support to the hypothesis that prejudice is related to status inconsistency. But these results may be already predictable from the known independent effects of income and education on racial attitudes. In this instance, Treiman showed that those whose education was consistent with their income stood midway in their attitudes between those whose education was higher than their income and those whose education was lower. But this was almost exactly what would be predicted from the additive association of income and education taken separately. To cite such a result, therefore, as support for a 'theory' of status inconsistency is unwarrantable.[1]

---

[1] Geschwender (p. 168 n. 25) attempts to counter Treiman's argument on the grounds that (i) he limited his enquiry to discrepancy between education and income; (ii) he used family and not individual income as his criterion of economic rank; (iii) some of

In summary, we suggest that an association between status inconsistency and social or political attitudes will be best explained not by reference to some highly generalised 'theory' of 'dissonance' but by reference to the psychological generalisations which, when brought to bear on the particular social context, will show how the results could be replicated by the test of further predictions. Often, indeed, the necessary psychological generalisations can be well enough put in the traditional language of jealousy, insecurity, conflict of loyalties and the rest without any recourse to the terms of experimental social psychology. No doubt the traditional language can be much refined and improved upon, and will need to be if the generalisations of 'commonsense' psychology are to be fully explained in their turn. But for the purposes for which a 'theory of status congruence' is advocated, to suggest that the common fact of incongruence furnishes an adequate explanation is misleading where it is not simply vacuous. It is, in fact, the sort of argument that earns social psychology as bad a name among scientific ethologists as among literary humanists.

II

On what grounds, then, do we ourselves suggest that the notion of 'relative deprivation' might help to furnish some more useful generalisation? It would be equally misleading to suggest that there is a 'theory of relative deprivation' or 'reference group theory' from which the prediction of differences in social attitudes could be directly derived, and there will be the same lapse into circularity if 'choice of comparative reference group' is cited *post hoc* as a vindication of the claim that the reference group which defines the scope of a person's resentment was at the same time the cause of it. Its usefulness must lie instead in helping the investigator to formulate more precisely one or more particular generalisations which explain otherwise unexpected or puzzling differences in attitude. The first step must, of course, be to establish a consistent association between feelings of 'relative deprivation' and variations in attitudes or circumstances which are logically independent of this feeling. Once given this the investigator will want to show that under specified

his 'inconsistents' could plausibly have been classified as 'consistents'. These are not, however, very powerful counter-arguments. (i) is in fact incorrect, since Treiman uses education/spouse's education; (ii) is an objection which could as well be made the other way round, depending what view is taken of the tie between the individual and his household; (iii) is already recognised by Treiman who deliberately chose cutting points to make the total distribution as symmetrical around the mean diagonal as possible while retaining enough categories for analysis in each cell.

historical conditions a specified reference group comparison will impinge upon a specified group and therefore, given the psychological generalisations applicable in the particular cultural context, give rise to feelings of relative deprivation. These may then in turn be shown to be associated with attitudes or behaviour which may be more or less remote from the original reference group comparison; this is a matter for the investigator to explore.

It may again be useful to offer one or two examples. In the well-known discussion by Merton and Rossi (1957) of a finding put forward in *The American Soldier*, the satisfaction of soldiers with promotion was suggested to be an inverse function of actual rates of promotion because of the unflattering comparisons which force themselves on a man who is not promoted as an increasing number of his erstwhile equals are moved into ranks above him. It needs to be emphasised that this suggestion, however plausible, cannot claim the validity of an experimental result; nor is it likely that, even if it is correct in the particular case, it can be generalised to a projection of the relationship between rates of promotion and frequency of satisfaction with promotion for the whole range of possible rates from 1 per cent to 99 per cent.[1] But if the explanation is valid in the particular instance, it shows how a difference of attitude can be explained not by the discrepancy between status ranks, but by the obtrusiveness of a reference group comparison which, given what we know about the culture in question and human motives and dispositions in general, generates the otherwise puzzling association between frequency of discontent and opportunities for promotion.

A second example may be taken from the hypothesis which, as we have already remarked, can be traced back to Aristotle, about the resentments of those whose political status is less than they feel entitled to by their education. There is nothing paradoxical about this example—it is no more than common experience would lead one to expect. But if we ask how it is to be explained, whether obvious or not, it is apparent once again that it is not the mere fact of discrepancy between status ranks which furnishes the explanation. It is the nature of the status accorded by the culture in question to education, and the consequent grounds of entitlement to authority claimed and conceded, which furnish the reason for a sense of relative deprivation among the educated but powerless. It is interesting in this context to contrast education with wealth. In some cultures wealth is likewise held to confer the right to political influence, but in others, or in the same cultures under other historical circumstances, it is not. Only

[1] Such a notional projection is in fact made by Davis (1959).

when the reasons for this are understood can the investigator confidently predict which groups whose economic status is higher than their political status will be relatively deprived on that account. It is simply not true to say that people always seek to bring all their ranks into equilibrium. It is rather that some, but by no means all, attributes that are relevant to the apportionment of status are held to carry an entitlement to status, or rank, in another field, and will therefore, if the entitlement is not fulfilled, give rise to a sense of relative deprivation.

In cases like these, a situation of relative deprivation is also a situation of status discrepancy. But it does not, of course, follow that every situation of status discrepancy is a situation of relative deprivation. Indeed, the question to be answered is precisely what causes a person whose statuses are 'inconsistent' to make, or not to make, the comparisons which will give rise to a sense of relative deprivation. Does, for example, a man who is rich but uneducated compare himself as a rich man with the uneducated poor and feel pleased that he is richer than they are, or with the educated rich and feel displeased that he is less educated than they? The question can only be answered by the sort of argument we sketched above, in which the individual's reaction to his social position is predicted from knowledge of the culture in question and such extrinsic psychological generalisations as may be shown to be applicable. The useful question, generally speaking, is not how many of the person's multiplicity of status ranks are discrepant, but which out of the multiplicity of the available comparisons he makes between himself and others, and what are the consequences of this for his other social attitudes.

On the topic of racial prejudice, with which this paper is implicitly concerned, there are two distinct ways in which feelings of relative deprivation, once known to have been engendered, might be connected with attitudes. It is obvious that a person who believes, correctly or not, that immigrants who are recognisable as such by skin colour, language, etc., and who have no better qualifications than himself, have been more successful in the search for a job or a house, will be likely to feel relatively deprived. A small proportion of the sample which we shall be discussing did claim (truthfully or not) to have had personal experiences of this kind. But the hypothesis which we wish to test is a very much more general one. Our suggestion is not simply that those with some overt reason to feel resentful of immigrants will express feelings of hostility towards them, but that those who in general view their position in such a way as to feel a sense of relative deprivation will be more likely to express hostility to out-groups and specifically to immigrants. They will, it is true, be incidentally in a situation of status discrepancy. But our argument is that only those particular situations of status discrepancy which are likely to give rise to feelings of relative deprivation will be found to be associated with a higher frequency of negative attitudes towards immigrants than a purely arithmetical argument would already suggest.

But among what groups should we expect to find these feelings of relative deprivation? One answer is to say that any person who feels relatively deprived by reference to whatever group or class he sees as more advantageously placed in the social structure than himself will be more likely to express a negative attitude to immigrants; and this is the first hypothesis which we shall try to test on the data of the sample survey. Even if such an association is found, it will not entitle us to say that these people are more likely to express hostility to immigrants *because* they suffer from feelings of relative deprivation in general. It may be not that their social position gives rise to feelings of relative deprivation which in turn predispose them to hostility to immigrants so much as that they are personally or psychologically predisposed to a resentment of others which finds expression *both* in their overt choice of reference group and consequent feeling of relative deprivation *and* in their hostility to immigrants. But whatever the explanation, it is still worth testing the initial presumption that an association will be found between hostility to immigrants and feelings of relative deprivation overtly expressed.

More specifically, we also want to see whether there is not at least one particular discrepancy of status which we might predict to be such as to engender feelings of relative deprivation and therefore, *in contrast to* other discrepancies of status, be associated with a higher frequency of hostility to immigrants than the additive effect of the 'status factors' taken separately would lead us to expect. The discrepancies for which the survey to be discussed in the following section furnishes the data, are necessarily limited. We are concerned only with those who are white, and therefore by definition of 'high' ethnic status. There is not, in our culture, sufficient warrant for treating sex or age as 'status factors' such that male/female or old/young can be taken as valid dichotomies of the kind we need. We are left, therefore, only with education, occupation and income. But it should be possible to suggest which discrepancies between these should, and which should not, be such as to engender feelings of relative deprivation. We have earlier remarked on the status of other kinds to which education is generally held to constitute an entitlement. Accordingly, if it is correct to suppose that this attitude is characteristic of contemporary England, we should expect those of high education and low income to feel in general a sense of relative deprivation, but those of low education and high income to feel relatively gratified. We must remember that education as such has a strong negative effect on the likelihood of hostility to immigrants. But we may expect, on our argument, that this will be modified by the sense of relative deprivation which will result if educational and financial status are not 'congruent'.

This hypothesis may, however, need to be further modified before we can predict an association with hostility to immigrants. Reflection on the category of the well-educated but ill-paid at once suggests that among their number will be found some whose occupations are indeed ill-paid but are nonetheless of 'incongruently' high status. Many practitioners of intellectual and artistic skills are, as is well known, highly esteemed but not very highly paid. It may well be, therefore, that although members of this group will take the holders of better paid non-manual jobs as their comparative reference group in the matter of income, they will not be the sort of people likely to feel in any sense resentful of immigrants. If there is a single definable group whose reference groups are likely to be such as to give them a sense of relative deprivation which will find expression in hostility to immigrants, it is those of high education and low income who are also in manual as opposed to non-manual jobs and therefore sufficiently close in social distance to the majority of immigrants to be moved to feel hostility towards them. Accordingly, we suggest that our second hypothesis might be framed as follows: people in manual jobs whose statuses are discrepant in that they are educated but not well paid are more likely to express negative attitudes to immigrants than those who are not well-educated, but are well paid; and they are at the same time more likely to express these attitudes than would be predicted from the additive effects of education, occupation and income as known to be independently associated with these attitudes.

III

Our findings are taken from a national sample survey drawn in England and Wales in 1962,[1] which contained a question worded as follows: 'What about foreign immigrants to this country such as the Irish or West Indians—some people think they are doing too well at the expense of British people. Do you think this is so or not?' Out of the total sample, 2 per cent were themselves immigrants to whom the question was not put and of the remainder 9 per cent answered 'Don't Know' and have

---

[1] The sampling method is described in Runciman (1966), Appendix 1.

accordingly been excluded from the subsequent analysis. This leaves a total of 1254 respondents, of whom 71 per cent answered 'yes' and 29 per cent 'no'.

It is clear that only limited weight can be rested on any conclusions drawn from these replies as to the relation between status consistency, relative deprivation and attitudes towards immigrants. First of all, the question was not phrased with the diagnosis of racial prejudice in mind. Second, the data on income may well be inadequate. Respondents have been divided into 'high' and 'low' income in terms of a division at the median of stated net income after deductions (or for married women, husband's income) of £12 10s. a week. But quite apart from the uncertainty how far people's own replies can be relied on in the absence of independent check, a substantial minority of the sample refused to answer at all, notably among non-manual workers and their wives. Third, there is the possibility that the cut-off points used may be such as to affect the results to a more than trivial degree. 'High' and 'low' educational status has been taken in terms of whether or not the respondent stayed on at school beyond whatever was the minimum age then in force; 'high' and 'low' occupational status has been taken in terms of manual or non-manual occupation, or husband's occupation; 'high' and 'low' economic status has been taken as described above. All three of these dividing lines could, perhaps, be differently drawn, and it may in addition be the case that a three, four or fivefold division would bring out correlations of attitudes with different degrees of 'status inconsistency' which are as it is submerged entirely. It would, however, be a mistake to try to make up for the limitations of the evidence by subjecting it to a more sophisticated analysis then it deserves. We suggest no more than that our results may produce some limited and tentative support for our argument up to this point.

Aside from differences which might have a bearing one way or the other on our present argument, distinct associations were found between the frequency of negative attitudes to immigrants and characteristics which, as we suggested earlier, have no direct and widely-held status rank assigned to them. There were no significant differences between men and women or between Conservative, Labour and Liberal supporters; but it was found that negative attitudes were less frequent among those under 45[1] than among older respondents, and very much less frequent among Low Church members than among members of other religious denominations.

[1] That those under 25 are an exception to the generalisation that prejudice increases with age has been shown elsewhere by Hill (1965).

These differences do not suggest any implications for status consistency or relative deprivation, but we present them in Tables 1 and 2 as having a certain interest of their own.

Our figures for intergenerational mobility in relation to perception of immigrants are of interest more as regards the upwardly than the downwardly mobile. There is certainly no support for the hypothesis that the

Table 1. *Age and Hostile Perception of Immigrants*

Age group	21–29	30–39	40–44	45–49	50–59	60–69	70–79
Per cent with hostile perception of immigrants	71·6	56·4	68·1	69·2	72·4	80·3	81·8
Number of cases	134	218	160	107	290	218	121

Table 2. *Religious Affiliation and Hostile Perception of Immigrants*

Religion	Church of England	Roman Catholic	Low Church	None	Other
Per cent with hostile perception of immigrants	75·5	70·3	13·5	68·7	56·0
Number of cases	1000	111	74	32	25

manual children of a non-manual father are any more likely to express hostility to immigrants than those whose manual occupational status is 'consistent' with that of their fathers. But the low percentage of the upwardly mobile who expressed hostile perception is striking. Any suggested explanation would, without further evidence of some kind or other, be purely speculative; but again, it seems worthwhile to present the figures for their own sake.

The test of our first hypothesis, that negative attitudes to immigrants would be associated with generalised feelings of relative deprivation, was done by means of an earlier question in the interview worded as follows: 'Do you think that there are any other sorts of people doing noticeably better at the moment than you and your family?' This was followed up, for those who answered 'yes' with the two further questions 'What sort of people do you think are doing noticeably better?' and 'What do you feel about this, I mean, do you approve or disapprove of this?' A wide variety of answers was given to the question 'What sort of people?' but no respondent in fact cited immigrants, or any particular immigrant group, as 'doing noticeably better' than themselves, so that anyone who answered 'yes' to the initial question may, for our purposes, be taken to have expressed a sense of relative deprivation not related in the first instance to immigrants as an overt reference group. Those 53 respondents who fell into the category which we discussed earlier of claiming objective

Table 3. *Intergenerational Occupational Mobility and Hostile Perception of Immigrants*

Mobility situation	Father and child manual	Father non–manual, child manual	Father and child non–manual	Father manual, child non–manual
Per cent with hostile perception of immigrants	76·1	73·9	55·5	45·6
Number of cases	662	115	209	138

experience to justify their negative attitude have first of all to be excluded. When this has been done, our hypothesis is still vindicated, as shown by the figures in Table 4; but the effect is not startling. If we suppose that it is to be explained not so much by the connection between a social situation leading to feelings of relative deprivation and hostility towards out-groups as by a psychological, rather than social, predisposition, then we might expect that those who expressed disapproval of those whom they saw as doing noticeably better would be more likely still to express a negative attitude to immigrants; and this is likewise borne out by the table. However, we are in no position to do more than speculate in the most general way about what may lie behind these figures. We would claim only that they suggest that although it is mistaken to assert that any kind of inconsistency between statuses presupposes these respondents to express a negative attitude to immigrants, there is at least some *prima facie* support for the claim that any feeling of relative deprivation of a broadly economic kind does accompany such a predisposition. The Don't Knows are not shown, but there were a substantial number: 180 in answer to the first question and 33 in answer to the second.

Table 4. *Relative Deprivation and Hostile Perception of Immigrants*

'Do you think that others are doing better than you are?'	Yes	No	
Per cent with hostile perception of immigrants	72·3	62·7	
Number of cases	694	319	

If respondent considers that others are doing better, how does he feel about this?	Approves	Indifferent	Disapproves
Per cent with hostile perception of immigrants	63·9	78·4	81·8
Number of cases	327	153	181

The test of our second hypothesis calls for slightly more discussion. The data on income, education and occupation are presented elsewhere by Bagley (1970), who points out that if the null hypothesis is interpreted as saying that no significant differences are found between those whose statuses are inconsistent and those whose statuses are not, then the null hypothesis can be rejected. But at the same time, if we suppose the 'theory of status congruence' to assert that those who are inconsistent will be more likely to express negative attitudes to immigrants than those who are not, it is at once seen to be falsified. The conclusion which first suggests itself from our data, which are summarised below in Tables 5 and 6, is that the expression of negative attitudes to immigrants is to be explained by the independent effect of the three variables. It has of course to be demonstrated that the three do have an independent effect; but this is amply confirmed from Table 6. The less educated are more frequently hostile to immigrants than the better educated, the less well-paid more frequently hostile than the better-paid, and those in manual occupations more frequently hostile than those in non-manual occupations, even when the other two variables are held constant. On what grounds, therefore, might we be entitled to argue that either status discrepancy or relative deprivation produces a greater likelihood of negative response?

Table 5. *Education, Income, and Occupation and Hostile Perception of Immigrants*

	Education		Income		Occupation	
	Low	High	Low	High	Low	High
Per cent with hostile perception of immigrants	75·2	51·8	75·9	60·3	75·9	61·5
Number of cases	960	253	596	398	808	444

Table 6. *The Independent Effects of Education, Income, and Occupation upon Hostile Perception*

	Education		Income		Occupation	
	Low	High	Low	High	Low	High
Per cent with hostile perception of immigrants	73·8	52·7	74·7	60·1	74·6	56·9
Number of cases	728	188	588	328	649	267

Note: The effects of any one status in the above table are calculated holding the effects of the other two statuses constant by means of a 2^3 interaction table (Maxwell, 1961, ch. 6).

The analysis is based on the 916 respondents for whom information on all three statuses was available.

If a discrepancy between education and occupation can already furnish a test of either or both of the two approaches, then it will be possible to include the whole of the relevant sub-category of the sample without the risk that the results are biased by the absence of those who failed to disclose their (or their husbands') income. But the results of this tabulation in fact tell against both approaches equally. Both those of 'high' occupation but 'low' education and those of 'low' occupation but 'high' education are almost exactly as likely to express a negative attitude to immigrants as would be predicted on the basis of the independent effects of occupation and education,[1] as is shown in Table 7. Furthermore, this finding is borne out by the results of a quite different study which allows these combinations of status ranks to be tested for their effects on the proportion of respondents with high scores on a test of racial prejudice.[2] These figures are shown in Table 8.

Table 7. *Combinations of Status Rank and Hostile Perception of Immigrants*

	Occupation low Education low	Occupation high Education low	Occupation low Education high	Occupation high Education high
Actual proportion with hostile perception of immigrants	76·9	65·0	63·0	44·7
Predicted proportion from additive model	75·5	68·3	63·8	56·6
Number of cases	748	131	92	143

Table 8. *Combination of Status Rank and Prejudice in a 1967 Survey*

	Occupation low Education low	Occupation high Education low	Occupation low Education high	Occupation high Education high
Actual proportion prejudiced	50·3	46·8	44·2	33·8
Predicted proportion from additive model	49·6	42·5	44·9	37·9
Number of cases	1460	525	147	260

[1] We have calculated the additive predictions by means of a simple average: the proportions with hostile perception in the two (or more) categories in question have been added and the result divided by the number of categories.

[2] The sample in question is a random sample of 2492 residents of Lambeth, Ealing, Wolverhampton, Nottingham and Bradford. The survey was carried out by Research Services Ltd, for the Survey of Race Relations and the figures shown are taken from a preliminary analysis carried out by C. R. Bagley. 'High Prejudice' denotes respondents who scored above the median on a six-item test of prejudice as disclosed in attitudes to discrimination in employment and the admission of coloured immigrants into Great Britain, and responses to open-ended questions relating to immigrants in general.

A possible vindication of the relative deprivation as distinct from the status consistency approach comes only when occupation is held constant and 'high' and 'low' incomes are introduced into the analysis. The decisive comparison for the test of the two approaches against each other is between those of high education but low income and those of low education but high income among those who, on our argument, are sufficiently close in occupational status to immigrants for their feelings of relative deprivation to be likely to predispose them to hostility to immigrants. On the additive argument, we would expect those of high education but low income to be slightly less likely to express a negative attitude than those of low education but high income alike in the manual, and the non-manual category. On the status inconsistency argument, we should presumably expect no difference between those of high education but low income and those of high income but low education, but merely a higher frequency of hostility expressed by the 'inconsistents' than the additive argument would already predict. In fact, the figures shown in Table 9 seem impossible to reconcile with any plausible version of the status inconsistency argument. Among the non-manual respondents, the percentage of those of high income but low education who expressed hostility is exactly what the additive argument would predict, whereas

Table 9. *Hostile Perception of Immigrants in Groups with Differently Ranked Statuses*

	Non-manual		Manual	
	Education low Income high	Education high Income low	Education low Income high	Education high Income low
Actual per cent with hostile perception of immigrants	65·9	55·8	68·7	76·5
Per cent predicted from additive model	65·7	63·0	70·4	67·8
Number of cases	47	52	179	34

those of high education but low income are markedly less likely to do so. From this it would seem, if the responses of non-manual workers and their wives about income are accurate and are not too much biased by the omission of those who refused to answer at all, that the combination of high education with high occupation is relatively impervious to the known effect of income. Among manual respondents, by contrast, the difference between the two categories is reversed: education fails to have the arithmetically predicted effect on those of low income, and those of high education but low income are 8 per cent more likely, instead of 10 per cent less, to express hostility. Some explanation, therefore, is called for beyond the independent effect of income, occupation and education, and although we cannot make any decisive claim on behalf of an interpretation in terms of relative deprivation, it does at least appear that such an interpretation would be compatible with our results.

There is no need for us to emphasise that very much more evidence is called for than we have presented in this paper before it might be possible to show just which situations of status discrepancy do, and which do not, have a causal relation to attitudes towards immigrants. By comparison with what might emerge from a study specifically designed to test the two hypotheses we have suggested, the results which we have presented are very limited indeed. We do, however, suggest that they may furnish at least some provisional support for our argument that it is a mistake to override the distinctive circumstances by which social attitudes are conditioned in the simple-minded pursuit of higher theoretical generality, and that 'status inconsistency' is better abandoned as an independent variable purporting to explain variations in the frequency (or, for that matter, the intensity) of such attitudes.

BIBLIOGRAPHY

ABRAMSON, J. H. 1966. *Emotional Disorder, Status Inconsistency and Migration. Milbank Mem. Fund Quart.* XLV, 23–48.

BAGLEY, C. R. 1970. Race Relations and the Equilibrium of Status Ranks. *Race* XI (1970), 267 ff.

BENOIT-SMULLYAN, EMILE E. 1944. Status, Status Types and Status Interrelation. *Amer. Sociol. R.* IX, 151–61.

BETTELHEIM, BRUNO and JANOWITZ, MORRIS 1964. *Social Change and Prejudice.* New York, The Free Press.

DAVIS, JAMES A. 1959. A Formal Interpretation of the Theory of Relative Deprivation. *Sociometry,* XXII, 280–96.

GESCHWENDER, JAMES A. 1967. Continuities in Theories of Status Consistency and Cognitive Dissonance. *Social Forces,* XLVI, 160–71.

GOFFMAN, IRWIN W. 1957. Status Consistency and Preference for Change in Power Distribution. *Amer. Sociol. R.* XXII, 275–81.

HILL, CLIFFORD 1965. *How Colour Prejudiced is Britain?* London, Gollancz.

HOMANS, GEORGE C. 1961. *Social Behaviour: Its Elementary Forms.* London, Routledge and Kegan Paul.

HODGE, ROBERT W. and TREIMAN, DONALD J. 1966. Occupational Mobility and Attitude Toward Negroes. *Amer. Sociol. R.* XXXI, 93–102.

JACKSON, ELTON F. 1962. Status Consistency and Symptoms of Stress. *Amer. Sociol. R.* XXVII, 469–80.

KELLY, K. DENNIS and CHAMBLISS, WILLIAM J. 1966. Status Consistency and Political Attitudes. *Amer. Sociol. R.* XXXI, 375–82.

KENKEL, WILLIAM F. 1956. The Relationship Between Status Consistency and Politico-Economic Attitudes. *Amer. Sociol. R.* XXI, 365–8.

LENSKI, GERHARD E. 1954. Status Crystallization: A Non-Vertical Dimension of Social Status. *Amer. Sociol. R.* XIX, 405–13.

LENSKI, GERHARD E. 1957. Comment on Kenkel's Communication. *Amer. Sociol. R.* XXI, 368–9.

MAXWELL, A. 1961. *Analysing Qualitative Data.* London, Methuen.

MALEWSKI, ANDRZEJ, 1966. The Degree of Status Incongruence and its Effects, in Bendix, R. and Lipset, S. M., eds., *Class, Status and Power.* New York, Free Press, 303–8.

MENZEL, HERBERT 1957. Public and Private Conformity Under Different Conditions of Acceptance in the Group. *J. Abnorm. Soc. Psychol.* LV, 398–402.

MERTON, R. K. and ROSSI, A. S. 1957. Contributions to the Theory of Reference Group Behaviour, in Merton R. K., *Social Theory and Social Structure.* New York, The Free Press, 225–80.

RINGER, B. B. and SILLS, D. L. 1953. Political Extremists in Iran. *Public Opin. Quart.* XV, 689–701.

RUNCIMAN, W. G. 1966. *Relative Deprivation and Social Justice.* London, Routledge and Kegan Paul.

RUNCIMAN, W. G. 1967. Justice, Congruence and Professor Homans. *Archiv. Europ. Sociol.* VIII, 115–28.

RUSH, GARY B. 1967. Status Consistency and Right-Wing Extremism. *Amer. Sociol. R.* XXXII, 86–92.

SEEMAN, MELVIN; ROHAN, DENNIS; and ARGERIOU, MILTON 1966. Social Mobility and Prejudice: A Swedish Replication. *Social Problems*, XIV, 188–97.

SHILS, EDWARD A. 1954. Authoritarianism: 'Right' and 'Left', in Christie, R. and Jahoda, M. (eds.), *Studies in the Scope and Methods of the Authoritarian Personality.* Glencoe, Ill: Free Press, 24–49.

SILBERSTEIN, FRED B. and SEEMAN, MELVIN 1959. Social Mobility and Prejudice. *Amer. J. Sociol.* LXV, 258–64.

TREIMAN, DONALD J. 1966. Status Discrepancy and Prejudice. *Amer. J. Sociol.* LXXI, 651–64.

PART III

8. *Misdescribing Institutions**

Two anthropologists, Smith and Jones, are comparing their field-notes on a ritual which they have observed. Their notes are in exact agreement as to what they saw, the accounts of their respective informants corroborate each other, and there is no further question which either Smith or Jones wishes to put to those whom they have witnessed performing the ceremonies. Smith, however, wishes to describe the ritual as magical; Jones wishes to describe it as religious. What sort of disagreement are they having?

A possible answer is that one or both of them is making a value-judgement. But this is not in fact very likely. It may be that to Jones, who believes in God and attends every Sunday at his parish church, praying for rain is a sensible and therefore a praiseworthy thing to do. To Smith, on the other hand, all forms of belief in the supernatural are ridiculous, and his use of the term 'magical' is a device for casting discredit on the kind of beliefs which Jones holds. But there will be few cases, if any, where neither Smith nor Jones can advance a better reason for describing the ritual as one or the other.

On the other hand, the disagreement may be one of simple definition. In Jones's textbook of social science, a necessary feature of 'magic' is a conscious attempt to manipulate the unseen powers. Smith, while agreeing with Jones that they have not been watching such an attempt, uses a textbook which classifies as 'magical' any ritual in which the participants act out a symbolic relation with the unseen powers, whether attempted manipulation is involved or not.

Alternatively, the disagreement of definition may hinge on a point of degree. Smith may agree that attempted manipulation of the unseen powers is a necessary feature of magic; but he may require that statistical content analysis of the supplications made should show a higher frequency of requests for direct intervention in the processes of nature than he and Jones in fact observed. In this case, the disagreement is one of a slightly different but still familiar kind. Is Theaetetus a shoemaker? Not unless he can turn out more well-made shoes in a day at the last. Is he bald?

* The first of these connected papers was published in the issue of *Analysis* of January 1967, and the second in the issue of January 1968 in reply to Martin Hollis, 'Runciman's Misdescriptions', which was published in the issue of October 1967.

Not if he has as many hairs on his head as that. Is he tall? Not unless you call five foot six tall. And so on.

But perhaps the disagreement of definition is more substantial. Suppose Smith's textbook adheres to a theory according to which all rituals which constitute an attempt to manipulate the supernatural (and which are accordingly subsumed under the rubric of 'magic') share a common origin. In describing the ritual in question as 'magical' Smith is asserting a hypothesis about its history. It may be that in the absence of oral or literary tradition, or adequate archaeological evidence, the hypothesis cannot be tested; but in arguing that manipulation is a necessary feature of magic, Smith is committing himself to an account of the origin of all such rituals which, he would concede, would be falsified if this particular ritual could be shown to have originated differently. (Indeed he might then say: the definition of magic which I learnt from my textbook was a mistaken one.)

But these several possibilities are not by any means exhaustive. For Smith and Jones can continue to disagree although both accept that (1) none of the alternatives so far suggested applies, (2) there is no further evidence to which they could appeal which would settle the difference between them, and (3) the participants in the ritual are not liars, or practical jokers, or madmen, or under the influence of drugs. Nonetheless, each still accuses the other of misdescribing the ritual. This alleged misdescription is not, of course, a misdescription of what they have literally seen and heard, for their field-notes agree precisely about the movements made, sounds uttered, the intervals between one movement or sound and another, and so forth. It is a misdescription of an institution, ritual or practice which has a meaning to its performers and is enacted according to rules. (Some philosophers might want to say: practices of this kind are *defined* by their rules.) There accordingly remain four related but distinguishable possibilities about the nature of their disagreement.

1. Jones wants to describe the ritual as religious because the participants themselves describe it as such. Surely, he says, if what they think they are doing is performing a religious act (and there are no difficulties of translation between languages) then they *are* performing a religious act, whether or not Smith prefers to label it 'mumbo-jumbo'. But Smith objects that just as 'In their culture, that gesture is held to be rude' does not entail 'That gesture is rude', so 'In their culture, that ritual is held to be religious' does not entail 'That ritual is religious'. Why, therefore, are we bound to accept their terms? Jones replies that he is not claiming any such relation of entailment, but merely that if we have understood the

meaning of their ritual to them, the proper way to describe it is in terms of that meaning. Smith may then counter by asking whether Jones would in fact accept *any* (sincere) account which they might give of their institutions and beliefs: suppose, for example, they were to give as their reason for propitiating the unseen powers their belief that the moon was made of green cheese, and then to say 'Isn't this a religious belief just like the religious beliefs you describe to us from your own culture?'. Would Jones then be content to describe this belief as 'religious'? To which Jones may reply, 'Not if the belief were actually nonsensical' or 'Not if they couldn't give *some* further account of why that constitutes their reason', or perhaps even 'Yes, as long as I had adequate evidence to vindicate our assumption that these people are sane'. Whichever line he takes, however, the argument will not be either vacuous or trivial, which is all that these examples are intended to show.

2. Smith and Jones agree about what, in normal circumstances, constitutes a religious ritual and what a magical one; but they have both to recognise that where institutions are being described there is no way of establishing beyond the possibility of dispute that the circumstances *were* normal. Now this might mean simply that the movements and utterances observed could not be proved to constitute a ritual at all. But there might also be a case where a disagreement on whether circumstances were normal underlay Jones's willingness, and Smith's refusal, to describe the ritual as 'religious'. It will be useful here to borrow from Miss Anscombe's discussion of 'Brute Facts' (*Analysis* 1963). Smith and Jones are agreed that (i) there exists the institutional background which is presupposed by the description 'a (religious or magical) ritual took place'; (ii) a set of observable ('brute') facts holds out of the range of sets one or more of which must hold if it is to be true to say that a ritual was performed; (iii) there is no warrant to suppose that the ritual did not take place within a normal context of ritual procedure (i.e. the performers were not playing a game, rehearsing for a film, etc.; as Miss Anscombe says, 'one *cannot* mention all the things that were *not* the case, which would have made a difference if they had been'). It might be, however, that even though Jones and Smith agree on a definition of 'religious', Jones is satisfied, but Smith is not, that the normal circumstances of a *religious* ritual in fact obtained. Smith accepts that the ritual was at least magical, because he is satisfied that nothing was the case which, if true, would entail that the ceremony was not a genuine attempt at the manipulation of the supernatural. But he is not sure that nothing was the case which would entail that the performers were not also genuinely *worshipping*

the unseen powers (and this is essential to the agreed definition of 'religious'). Jones's claim that no such thing *was* the case cannot be vindicated by appeal to any further facts. Nor can Jones produce a complete list of everything which was not true of the state of mind of the presumed worshippers and which would, if true, cast doubt on the description of the ceremony as 'worship'.

3. The disagreement continues because of the inability of Smith and Jones to arrive at a closed definition of either 'religion' or 'magic'. (Some philosophers might say: such concepts are inherently open-textured.) This problem is heightened where the observer is studying a culture very different from his own, but it will arise in any case—not even an English anthropologist can give a closed definition of 'joke' or 'snobbery'. There are familiar analogies from jurisprudence such as 'negligence', where the scope and limits of the concept are defined by an agglomeration of precedents. Now it is possible that a dispute about the implications of previous precedents might turn out to conceal a value-judgement after all, for Smith or Jones might be latching a commendatory or disparaging implication onto one or other of the lists of defining characteristics which have turned out to be inadequate to settle this particular case. But this need not be so. A concept like 'religion' can quite well be open-textured without being either commendatory or disparaging, and it may never be possible to specify in advance what features of a ritual will or will not qualify it for admission to the subclass of 'religious' rituals. The disagreement between Smith and Jones is accordingly whether or not to set the precedent that the concept of 'religion' shall cover the case in question; and it is a decision which will have to be reached on *a priori* grounds.

4. Finally, Smith and Jones may each have put forward a complete but different list of both sufficient and necessary characteristics of 'religious' rituals, and they may find that the overlap, although extensive, is not enough to bring them to agreement. Furthermore, the reasons which each gives for his list may be neither arbitrary (in the sense that any criterion of classification whatever is legitimate if it is consistent) nor substantive (in the sense that a testable hypothesis is embodied in the choice of sets of defining characteristics). In other words, their difference is one of emphasis; but that emphasis is part of the descriptive job which the term 'religious' is being required to do. Jones wishes to stress some distinctions more than others, Smith others more than some. The only hope which either has is to make the other's emphasis appear so strained that the assumptions on which it rests become discredited.

I don't know whether this particular example of religion and magic is in fact well-chosen, since I don't know whether this is a dispute which arises at all often, between anthropologists. But two morals nonetheless suggest themselves from it. First, it is dangerous in discussing institutional practices to dismiss ostensibly definitional disagreements as either trivial or arbitrary, even if no empirical hypothesis is implicit in the term applied to the behaviour in question. Second, perhaps too much attention is devoted by philosophers to the differences between explanation in the natural and in the social sciences; it is at least as problematical to say what we are doing when we describe (or, therefore, misdescribe) sequences of self-conscious behaviour performed in an institutional context.

Misdescribing Misdescriptions

In *Analysis* for January 1967, I discussed the nature of the disagreement between two hypothetical anthropologists, Smith and Jones, whose field-notes agree about a ritual but who differ over whether it should be called 'magical' or 'religious'. In the issue for October 1967, I am taken to task by Mr Martin Hollis for allowing the pair of them to start quarrelling about terms instead of exploring further the beliefs, as against the actions, of the performers. Mr Hollis's objection does not, I think, invalidate the point I was concerned to make. But the issue which he raises calls for two short comments.

Hollis supposes the performers to say 'In what follows we invoke Kwoth (or the Spirit of the Above) in an act of worship'; and he argues that if Smith then disputes that the ritual is religious he can only question the translation of 'Kwoth'. But in what sense is the problem one of translation? As Hollis says himself, the fact that Smith and Jones are English speakers is merely an empirical nuisance; it has no philosophical relevance. We can just as well bring them back from Darkest Africa and set them on Brigadier Lord Hunt, who believes, or says he believes, that 'There is no height, no depth, that the spirit of man, guided by a higher Spirit, cannot attain' (*The Ascent of Everest*, p. 232). Does he mean Kwoth? Perhaps he does. Or perhaps he doesn't really know what he means. Smith and Jones, following Mr Hollis's injunction, can ask him any question they can think of. They are perfectly well aware that they cannot settle what are his beliefs simply by spying on him during morning service in the regimental chapel. But it may turn out to be very difficult—much more so, indeed, than it was among the outspoken and clear-headed worshippers of Kwoth—for them to settle either whether his beliefs (feelings, attitudes, etc.) can plausibly be argued to be equivalent to those of Kwoth-worshippers or how well 'worship' (and therefore 'religion') fits them. And Smith and Jones may, therefore, find themselves embroiled once again in a non-empirical but non-trivial argument.

In any case, how far is Hollis right in suggesting that a sufficient description of rituals and institutions can be established by reference to beliefs? Suppose we send Smith and Jones off to White Hart Lane to watch Spurs play Chelsea. How far will it help them in their attempt to describe what is going on if they ask the players and spectators about their beliefs? Hollis says that 'what we are doing depends on what we are trying to do'. But can everybody at White Hart Lane tell Smith and Jones what exactly they are trying to do and are therefore doing? True, Smith and Jones will not expect either of the two centre-forwards to say 'I don't know if I'm trying to score a goal or not'. (True also, if the game is not Spurs v. Chelsea but Liverpool v. Everton, they will find that the religious beliefs of the spectators are by no means irrelevant to what takes place.) But when they come to argue about which to choose out of all the (non-evaluative) terms by which they may think of describing the institution of football, what questions can they ask the participants about their beliefs which will decide for them?

How anthropologists (or historians, or sociologists) should in general proceed with the study of ritual it was beyond the ambition of my paper to suggest. But Mr Hollis need not suppose that I and my two 'lackeys' (as he chooses to describe them) are making the mistake which he has in mind about the relation of institutions to beliefs. Smith and Jones need not, to get into the difficulties I recounted, be anthropologists of quite so coarse and philistine a kind as Mr Hollis suspects. They are, of course, admirers of Professor Evans-Pritchard, as are we all. But they don't (does Mr Hollis?) believe that their difficulties can be dismissed merely by saying, as Evans-Pritchard once did, that 'The facts will be the same without their labels' (*Witchcraft among the Azande*, p. 11). Indeed, this is one reason why they realise that the description of institutions poses the philosophical problems which it does.

9. 'Social' Equality*

Of the many inequalities between one person or group and another which are social in the sense opposed to individual, I am concerned in this paper only with those which are social in the sense opposed to economic or political (or, in other words, with inequalities of status as opposed to wealth or power). My purpose is to suggest that the sense in which men should treat each other as 'social' equals can be derived from the distinction between (as I shall use these terms) praise and respect, and that this in turn makes it possible to circumvent some of the familiar difficulties raised by what can loosely be called Kantian notions of equality between men as such.

It may sound odd to propose that the difficulties of a Kantian formulation can be circumvented by reference to the notion of respect, since it is precisely this notion, and the impossibility of a satisfactory definition of it, which bedevils Kant's doctrine about treating people as ends and not means. It is easy to see some sort of meaning in phrases of this kind. But as soon as closer definition is attempted, the idea of equal respect for the dignity of the individual (or however it is put) turns out to be as elusive as ever. The solution, however, does not lie in attempting yet another definition of respect. It lies in laying down initially that all inequalities of respect are illegitimate, and then stipulating that all inequalities of status are to be taken as inequalities of respect unless they can be shown to be inequalities of praise. The merit of this oblique approach is that inequalities of praise present much less formidable difficulties of diagnosis. The sense in which men should treat each other as 'social' equals can then be summarised in the maxim: free inequality of praise, no inequality of respect.

One way of both deriving the maxim and illustrating the nature of the distinction which it embodies is by reference to the contractual model of justice developed in a series of related papers by John Rawls.[1] The essence of Rawls's model is that rational men in a state of nature who are ignorant of what will be either their personal characteristics or their starting

* This paper was first published in the *Philosophical Quarterly*, XVII (1967). It is criticised by Norman S. Care, 'Runciman on Social Equality', *ibid.* XVIII (1967), 151–4, but see chapter 10, section III, below.
'Justice as Fairness', *Philosophical Review* LXVII (1958), pp. 164–94; 'The Sense of Justice', *ibid.* LXXII (1963), pp. 281–305; 'Constitutional Liberty and the Concept of Justice', *Nomos* VI (1963), pp. 98–125; 'Distributive Justice', in P. Laslett and W. G. Runciman, eds., *Philosophy, Politics and Society*, 3rd ser. (Oxford, 1967), pp. 58–82.

position in their eventual society are supposed to be required to agree on principles by reference to which they will both claim and concede their rights. If, accordingly, we picture them debating the principles according to which inequalities of status should in due course be regulated, it is evident that they will settle on principles which will admit some, but not all, inequalities of status as just. It might at first glance seem tempting to argue that they would want a strict egalitarianism of status; the implication of such phrases as 'equal before God' or 'equal as human beings' is, it might be said, that all men share some absolute, primordial equality of status which is subsequently perverted by the formation of vested interests. But this is just where such phrases are misleading. What objection would be advanced by rational men without vested interest to a system in which they would be free to bestow esteem upon others and be esteemed by them in turn, wherever they might turn out to be placed and whatever talents or attributes they might turn out to possess? And if such persons would have no objection to such a system, is not a strict egalitarianism of status not merely impracticable but unjust?

But at the same time, Rawls's model makes clear that some restrictions, at least, of inequality of status would have been agreed by the parties to a primordial contract. To elucidate the kind of inequality of status which they would certainly have wanted to disallow, it is easiest to start from an example. Let us suppose the parties to the contract to be considering the possibility of a society in which different people will have different colours of skin. This is a personal characteristic which, they will say, everyone must be free to admire or not as he chooses. There will be no social injustice involved if one man admires a white skin more than a black one. Even if such a sentiment is unanimous among those whose skins are white, this will still be no more of a social injustice than if they all admire blonde hair or athletic prowess or dialectical skill. But now suppose that the parties to the contract envisage a society of white supremacists and the mode of social relations which (quite apart from inequalities of wealth and power) obtains there. Having, as far as they know, an equal chance of turning out to have a skin of either colour themselves, they will hardly be disposed to accept that mode of social relations as just. And to establish that the inequalities of status in such a society are inequalities of respect rather than praise, it is enough merely to try to account for them in terms of praise. To say that white supremacists are *praising* each other for the colour of their skins is absurd; what they accord to each other, and deny to those with black skins, is equality of respect.

The white supremacist may, of course, reply that his attitude is directed not towards black or white skins as such but towards those attributes with which he has observed a black skin to correlate and which justify him in refusing to treat those with black skins as his social equals. To take another example, Aristotle's unwillingness to accord equal status to women might be defended by the same sort of argument. His denial that women are fully eligible for friendship with men rested on a sincere conviction of the impossibility that any woman should possess those admirable qualities of intellect and temperament which were, for him, a necessary condition of friendship.[1] In the society in which this view was widely held, would not the resulting inequality of status between men and women be defensible as an inequality of praise? The answer to this objection, however, is easy enough. For if the unequal treatment meted out to Negroes, or to women, is defended on the grounds of such a correlation, then the supremacist must abandon his argument the moment that the correlation is shown not to hold. And once he concedes that he would refuse to admit even gifted and cultivated Negroes, or women, to an equality with himself, then he is once again exposed as having an attitude to colour or sex which cannot be plausibly defended in terms of praise.

There remains, however, a more serious difficulty. The example of colour may serve as a useful illustration of the distinction between praise and respect, given the absurdity of speaking of white supremacists as praising each other on account of their skins. But many social inequalities are based on attributes which can much more plausibly be regarded as meriting either praise or blame. Suppose, indeed, that it were in fact the case that all women were less gifted than men, or all Negroes less intelligent than Whites. This would surely not acquit those who practised social discrimination against them; but to establish that it did not, it would have to be shown that the attitude to lack of talent which engendered this discrimination was not merely dispraise but disrespect; and this is by no means as easy. It is seldom that the nature of the attribute which gives rise to an unequal apportionment of status is enough to expose such an inequality as a violation of respect. It is rather the treatment itself which needs to be diagnosed as the manifestation of an inequality of either respect or praise. A 'social' inequality—that is, any pattern of rule-governed behaviour whereby a group or class is visibly accorded either higher or lower esteem by the other members of a social system—finds

---

[1] Further, there is on Aristotle's view no denial of justice in unequal relations between men and women because both benefit in proportion to the merits which they bring to the relationship (*Eth. Nic.* 1161a).

expression in actions which are either, on the one hand, noticeably flattering or deferential or approbatory or obsequious or, on the other hand, noticeably disparaging or deprecatory or insulting or humiliating. What is the test which will show whether such behaviour is the expression of praise and dispraise, or respect and disrespect?

There is, to begin with, a logical difference between respect and praise. In the language of games theory, praise is a zero-sum concept. Respect, whatever it means, is not. Where two people are accorded unequal praise, it is (logically) impossible to accord more or less praise to one without thereby increasing or diminishing the praise accorded to the other. Universal equality of praise is equivalent to no praise at all; but where one person is accorded respect and another is not, it need not constitute a disrespect of the one if the other is subsequently accorded equal treatment.

It might be objected at this point that although praise is in some sense a relative concept, it is not in fact a zero-sum concept any more than, for example, height. Praising, it might be said, is like assigning a score on a standard test: if A scores 8 out of 10 for excellence, then this will not be altered by the fact that B also scores 8. On this view, to accord equal praise to A and B is like saying that A and B are both six feet tall—the excellence attributed to the one is not at the expense of the excellence attributed to the other. But is praising like that? Praising is, as I shall maintain, importantly related to scoring; but the whole point of praising is surely that it is not like saying 'A is six foot six' but 'A is tall'. And if everyone is six foot six, nobody is tall (or short either). An inequality of praise can be *represented* as an interval between scores on a scale; but this is not the same thing.

The alternative approach to the distinction between praise and respect is by way of the forms of behaviour in which praise is expressed. These will, of course, be culturally conditioned. But in our own culture, at least, to clap or cheer is to express praise; whereas to bow or kneel is (in the absence of special explanation) to express respect. This is not a hard and fast rule, for a bow (if not a genuflection) is sometimes as neutral an expression of courtesy as a nod or a handshake. But once a bow appears to be symbolic of an inequality of esteem, then there is at once a provisional suspicion of inequality of respect. An anthropologist who is investigating any such apparent inequalities of status will have to make sure that information is not being withheld from him, that the behaviour in question is not random or in jest, and that he has grasped the meaning to the members of the society under study of their language, rituals and customs. But he will thereafter be in a position to sift out at least some inequalities of praise and respect by observing the forms of behaviour in which inequalities of status are in fact regulated and expressed.

Even with the clues furnished by fieldwork, however, many inequalities of status may remain ambiguous. The experienced anthropologist may be able without too much difficulty to isolate behaviour symbolic of differential esteem.[1] But there will be few cases where the form of behaviour will by itself be sufficient to make clear whether this inequality should properly be classified as inequality of praise or of respect—as few, perhaps, as where the nature of the attribute in question can by itself supply the answer. Suppose, for example, that an anthropologist discovers a society in which the strong habitually behave in an insulting manner towards the weak. Let us assume that he has established that the one-sided pattern of insults is not random or in jest,[2] and that he has discarded the hypothesis that everyone in this society despises everyone else, but only the strong dare express their contempt for the weak. He is still faced with a choice of interpretations of these insults. How is he to categorise them as expressions of dispraise or disrespect?

At this point, it is rewarding to go back to the logical difference between the two. If the strong, in this society, are only dispraising the weak (and the social inequality between strong and weak is therefore a just one), they must be doing no more than ranking them by comparison with others on some (at least ordinally) measurable attribute. They must, as it were, be assigning them a score. They must not be in any sense further degrading them on account of the score which they give. If, therefore, the strong sincerely disapprove of physical weakness, and are insulting the weak from the same sort of motive as inspires a theatre audience to boo an actor whose performance they think inadequate, there is no violation of social justice. The strong are merely assigning to the weak an unflattering strength-rating. But if the behaviour of the strong to the weak humiliates or dishonours them in some additional respect, or if the strong abuse or vilify

---

[1] This can, however, itself be argued by reference to some wider social theory. Hobbes, for example, says in chapter 10 of *Leviathan* that 'The manifestation of the Value we set on one another, is that which is commonly called Honouring, and Dishonouring. To value a man at a high rate is to *Honour* him; at a low rate, is to *Dishonour* him'. But because of his preoccupation with inequalities of power, Hobbes's list of the acts by which honour and dishonour are expressed includes several which not everyone would accept: for example, to pity someone is, according to Hobbes, to 'dishonour' him, while to be either loved or feared by others is 'honourable' because these are 'arguments of Power'.

[2] This too may sometimes remain arguable, since in many cultures there are games and contests in which the boundary between play and a serious dispute over status is very difficult to define—for example, *'joutes de jactance'* and slanging-matches (on which see J. Huizinga, *Homo Ludens* [English edn.; London, 1955], pp. 65 ff.).

or disparage the weak in a manner which goes beyond that in which they would express dispraise of each other with regard to some other attribute than strength, then there is at once strong *prima facie* evidence of an inequality of respect.

Now it may seem too large a concession to allow *all* expressions of praise to be legitimate: what, for example, are we to say if dispraise of the weak by the strong is expressed not merely by words but by physical violence? Assault is not, it may be argued, easy to construe as no more than the expression of an unflattering strength-rating. But there could very well be a society in which physical violence was the mere equivalent of a catcall or a boo—where, in fact, the audience had to be requested not to shoot the pianist. So radical an expression of dispraise might be thought reprehensible on a number of other grounds; and if it were to have the sanction of the law, or if the murder of pianists were to be regarded *more* lightly than the murder of any other sort of person, then there would indeed be a social injustice at issue. But the misuse of superior strength is not of itself a violation of respect. (Consider, as a further example, the duellist who challenges only his peers.) No unjust social inequality need be implied in the murder of a bad pianist. There may be an *individual* injustice, if the murdered pianist played no worse than another who was merely booed on the previous night. But this still would not turn an expression of dispraise into an expression of disrespect.

A different objection might be that the notion of praise is not too strong, but too weak. It is generally agreed among writers on justice that the essence of justice, whether individual or social, lies in treating like cases alike, or in other words in not treating people differently except where there is some demonstrable, relevant difference between them.[1] Surely, it could be said, the notion of inequality of status covers more than can be brought within the ambit of praise or dispraise? How can the notion of praise help to show whether the differences on which unequal status is based are relevant ones? Are not some of the inequalities which most clearly constitute a violation of respect[2]—for example, slavery—inequalities to which the notion of praise is not so much inappropriate as irrelevant?

This sort of objection, however, is likely to rest on a confusion of inequalities of status with inequalities of power. Inequalities of status may

---

[1] The procedural injunction to treat like cases alike is of course distinct from, and logically prior to, the 'shifting and varying criterion used in determining when, for any given purpose, cases are alike or different' (H. L. A. Hart, *The Concept of Law* (Oxford, 1961), p. 156).

[2] There may, of course, be violations of respect, however respect is defined, at a purely individual level—say, in a sado-masochistic relationship between two social equals.

both overlap with and derive from inequalities of power; but the justice of the one is independent of the justice of the other. Whether an inequality of power is just depends on whether the subordination of those who take orders to those who give them is such that rational men without vested interest could have assented to it in principle before knowing whether they would turn out to be the givers or the takers of orders. This does not determine one way or the other whether an inequality of status deriving from this system of authority is just. It is true that the stability of a system of authority may depend on whether those in power are sufficiently esteemed by those beneath them for them to be able to secure their obedience without coercion. It is also true that 'respect' can be used in contexts where it is virtually synonymous with obedience, as in the injunction that officers should have the 'respect' of their men, or that children should 'respect' their parents. But it does not follow either that (*pace* Hobbes) obedience entails esteem, or that where esteem is a concomitant of obedience it should for that reason be classified either as praise or as respect. Thus slavery does often denote a violation of respect, since it often brings about unjust inequalities of status as well as of power. But there might be a society where it didn't. In a society where the accepted penalty for losing in some recognised kinds of contest or dispute was that the loser should become the slave of the winner, slaves might not suffer any more loss of esteem than the disesteem attached to losers' lack of skill. To be sure, the inequality of power between masters and slaves is not one which would commend itself to men in a state of nature who did not yet know their eventual positions in society and were debating what inequalities of power should in due course be permitted as just; but its relation to inequality of esteem is a contingent one.

The notion of praise serves also to bring out what is important in the connection sometimes drawn between the notion of social equality and the notion of role. It is sometimes said that equality requires not that all men should be classified alike, but that they should not be differently valued by reference to their roles, titles or positions as distinct from their persons. This sort of injunction is apt to lead to difficulties similar to those involved in any Kantian doctrine of equality between men as men, or as moral beings. But it can be made more useful and precise if it is linked to the maxim: free inequality of praise, no inequality of respect. For if esteem (or disesteem) is accorded to a man in virtue of his occupancy of some particular role, title or position, it will be impossible plausibly to categorise this as praise or disprise except where the role, title or position is direct evidence of a high (or low) score on a definable attribute to which esteem is attached by some or all of his fellow-citizens. Nobody claims to praise the occupant of a role for no other reason than that he occupies it.[1] Someone might, for example, accord praise to all the generals in his society because they are all good generals (this is the sort of example usually cited to illustrate Kantian injunctions about seeing men from a human rather than an institutional point of view); or because, in the praiser's view, nobody can rise to be a general without exceptional gifts of character or intelligence; or because the generals have, as a body, performed some one or more praiseworthy acts. But the moment that the generals are accorded esteem, as evidenced in the behaviour of others towards them, which cannot be classified as the collective expression of praise, then there is an equality of respect and (by definition) a social injustice.

Consider three hypothetical societies: first, a society in which soldiers, and only soldiers, are awarded medals; second, a society in which soldiers, and only soldiers, are accorded honorific titles by which they are habitually addressed; third, a society in which civilians never initiate conversations with soldiers, but only soldiers with civilians. In the first society, the inequality of status between medallists and non-medallists is at once defensible as an inequality of praise. The award of medals symbolises a high rating on whatever attributes (in this case, military attributes) the society or institution awarding the medal thinks praiseworthy. There is no social injustice in the implied disparagement of the non-military, any more than the award of medals to Olympic runners is a social injustice to those who cannot run so fast. Furthermore, the inequality is zero-sum: the esteem which a medal bestows is in inverse proportion to the number of people awarded it. The inequality between medallists and non-medallists could only be described as an inequality of 'respect' where 'respect' was being used as a synonym for praise—as when, for example, to avow 'respect' for a person's intelligence is synonymous with praising him for being intelligent.

In the second society, the status apparently accorded to soldiers is on the borderline. If the bestowal of a title upon selected soldiers can be argued to be equivalent to the award of a medal (or a citation, or a public eulogy), then it is no more than the expression of praise. But if *all* soldiers are so addressed, or if the title carries further privileges of status (if, say, it is hereditary), then to describe the esteem attaching to it as praise becomes proportionately less plausible. The award of such titles might, of course,

Although there are, of course, people who deceive themselves into thinking that they value dukes for their wit and not their dukedoms: as Proust says, this is precisely what snobbery consists in.

be defended on the grounds that they are a *reward*. Are they not, it might be said, equivalent to a land grant or a cash donation, by which the services rendered by soldiers to the state can be recompensed? And surely there is no social injustice in these? But although the element of reward may explain such privileges, it does not thereby justify them. From whatever motives a government offers privileges to its veterans, this will not by itself have anything to do with whether those privileges are socially just. It is no defence of the justice of slavery to say that the slaveholders were all promised the privileges of slaveholding as a recompense for their services to the state. And where the privileges offered in recompense are privileges of status as distinct from (or as a separate concomitant of) privileges of wealth or power, the implausibility of describing them as the bestowal of praise is the measure of their injustice as an inequality of status.

Where, finally, civilians never speak to soldiers unless spoken to, there is evidence of an inequality of status which could not be described in terms of praise and dispraise without extreme implausibility;[1] and this inequality is not strictly zero-sum. True, if civilians began to violate the convention, this might be taken by the soldiery as a sign that their status was no longer what it used to be. But there is no necessary connection between the status enjoyed by the soldiery and their conversational exclusiveness; whereas a society which awarded no medals to soldiers which it did not also award to civilians could scarcely be claimed to be putting any higher value on soldierly than non-soldierly virtues.

There remain two categories of example where there appears to be, but isn't, an inequality of status which is legitimate without being an inequality of praise. The first is where behaviour of an ostensibly deferential kind is motivated by a difference between persons which is not, or at any rate not necessarily, a social inequality. An example is the deference accorded in many societies to the old. Sometimes, this may turn out to be an expression of praise, as where the old are credited (rightly or wrongly) with superior wisdom or even magical powers; in such societies, admiration for the old could well find expression in, say, asking them to speak first in council, or cheering their public appearances, without any overtones of unequal respect. Conversely, there may be gerontocratic societies where the deference accorded to the old is indeed an illegitimate inequality of respect. But there may also be societies where 'deference' to the old is not

[1] One could, of course, construct an example: in a society in which philosophers were extravagantly admired and were assumed to be unstintingly devoted to philosophy, non-philosophers might hesitate to address them through unwillingness to break into their (praiseworthy) reveries. But this is just what one means by 'special explanation'.

in fact a symptom of any social inequality at all. To bring an old person his food, or to come to him whenever summoned, or to give way to him in the street might all appear to be 'deferential' acts. But they could well signify nothing beyond the awareness that physical infirmity entitles those handicapped by it to such services as they cannot perform for themselves and such special treatment as naturally follows from a recognition of physical needs. A charitable and kindly society where such behaviour was strongly entrenched by custom might deceive the visiting anthropologist into thinking that he had disclosed an inequality of respect. But he would be making a mistake if he were to deduce an (unjust) social inequality from behaviour which was deferential only in this special sense.

The second kind of example is where inequalities of status are purely matters of protocol. Where, for example, there is an established order of precedence such that diplomatic representatives are seated at receptions in order of the seniority of their delegations, there may seem to be a legitimate inequality of status which has nothing to do with praise. But such differential treatment is an inequality of status only in the most formal sense; and as such, it need only conform to the canons of purely *procedural* justice. Where some order of preference is desirable, but it doesn't matter what it is, any convention which will conveniently cover all contingencies could be readily agreed by the parties to a contract made before vested interests had been formed. Where protocol only is at issue, even a random order would be just (however undesirable on the grounds of practical convenience). Indeed, the test of whether such orders of precedence *are* purely matters of protocol is whether they could, in principle, have been left to chance by men without vested interest having to decide what inequalities of status they would permit in advance of knowing their own positions.

Inequalities of social esteem are, therefore, only just if they can be plausibly interpreted as inequalities of praise. But if this is so, why have political and moral philosophers given so much importance to the notion of respect? Perhaps the best answer is to say that it has seemed to them to entail the notion of *valuing* and the notion of valuing has seemed to entail an obligation to behave in some specifiable way towards other people. They have accordingly tried to extract from the principle of formal justice at least one principle of substantive justice: if it is a rule that like cases are to be treated alike, then human beings must be treated as human beings; and to treat people as human beings must mean at the very least acting towards them in a way which manifests some sort of positive regard for them. The force of the injunction about respect is, however, better interpreted in a negative (but not therefore vacuous) sense. It means that we should not, where collective inequalities of status are at issue, permit a system which would not be defensible by appeal to principles which could have been settled in the state of nature by rational men who were as yet ignorant of what their own tastes or situations would be. Such men would have agreed that any inequality of status would be legitimate if it could be shown to be an inequality of praise. They would also have agreed that no matter how strongly they might come to disapprove of a class of their fellow-citizens on either aesthetic or moral grounds, they would have no warrant for complaining that it was socially unjust that other people should admire them, even if such admiration was degenerate, or perverse, or tended to corrupt the young, or any number of undesirable things. But they would not sanction any behaviour symbolic of collective esteem or disesteem which was not of a kind defensible as praise.

Now it is perfectly possible that in a society whose system of status was just, and in which all 'social' inequalities (which might be very wide) were therefore defensible as inequalities of praise, much discontent would be engendered. Such a society might be less stable, less efficient, or even less happy than one in which many differences of status were preserved which could only be classified as inequalities of respect. But this is another question. There can always be good reason for saying than an unjust society is preferable to a just one. But a society in which all inequalities of prestige or esteem were inequalities of praise would to this extent be just; and this aspect of social justice is what all the phrases about human dignity, equality before God, and equality as moral beings are in their different ways trying to express.

10. 'False Consciousness'*

It may be as well to begin from the *locus classicus*, Engels to Mehring, 14 July 1893: 'Ideology is a process accomplished by the so-called thinker consciously, it is true, but with a false consciousness. The real motive forces impelling him remain unknown to him; otherwise it simply would not be an ideological process.'

In this paper, I shall first of all argue in defence of what I take to be Engels's view. I shall then suggest how it may have a useful bearing on the problem of social choice.

I

It will hardly be disputed that Engels's sort of language has fallen into general discredit; and it is not difficult to see why. Psychology has made some progress, at least, since Engels's day, and 'ideological processes' and 'real motive forces' are not the sort of terms to be found in the technical vocabularies of the more prominent contemporary theorists. But perhaps it is only a question of phrasing Engels's notion a little more carefully. It would, of course, be possible to give 'false consciousness' a respectable, not to say innocuous, meaning by equating it with a simple deviation from majority opinion, or sentiments expressed under duress, or impressions mistakenly derived from an unreliable source. But it is not one of these that I take Engels to have had in mind. The sense which Engels gave to it, and which to my mind it retains, derives from a distinction between those sincerely held attitudes or beliefs which are, and those which are not, related in a causal sense to the social situation and thereby to the interests of the believer.

Now such a relation between interests and attitudes or beliefs may be of two kinds. A person may, on the one hand, hold views which would be different if his interests were not what they are; or he may, on the other hand, *not* hold views which he *would* hold if only he *knew* what his interests are. It is one thing to be blinded *by* one's interests; it is another thing to be blind *to* them. 'False consciousness' is often used to stand for the second of these, as, for example, when a blindness to their 'true' interests is attributed to proletarians who fail to see the impending collapse of capitalism as Marxists see it. But blindness to one's interests is, in effect, merely ignorance of the facts of the case; or if the facts are in dispute, then

*This paper was first published in *Philosophy* (1969).

we are back with the first sense—the view which a person takes of the future of capitalism may, like anyone else's views, be influenced by Engels's 'real motive forces', and it may accordingly be these forces which induce him to put his allegedly mistaken short-term interest in accommodating to capitalism over his allegedly demonstrable long-term interest in demolishing it. For the purposes of this paper, this well-known example is simply one of many variants of the question: how far, and in what sense, can a person's attitudes or beliefs be causally explained by his circumstances?

There are a number of objections which are likely to be raised by the attempt to talk of causal connections in this context. Beliefs, some one will say, are not the product of interests or anything else in Engels's sense; and although there may be some *logical* connection between some of a person's attitudes or beliefs and his interests—a point to which I shall have to return in a moment—it would be a gross philosophical error to treat this as though it were a relationship of a so-called Humean kind, or to talk like John Stuart Mill about the same causes which make a man a Churchman in London making him a Buddhist or Confucian in Pekin.[1]

A whole gamut of interconnected controversies might be allowed to obtrude here on which there seems to be no general agreement among philosophers. But it is not, fortunately, necessary before proceeding further to resolve what we mean by mental acts, whether beliefs can ever be the outcome of decisions, how motives relate to dispositions, or in what contexts the term 'reason' is properly interchangeable with the term 'cause'. It is quite possible to accept a logical connection between one belief and another and still to ask how the first belief in the chain came to be accorded credence and by persons of what kinds and circumstances it continues to be held. Whether or not the reasons which I give for either my actions or my beliefs can properly be labelled causes, it is still quite proper for someone to ask: what has caused me to act or to believe as I do for the reason I have given? It is true that some questions of this kind may appear trivial and even foolish: it is not an interesting question to ask the cause of my belief that the square of the sum of two numbers is the sum of their squares plus the double of their product, since there is not an interesting class of contrasted cases such as is presupposed by a request for the cause. But it still does not follow that it is illegitimate to ask under what necessary or sufficient conditions we can reliably predict that a belief of this kind will be held; in a different academic context, it

[1] *On Liberty*, ch. II.

might be a question of serious scientific interest what minimum age in the human child is a necessary condition of it.

For the purposes of this paper, therefore, the antithesis between reasons and causes can be effectively dissolved. Where reasons *are* causes, there is no difficulty anyway; where they are not, they are simply to be elided into the beliefs. The seeker after causes will (quite properly) replace the question 'what are the reasons for this belief?' with the question 'what are the causes of the acceptance of these reasons by those who do accept them?'. The fact that 'why do you believe X?' is often satisfactorily answered without mention of causes doesn't mean that there aren't any. It merely shows that reference to causes is likely to be inappropriate if it is the *justification* of a belief which is being asked for. It is true that we do not yet have the psychological laws which are somewhere presupposed by references to the various causes of various beliefs, and Engels himself hardly helped us to discover them. But this is a matter of doing more thorough and sophisticated research into the subject than Engels did.

A second, and different, objection which might be made is that a statement purporting to link a man's interests to his beliefs is necessarily incapable of validation. How, someone might want to ask, can empirical research ever demonstrate that if a man's circumstances and therefore interests were not what they are, he would not hold the views which he does? This objection, like the first raises a number of unresolved philosophical (or in this case logical) controversies. But again, for the purposes of this paper it is necessary only to observe that it is enough that statements of this kind should be no more vulnerable than statements of similar form in the established sciences. The problem of counterfactual conditionals has not inhibited the discovery of well-tested causal generalisations in other fields, and it is not on these grounds, therefore, that Engels or his successors should be deterred from the attempt to arrive at causal generalisations linking interests to attitudes and beliefs. It has, no doubt, to be conceded that in idiographic explanations of the kind commonly put forward by writers of history the reliance to be placed on counterfactual conditionals is relatively weak. We are on much safer ground with 'If the length of the pendulum had been shortened by three-quarters, its period would have been halved' than we are with 'If Napoleon had trusted the intelligence which his spies reported to him on the eve of the battle, he would again have become master of Europe'. But this is to do with the state of our knowledge, not with the logic of explanation. We may not be able to state the laws in question, any more than Old Mother Hubbard, who knows quite well that the pot will boil if left on the fire, may be able to formulate the appropriate generalisations about temperature and atmospheric pressure. But our inability to say precisely and over a wide area how men's interests will affect their attitudes and beliefs has nothing to do with the logical problems raised by a comparison of 'butter melts at n degrees' with 'all the coins in my pocket are silver'.

A third possible objection might be derived from the notion of the person. It is all very well (someone might argue) to say that my attitudes and beliefs are a function of my social and personal attributes. But there will come a point at which it is misleading and even meaningless to claim that I am still, so to speak, I. There may be no impropriety in such a hypothesis as that 'The Minister would not now be taking the same view of the need for a wage-freeze if he were still in Opposition'. But if taken too far, will not such conjectures lead to fancies like those of the nineteenth-century ethnographers which Professor Evans-Pritchard has effectively ridiculed as deriving from 'psychological suppositions of the "if I were a horse" sort'?[1] There is, however, a simple and adequate distinction which can be made between the first and the second. George Orwell asks somewhere, 'What do you have in common with yourself as a child?', and answers, 'Nothing, except that you are the same person'. And so you are, *whatever* has happened to you between now and then. It is admittedly possible that even a modest change in your circumstances would have transformed out of recognition your subsequent actions, characteristics, attitudes and beliefs; indeed, on Engels's view of the matter this is undoubtedly the case. But it would be odd to say that you would then have become a different person in any sense beyond the conversational hyperbole whereby this phrase is used to stand for a particularly profound or drastic transformation. The error which Evans-Pritchard is concerned to discredit springs from a failure to recognise that hypotheses of this kind must rest on a specified prior state of the person (or the organism or, more generally still, the system). To put it into quasi-scientific terms, there must be stated values of the state coordinates of the system in question at t_1 as well as t_2. Once this condition is satisfied, the empirical credentials of a hypothesis linking characteristics at t_2 with characteristics at t_1 are guaranteed. The difficulties to which it gives rise are not those of formulation but those of adequate experimental or statistical test.

[1] E. E. Evans-Pritchard, *Theories of Primitive Religion* (Oxford, 1965), p. 108.

II

But what is meant by interests? It may be conceded that some antecedents of beliefs may be properly regarded as causes and yet disputed that interests can function as such causes in the sense that a vindication of Engels's language will require. There are two possible sources of difficulty. First, might not the notion of having an interest be logically tied to the notion of having the relevant attitudes or beliefs, rather in the way that for some philosophers, at least, the notion of having an intention is tied to the performance of the relevant action? Second, even if the logical independence of interests from beliefs can be satisfactorily established, can they effectively be distinguished not merely from wants, but from tastes, pleasures, opportunities or even claims?

The first question is the easier to dispose of. It appears to pose a difficulty not because the notion of interest is in fact logically tied to the relevant belief, but because the notion of *dis*interest is often so used as to follow from the *absence* of certain beliefs. What, in practice, leads us to feel confident that a man is disinterested? Usually, that he doesn't express a view which, if he did, would lead one to suspect him of bias. But to take such an argument seriously merely raises the spectre of circularity which haunts every theory purporting to rest on the 'ideal observer' or the 'impartial spectator'. It may be tempting to assert in one breath that Solomon is shown to be disinterested by the verdict which he gave and that the verdict was obviously correct because Solomon was so clearly disinterested. But you cannot establish the disinterestedness of a verdict, or an attitude, or a belief by deduction from its content, or vice versa. Only when interest is so defined that it is possible for a man not to want his interests will the answer to the question whether his interests do influence his views be something to be demonstrated and not assumed. (Dr Johnson: 'We are all more or less governed by interest. But interest will not make us do every thing.')

To answer the second and more difficult question, therefore, I have to make much clearer what it is that should be meant by 'having an interest'. It is not enough to say merely that something can be in a person's interest whether he wants it or not. It has also to be shown just how we are to decide whether it *is* in his interest; and there are several things besides wants from which interests need effectively to be distinguished. First, a man's interests are not his 'real will' in the idealists' sense; this suggestion would not only revive the notorious difficulties of the idealist position but also recreate with 'ideal' wants the difficulties which already arise over actual ones. Second, a man's interests are not his putative pleasures; something can be in his interests without his enjoying, or even expecting to enjoy, it just as much as without his wanting to have it. Third, a man's interests are not such claims as would, if he were to make them, be legitimate; there is nothing contradictory in saying that something is in his interests which it would be unjustifiable for him to claim.[1] Fourth, a man's interests are not his opportunities to get what he wants; this still leaves the matter to be decided by reference to what he *does* want (and if we amend 'what he wants' to 'what he *might* want' the move will be self-defeating: he might want anything whatever). None of these answers is adequate, because they all underemphasise the most important distinction implicit in the notion of having 'interests' at all—the distinction between advantages on one side, and wants (and with them tastes) on the other.

It might be said that one aspect of this distinction is already brought out by the suggestion that the furtherance of a man's interests requires the maximisation of his opportunities as opposed to his gratifications (or, to borrow Hobbes's definition of 'powers', his 'present means to obtain some future apparent Good').[2] But the connection with wants must be severed altogether. A 'future apparent Good' is still too close to a presently recognised want, even if for something not immediately attainable. If we are to achieve the necessary severance, we shall do better to borrow not from Hobbes himself but from Pareto—a latter-day Hobbesian in whose writings accusations of false consciousness are as frequent as in those of Engels, although not by this name. Pareto is not, unfortunately, anything like as clear in his discussion of 'interest' as one would wish. But what he appears to have in mind is a maximisation of opportunities in a fairly specific sense—the maximisation of a person's wealth, or power, or (in his own words) 'consideration and honours', to whose acquisition, he says, individuals and communities are likewise 'spurred by instinct and reason'.[3]

It is true that this familiar sociological trinity raises serious difficulties of definition in its turn.[4] 'Power', in particular, can be so broadly used as to become indistinguishable from opportunity in general, and it will be

---

[1] I owe this (to me) rather odd interpretation of 'interest', and also the objection against it, to Brian Barry, *Political Argument* (London, 1965), p. 175, where it is attributed to S. I. Benn and John Plamenatz. Barry's own definition is the one I list fourth, with the qualification that wants on behalf of others must be excluded.

[2] *Leviathan*, ch. x.

[3] See the *General Treatise of Sociology* (tr. Henderson as *The Mind and Society*), para. 2009, and Talcott Parsons, *The Structure of Social Action* (New York, 1937), pp. 263, 298.

[4] See chapter 4, above.

no advance to substitute for 'opportunities' 'opportunities to maximise opportunities'. But however difficult it is to offer a wholly satisfactory definition, what I take to be meant by the attribution of more power to A than to B is that A can determine the actions of more people against stiffer resistance on their part than can B. Thus it is possible in principle to rank the members of a community in order of power, just as it is possible in principle to rank them in order of prestige (by a scale of social distance) and of wealth (by expressing their net resources and income in cash terms). To say, therefore, that something is in a man's interest is to say that it will result in an improvement in his position with respect to one or more of these three; and this is a matter which will be established by qualified observers quite independently of his wants and tastes and of how he may happen to choose to employ such wealth, power and social prestige as he has already.

Now it is a matter of common observation that people do, in general, want to augment their wealth, power and social prestige; and it is also a matter of common observation that their desire for their interests sometimes influences their beliefs although they are either unable or unwilling to acknowledge it. We are all sufficiently familiar with such situations in both public and private life for it to be unnecessary to offer examples. It may, however, be useful to offer an example to illustrate how a man's interests are conceptually distinct from his attitudes and beliefs in a way that his wants and tastes are not. Contrast (1) 'You are a supporter of Communism because you are temperamentally hostile to individual freedom' with (2) 'You are a supporter of Communism because you believe that a Communist government would effect a redistribution of wealth in favour of such people as yourself'. (1) is a matter of taste, (2) of interest, and where the first is not an empirical matter, the second is. If we may suppose, for the purposes of this rather crude example, that a central tenet of Communist doctrine is that as many as possible of the individual citizen's actions should be under the control of the State, it would be a contradiction to say without qualification 'I am temperamentally hostile to individual freedom but I am not a supporter of Communism'. It would not be a contradiction to say without qualification 'I am aware that I would benefit from the redistributive policies of a Communist government but I am not a supporter of Communism'. To link a person's preference for an authoritarian party to his dislike of individual liberty is not to advance a hypothesis of cause and effect; to link his interest in redistribution of wealth to his support for a party pledged to redistribution is.

This line of argument can, of course, be extended from examples of this kind both more broadly into the sociology of knowledge and more deeply into individual psychology. More broadly, the assertion that beliefs are the product of circumstances (or, as Marx himself put it, 'social being determines consciousness') can generate ambitious generalisations about the content of the religious and political ideologies of different social strata. More deeply, the assertion that a person may be unaware of the influences acting on his attitudes and beliefs can generate elaborate psychoanalytic conjectures about the unconscious. These, however, lie well beyond the scope of this paper. I have merely been concerned to vindicate the view that there can be a causal connection between interests (as I have defined them) on the one hand and attitudes and beliefs on the other, and to suggest that this gives a useful and legitimate sense to the 'real motive forces' of Engels's phrase.

III

If I am right in this, then the importance of interests in the explanation of attitudes and behaviour is a straightforward matter for sociological and psychological research, and an ostensibly philosophical paper such as this one becomes redundant. But what are the implications of this for the problem of social choice? As is well known, the problem of social choice arises because the aggregation of individual choices can be satisfactorily effected only when there is one policy alternative which will make every individual better off than at present. An impasse is reached as soon as either (1) some people can be made better off only by making others worse off, or (2) there is a choice of policies all of which will benefit an equal number, but of different people, or (3) one policy will make everyone considerably better off, whereas another will make some people a little, but others very much better off. The only way out of the impasse is to invoke the fiction of the social contract, according to which the members of society have all agreed in advance what principles are to govern the decisions of social policy with which they will be faced once society has been brought into being. In other words, we must go behind the formation of vested interests to what is called by Professors Buchanan and Tullock 'the stage of constitutional choice'[1] and by Professor Rawls 'the original position'.[2] Once the members of society *have* interests—and they

---

[1] James M. Buchanan and Gordon Tullock, *The Calculus of Consent* (Ann Arbor, 1962), pt. II.

[2] John Rawls, 'Distributive Justice', in P. Laslett and W. G. Runciman, eds., *Philosophy, Politics and Society*, III (Oxford, 1967), 58–82. (This paper is one of several which develops a contractarian theory of justice first put forward in 'Justice as Fairness', *Philosophical Review* LXVII (1958), pp. 164–94).

cannot but have them from the moment that society is formed—they cannot be expected to agree on principles by which conflicts between these interests are to be resolved. But if we suppose that such principles had had to be established before anybody could know what their interests might be, then agreement is altogether less implausible.

A device of this kind can, it will be clear, be employed in a purely *a priori* fashion. If we ask what criteria for collective decisions would have been adopted by rational men at some hypothetical time of constitutional choice, the question can be answered by simply eliciting the covert implications of 'rational'; and we shall again be confronted by the spectre of circularity which I earlier described as haunting all theories of the ideal observer. But why should the supposition not be framed in a deliberately empirical manner? If my earlier remarks are correct, it may be useful to approach the problem of social choice not by asking what principles it would be 'rational' to select in advance of the formation of interests, but what principles would *in fact* have been selected by persons 'rational' in a very much weaker sense who found themselves in such a situation.

The objection which this is likely to raise is not that rules for collective decision-making are never selected in advance of the formation of interests, since games, ballots, markets, courts of arbitration, or protection and indemnity associations can all be defined and regulated (and often are) by rules agreed among the initial participants before they can yet know how far they will stand to gain or lose by these rules. The difficulty is that where the rules of society itself are in question, the notion of the 'original position' appears to require that those supposed to be deciding on constitutional principles should not merely be without particular interests in any particular market, ballot, etc., but should be without any interests whatever that would enable them to see what sort of rules would work out in their favour. And this means that they must, in effect, be persons without attributes. For how, after all, could someone conceivably be put in a situation where it was not evident that *some* social arrangements could be made that would be more likely than others to augment his power, wealth or social prestige?

This point is, indeed, urged by a recent critic of Rawls, who argues that agreement would not be reached in the original position precisely because 'it would be reasonably well known to each person what his talents and abilities were relative to his fellow-citizens'.[1] But it is not at all as decisive a

---

[1] R. P. Wolff, 'A Refutation of Rawls's Theorem of Justice', *Journal of Philosophy*, XIII (1966), 188. The same argument is put by Norman S. Care, 'Runciman on Social Equality', *Philosophical Quarterly*, XVIII (1968), 151–4.

point as it seems. To evade it, it is not necessary to suppose the persons in the original position to be without attributes (which would admittedly make nonsense of the suggestion that the problem can be treated empirically). It is necessary only to suppose that they are *ignorant* of their attributes to the degree that their attributes give them a vested interest in one constitutional principle as against another. Once we suppose, as Rawls himself explicitly does, a 'veil of ignorance' which covers not only the future workings of the institutions on which they are to agree but also their own place in the distribution of natural abilities, this will be sufficient for the conditions of the 'original position' to be satisfied. They need not be wholly bereft of attributes. They need only be temporarily amnesiac: they may retain the use of their senses, the knowledge of their mother tongue, and an approximate familiarity with the range over which the mental and physical attributes of human beings can vary. They have, however, forgotten for the time being what their own tastes and talents are, and the veil is lifted only when they have agreed upon some constitutional principles or other and have thereby committed themselves without knowing about the interests which they will discover (when they remember their tastes and talents) that they have.

But to substitute ignorance of attributes for the absence of them still leaves the objection with some of its force, for the claim that the choices of these hypothetical amnesiacs are in principle susceptible of empirical investigation is plausible only at the cost of surrendering any serious prospect of acquiring the evidence in question. It is true that on some topics, at least, we may feel reasonably confident of the kind of agreement which they might reach. Difficult though it is, for example, to suppose that an experiment could be conducted in which the subjects were momentarily ignorant of the colour of their skins, it is plausible to suppose that if they *were* in this situation they would not settle on a principle which would permit automatic racial supremacy to be accorded to citizens of any one colour. But since psychologists are not (as far as I know) able to perform such physio-chemical manipulations as will render an experimental subject oblivious of his pigmentation, an argument purporting to show that he would as a matter of fact decide one thing and not another will have to be advanced without benefit of experimental grounds.

One possible source of experimental evidence does suggest itself if the constitutional choice is made vicarious—if, for example, prospective parents are required to decide on the rules by which the opportunities and rewards of their unborn children are to be regulated. Since they are wholly ignorant of what these children's attributes may be, they can have no known interests on their behalf; and thus if we suppose them to be deciding how educational facilities are to be apportioned within a community which they have decided to establish, we may safely predict that they will agree on some principle of equal access. But even here, it would be fanciful to suggest that we should be observing a decision taken in a state of 'true consciousness', for these parents would in practice be found to project from their knowledge of their own social circumstances to a guess about what their children's circumstances would be likely to be. What is more, they would be right, since there are reliable grounds for predicting many of the personal as well as social attributes of children from the acquired and genetic characteristics of their parents. Even this device, therefore, will not be enough to sever the subjects altogether from any known interest in the constitutional decision which they are to be required to take.

Even if, however, the decisive experimental conditions cannot be adequately satisfied, it does not follow that no purportedly empirical generalisations can be formulated. Amnesia aside, a man without any interests whatever is indeed a fiction. But a man without any *one* interest is not; and it is an entirely respectable scientific procedure to generalise from the aggregation and extrapolation of a sufficient number of partial examples to the 'pure' case. An argument of this kind may, of course, be a bad argument. Many arguments in the social sciences resting on the properties of 'ideal types' are bad arguments. But if they are good arguments—if, that is, they are properly supported by a well-tested theory— then they are as legitimate as the frictionless planes of classical mechanics. I do not know whether there will ever be such a well-tested theory as would enable us to extrapolate with confidence to the constitutional choices which would be made within specified limits by a hypothetical sample of men wholly without interests. But to answer this it would be necessary to anticipate the course which the programme of research implied by Engels's suggestion might take, once admitted how unlikely it is that we could settle the question at one blow. Our evidence for the causal effects of interests on attitudes and beliefs is, at the moment, exceedingly imprecise, and such effects are generally postulated *ad hoc* where the historian or the biographer finds them plausible. But it will hardly be questioned that there is an enormous amount of such evidence. We do not know precisely how the influence of interests operates. But we surely know that it *can* operate—that other things being equal, a person's attitudes and beliefs would, at least sometimes, be different if his interests were not what they are. Unless common observation is somehow proved totally erroneous in this, therefore, it cannot be other than an empirical matter how far a choice of constitutional principles would, and how far it would not, be determined by the influence of the desires of the persons in question to augment their wealth, power and prestige.

There is, to be sure, no reason to suppose that even within a common culture a representative sample of persons divorced from their interests would agree beyond a limited range of general principles and a small number of specific procedural arrangements. But the purpose of treating the question as an empirical one is precisely to try to discover how much the inability of already interested parties to agree on a constitution is as a matter of fact due to the influence of their interests on their attitudes and how much should be attributed to causes of another kind.[1]

Whether, once this has been ascertained, it is preferable that matters of social policy should be decided by reference to what would (or would not) have been agreed in an 'original position' is another matter. Those exercised with the problem of social choice would, I imagine, be likely to think so. But it is always open to someone to say that a choice of policy which passes this test better than another is not, even *ceteris paribus*, preferable to *him*.

---

[1] Cf. (apart from Dr Johnson) Mill, *System of Logic* VI, v, 4: 'It is a scientific proposition . . . that an interest on one side of a question tends to bias the judgement; not that it invariably does so'.

11. *Games, Justice and the General Will**

(WITH A. K. SEN)

In this paper, we argue that a useful sense may be given to the 'general will' and the 'common good' by reference to the theory of non-zero-sum non-cooperative games, and we suggest some possible implications of this for the notion of social justice.

I

We begin by looking at the two-person, non-zero-sum, non-cooperative game known as the 'prisoner's dilemma'.[1] Two persons are thought to be jointly guilty of a serious crime, but the evidence is not adequate to convict them at a trial. The district attorney tells the prisoners that he will take them separately and ask them whether they would like to confess, though of course they need not. If both of them confess, they will be prosecuted, but he will recommend a lighter sentence than is usual for such a crime, say six years of imprisonment rather than ten years. If neither confesses, the attorney will put them up only for a minor charge of illegally possessing a weapon, of which there is conclusive evidence, and they can expect to get two years each. If, however, one confesses and the other does not, the one who confesses receives lenient treatment for providing evidence to the state and gets only one year, and the one who does not receives the full punishment of ten years. From an egoistic point of view, the strategy of confession for either of the prisoners 'strictly dominates' over the strategy of non-confession, i.e. no matter what the other prisoner is assumed to do it is always better for this prisoner to confess. If, for example, this prisoner thinks that the other one is going to confess, then by confessing himself he gets only six years rather than the full ten years which he will receive if he does not confess. If, on the other hand, he assumes that the other prisoner will not confess, then by confessing he gets only one year

*This paper was first published in *Mind*, n.s. LXXIV (1965).
[1] First devised by A. W. Tucker, and discussed in R. Duncan Luce and Howard Raiffa, *Games and Decisions* (New York, 1957), pp. 94–102.

and by not confessing he gets two years. So no matter what this prisoner assumes about the other's behaviour, it is always in his interest to confess. The same, of course, holds for the other prisoner. Therefore, assuming egoism, both will confess and receive six years each, but if neither confessed, they would have received only two years each. So what seems rational from an individualistic point of view, i.e. each taking the other person's actions as given, produces a relatively worse overall result.

To clarify the picture for ready reference, we reproduce below in a summary form the consequence of alternative policies for the two prisoners. The rows represent prisoner 1's policies and the columns prisoner 2's policies. We can find the overall result by looking at the item that belongs to the appropriate row and the appropriate column. The first figure within each pair of brackets represents the consequences for prisoner 1 and the second those for prisoner 2, e.g. (10, 1) represents ten years for the first and one year for the second.

Prisoner 2

		Not confess	Confess
Prisoner 1	Not Confess	(2, 2)	(10, 1)
	Confess	(1, 10)	(6, 6)

As is clear, for prisoner 1 the second row is better than the first, no matter which column he is in, and for prisoner 2 the second column is better than the first, no matter which row he is in. So the self-seeking of the two will lead them to (6, 6), as a consequence of confession by each, whereas they would have been both better off at (2, 2), the consequence of neither confessing.[1]

It is important to recognise that even if the two prisoners are allowed to talk to each other and to conspire, this will not affect the outcome. Since both prisoners are self-seekers, and since the confession takes place separately, it will be in the interest of each to break the contract not

---

[1] Repetitions of this game over time, under certain circumstances, may take the two to the mutually beneficial solution, but this is not always the case (Luce and Raiffa, pp. 97–102). Besides, such pure repetitions are normally not possible in social games, with which we shall be concerned in the rest of the paper. In fact, in the case of the 'prisoner's dilemma' itself, pure repetitions will be difficult and many repetitions unlikely.

to confess which they might have made; and it will be in the interest of each to do this quite irrespective of whether each assumes that the other prisoner will also break his contract or not.

This conflict between what seems individually better and what seems to produce the best overall result contains, in our view, the essence of Rousseau's distinction between the 'will of all' and the 'general will'. The 'general will' of the prisoners, we can say, is to avoid confession, but each person's 'particular will' is to confess. Since, in the absence of successful collusion, their self-seeking will take them to a situation worse for both, what is needed is an enforceable contract between them. They would both be ready to appoint an agent who would see to it that neither of them confessed. In the absence of sanction (or, we might even say, of a Sovereign), each prisoner may be driven by rational self-seeking to break the contract which is to the common advantage of both.

This gives an immediate and plausible sense to Rousseau's notion of the members of a society being 'forced to be free', and can be claimed to correspond with what Rousseau says in the *Social Contract* about the general will. It is not our purpose to offer yet another reinterpretation of Rousseau as either totalitarian or liberal; but it seems worthwhile to point out how Rousseau's notion can be given a valid sense by reference to the model of the prisoner's dilemma. The purpose of the general will, says Rousseau,[1] is the good of all, or common good: the general will 'always tends to the public advantage'. What makes the general will general is not the number of citizens involved, but 'the common interest by which they are united'. The divergence between the general will and the will of all arises because the individual's personal interest 'may dictate a line of action quite other than that demanded by the interest of all'. The general will, though remaining unalterable, becomes subordinated to the encroachment of individual wills when 'each, separating his interest from the interest of all, sees that such separation cannot be complete, yet the part he plays in the general damage seems to him as nothing compared with the exclusive good which he seeks to appropriate'—an account which fits exactly the case of the prisoner who seeks to gain an advantage by breaking the contract. The general will is general not only in its origins but its objects, and is 'applicable to all as well as operated by all'. It tends always to equality: and all citizens being equal by virtue of the contract, 'none has the right to demand that another should do what he does not do himself'. It is, finally, the legislator who must persuade the people of

[1] The quotations which follow are taken from the translation in *Social Contract* (ed. Barker), World's Classics edn. (London, 1947).

their true interest: the average man 'finds it difficult to see what benefit he is likely to derive from the ceaseless privations which good laws will impose upon him', so that the good legislator is the legislator who will lead those 'to whom mere mortal prudence would ever be a stumbling block' (or who would, in other words, pursue what might well be their rational individual strategy, but at the cost of their real benefit).

These remarks of Rousseau's seem to us to make it possible for an interpretation to be given to the general will on the model of the prisoner's dilemma. This interpretation requires, however, to be distinguished from the interpretation of the general will given by Arrow in *Social Choice and Individual Values*. According to Arrow, 'The idealistic doctrine may then be summed up by saying that each individual has two orderings, one which governs him in his everyday actions and one which would be relevant under some ideal conditions and is in some sense truer than the first ordering'.[1] Our interpretation, by contrast, does not require us to impute to each person more than a single set of orderings. On our view, each person has (as in Rousseau) a single and consistent aim. The conflict between the will of all and the general will arises not because the individual must be required to change his preference orderings, but because of the difference between the outcome of individual strategy and of enforced collusion which arises under the conditions of the non-cooperative, non-zero-sum game.

We thus further assume that a substantive sense may be given to the common good (again, as in Rousseau). This is not to say that the general will enjoins a set of specific practices on specific persons. Rousseau makes clear at several points that this is not so. It does, however, mean more than the sense to which, it has been argued by Benn and Peters, the common good must be restricted, namely that all claims should have been impartially considered before legislation is passed.[2] The limit which must be imposed on the meaning of the common good is rather that it loses its meaning where there is a conflict of 'real' interests even in Rousseau's sense. That is to say, the common good may be taken to be substantively embodied in what the general will wills: but the general will does not will anything which requires that any person should be (in terms of his own preference ordering) the long-term loser, although it may, of course, require him to forego the pursuit of an individual advantage which, without enforced collusion, would leave him in the end worse off. We may

[1] Kenneth J. Arrow, *Social Choice and Individual Values* (New York, 1951), pp. 82–3.
[2] S. I. Benn and R. S. Peters, *Social Principles and the Democratic State* (London, 1959), p. 227.

say, if you like, that the general will always fulfils the conditions of Pareto optimality, although it is not suggested thereby that Pareto optimality is a sufficient criterion of justice. Whether or how far it may be useful to say that the general will wills justice will be considered in the second section of this paper.

There is, however, a difficulty which may arise even where Pareto optimality is satisfied. Even where a set of social arrangements may be envisaged whereby all individuals would benefit, there may be a choice where one class of persons would be better off under one possible set of arrangements and another class under another. Consider, for example, a country where some people have cars with a left-hand drive and others with a right-hand drive, so that the former would prefer a rule of driving on the right and the latter of driving on the left. Which law does the general will enjoin? It will be in the interest of both the two classes to have either of the two laws in preference to none at all, but one class will prefer one law and the other class another. We are here faced with a choice of cooperative solutions to a non-zero-sum game, and there does not appear to be any criterion by which one solution better embodies the general will (or, we may say, is more just) than the other. In other words, the appeal to the general will appears to yield weak but not strong orderings of aggregated preferences.

The problem, therefore, in such cases as these is to settle in advance the rules of a fair game by which the choice of cooperative solutions to a non-zero-sum non-cooperative game may be made. In the example offered, it could be claimed that the general will might require an appeal to the majority principle (with, perhaps, an agreement in the case of a tie to abide by the toss of a coin). Everyone could be assumed to be ready to accept a general method of resolving deadlocks which would be preferable to the pursuit by everyone of his atomistic rational strategy. The implementation of the law enacted on this basis would be consistent with the general will. In such a case, it could be said not only that the general will wills the common interest (either of two alternative laws being demonstrable as in the common interest in preference to no enforced collusion at all), but also that the general will wills the just resolution of conflicting interests. This formulation, however, directly raises the relation of the general will to the notion of justice, and the limits of the scope of the general will when applied to problems traditionally associated with the concept of social justice. It is to these questions that we turn in the following section.

I I

For this purpose it will be convenient to start from the contractual model of justice as fairness as developed by John Rawls.[1] It is the notion of the contract which, on Rawls's model as on Rousseau's, must link any notion of the general will to that of justice, since it is by virtue of the contract that all persons are to be viewed as equally subject to the general will, and it is by reference to the contract that assessment is made of the justice of demanding that the individual should surrender the right to act purely according to his atomistic strategy. As used by Rawls, the contract implicit in justice as fairness is not, of course, a historical contract. But it is a contract in that all parties seeking a 'just' aggregation or resolution of their individual interests are to be envisaged as having made, in Rawls's phrase, a 'firm commitment in advance'. This commitment is not on specific practices, but on 'principles of appraisal' mutually acknowledged by 'free persons who have no authority over each other'; and it is according to these principles that their competing claims are to be settled. This means, in effect, that every member of a society might as well have been party to a fictitious contract to abide by decisions of social policy to the extent that he would expect his own claims to be vindicated when in accordance with the principles agreed in advance. That this is the essence of justice, and that the social contract (in a modified form) does provide the model for it, seems to us to be adequately demonstrated by Rawls. It remains to consider the relation of the general will as we see it to this conception of justice.

On the model of the prisoner's dilemma, both prisoners partially share a common preference ordering—both, that is, prefer (2, 2) to (6, 6), since both wish to minimise their joint and equal sentences. Extending this, therefore, we must say that the model only applies to cases where social aims are up to a point unanimous.[2] However, even where aims may be said to conflict in that people may have conflicting preferences between cooperative solutions to a non-zero-sum non-cooperative game, but where each cooperative solution is better than no cooperation at all, we have seen that the general will may will a solution acceptable to both parties. The real difficulty comes when we are confronted with a case where cooperation cannot make everybody better off. Take, for example, zero-sum social games—games, that is, where the gain of one person or group

[1] John Rawls, 'Justice as Fairness', *Philosophical Review*, LXVII (1958), 164–94.
[2] Cases of this kind vary from such civic rules as not dumping rubbish on the street to important national economic decisions. For an example of the last, see A. K. Sen, 'On Optimizing the Rate of Saving', *Economic Journal*, LXXI (1961), esp. pp. 487–9.

must be the loss of another. By our sense of the general will, a person cannot here be 'forced to be free', except where his own long-run preference ordering can be shown to be better realised by his acceptance of the loss in this particular case. What this means is that when the rules of a zero-sum game are to be settled then the general will may be described as enjoining the rules of a game of 'fair' division to the extent that such rules can be shown to be in the long-term or 'real' interest of all the players relative to the outcome which would result without such rules. A 'fair' zero-sum game, to accord with the requirements of our sense of the general will, must in this sense accord with the preference orderings of all the players.

What will it mean, therefore, to say that (as Rousseau seems sometimes to imply) the general will wills social justice? It is clear that on our analysis the justification of either enforced collusion or of 'fair' rules for zero-sum social games will cover fewer cases than could be appealed to by Rawlsian justice. If justice is interpreted in Rawls's sense—and a case could perhaps be made for thus interpreting Rousseau's 'true principle of equity'—then justice corresponds to such solutions to zero-sum games as accord with principles to which the players, had they met before the game under conditions of primordial equality, *would have* jointly agreed. Our view of the 'general will', which rather follows Rosseau's emphasis on common interests than his implication of common principles, does not offer any way of establishing principles by which some players must accept to be losers except in so far as the acceptance of rules entailing loss accords with the players' long-term interest or preference. Interest does not mean here that terms of 'fair' contracts depend purely upon the threat-advantage of individual players—an objection effectively raised by Rawls against Braithwaite's *Theory of Games as a Tool for the Moral Philosopher*. But it does mean that we do not extend the general will so far as to allow persons to be 'forced to be free' by the criterion of any principle to which they could be supposed, if rational, to have been prepared to assent from the state of nature.

The initial difficulty in fitting the notion of a 'game of fair division' even to our limited sense of the general will is that there are occasions when such games as formally defined by game theory are manifestly unfair. This is the difficulty inherent in the attempt to apply the theory of games to the resolution of conflicting claims without (as Rawls shows to be necessary) introducing some further concept of fairness. The difficulty most obviously arises when one player in a game of 'fair' division is initially very rich and the other very poor. Nor, unless unanimity already exists, is it possible without a regress to make the rules of the game themselves a part of the players' desired outcome. By Rawlsian justice, we could perhaps settle the matter by establishing the principles by which rational persons would, before knowing if they would be rich or poor, have agreed to decide when a game of 'fair' division was in fact appropriate. But this involves the assumption, which we do not ourselves wish to make, that there are no conflicts between the principles of, say, needs and deserts, except those dictated by a vested position. We can, however, demonstrate that persons can be 'forced to be free' in the cases where their preference ordering of social states will be better realised as a result of their willingness not to pursue their atomistic strategy.

With the concept of 'social justice' which follows from Rawls's model of justice and that of the 'general will' as developed above, it becomes possible to make the following statements about their relationships in the context of rules that are used to compel individuals. The set of rules that satisfy the criterion of 'social justice' we refer to as S, and the set of rules that conform to an unambiguous 'general will' we refer to as G. Our contentions are the following:

(i) G is a sub-set of S.

(ii) The 'complement' of G in S, i.e. the set of rules that belong to S but not to G, may be non-empty. This means that it is possible that some rules may be socially 'just' without conforming to an unambiguous 'general will'.

(iii) Because of the possibility of a genuine conflict of principles about who should gain and who should lose, it may be difficult to decide whether a rule belongs to S or not, if it does not belong to G.

Statement (i) says that if a particular rule conforms to an unambiguous 'general will', it will pass Rawls's test of 'social justice'. If a certain contract will lead the persons concerned to a situation where everyone would be better off than they would be if they followed atomistic strategy, then it will be correct to say that everyone, if rational (as defined by Rawls), will accept the contract in a situation of primordial equality, i.e. even without knowing his own exact position in the game. In the example of the 'prisoner's dilemma', the contract of non-confession will conform to 'social justice' from the point of view of the two prisoners. Breaking this contract, moreover, can be regarded as 'unjust', and if either prisoner tries to break the contract he may be justly 'forced to be free'.

Statement (ii) can be understood by visualising a case where it is known that everybody concerned would have accepted a rule in a state of primordial equality, even though the rule in practice leads to the greater detriment of somebody than would result if he were to follow his atomistic strategy. If, for example, it were known that everybody would have supported a certain system of progressive taxation in a state where they had absolutely no idea what their own pre-tax income would be, then such a system of taxation would satisfy the Rawlsian requirement of justice, even though there might not be the necessary partial unanimity of interests required for the existence of a 'general will'.

Statement (iii) can be illustrated with the same example. Since there exist genuine conflicts of principles, e.g. between 'needs' and 'deserts', it will become difficult beyond a certain point to establish what principles people would have subscribed to in a state of primordial equality. Whether, therefore, a particular person's argument is attributable to his vested interest in the situation in which he finds himself, or whether it is attributable to a principle he would (if rational) have accepted even when he had no such vested interest, may be difficult to resolve. In contrast with this, cases that fit the 'general will' pose no special difficulty, since irrespective of a person's vested position, the enforceable contract is to his advantage.

We do not, therefore, wish to restrict the use of the notion of 'social justice' to the cases that conform to a 'general will'; but we do want to point out that in these cases there is no possibility of ambiguity in the interpretation of 'social justice', unlike the cases where the model of a 'general will' cannot be applied.

Index

233